C++ for Pascal Programmers

Ira Pohl

University of California, Santa Cruz

The Benjamin/Cummings Publishing Company, Inc.

Redwood City, California ■ Fort Collins, Colorado
Menlo Park, California ■ Reading, Massachusetts ■ New York
Don Mills, Ontario ■ Wokingham, U.K. ■ Amsterdam ■ Bonn
Sydney ■ Singapore ■ Tokyo ■ Madrid ■ San Juan

To Plato, Euclid, and Leibnitz

Sponsoring Editor: Alan Apt
Production Coordinator: Laura Kenney
Text Designer: Linda Seals,
    B. Vader Design/Production
Cover Designer: Juan Vargas
Copy Editor: Carol Dondrea
Compositor: Graphic Typesetting Service

© 1991 by The Benjamin/Cummings Publishing Company, Inc.

LIBRARY OF CONGRESS CATALOGING-IN-PUBLICATION DATA

Pohl, Ira.
    C++ for Pascal programmers / Ira Pohl.
        p.   cm.
    Includes index.
    ISBN 0-8053-0911-X
    1. C++ (Computer program language)   I. Title.
QA76.73.C153P65   1991
005.26'2−dc20   90-34502
    75116   CIP

ISBN 0-8053-0911-X

  BCDEFGHIJ-AL-9543210

The Benjamin/Cummings Publishing Company, Inc.
390 Bridge Parkway
Redwood City, California 94065

PREFACE

This book is intended as a gentle introduction to programming in C++ for the programmer or student already familiar with Pascal. Its approach is an evolutionary teaching process that uses Pascal as a starting point. With this approach, the programmer can stop at any point in the text and use the language facilities learned up to that point. We start with Pascal and end with C++. The book is an up-to-date description of C++ based on AT&T C++ release 2.0. Appendix C is an especially useful summary of the C++ language.

Pascal is the major teaching language for beginning computer science students. Designed by Niklaus Wirth in 1970, it is a small, powerful language, popular in both the academic community and the personal computer community. Many efficient and fast compilers exist for it— which, indeed, was one of its design goals. However, Pascal lacks some key features that limit its use in the professional community, where C is the dominant language.

C++ is a powerful modern successor language to C. It was invented at Bell Labs by Bjarne Stroustrup in the mid-1980s. C++ adds to C the concept of *class,* a mechanism for providing user-defined types also called *abstract data types*. It supports *object-oriented* programming by these means and by providing inheritance and run-time type binding. C is the present; C++ is the future.

By carefully developing working C++ programs, using the method of *dissection,* this book presents a simple and thorough introduction to the programming process in C++. Dissection is a technique for explaining new elements in a program that the student or programmer is seeing for the first time. It highlights key points in the many examples of working code that are used to teach by example.

v

This book is intended for use in a course in programming in C++. The audience is expected to know Pascal or have enough programming experience to follow this tutorial. It can also be used as a supplementary text in a comparative language course, software methodology course, advanced programming course, data structures course, or other courses where the instructor wants C++ to be the language of choice. Each chapter presents a number of carefully explained programs. Many programs and functions are dissected.

All the major pieces of code were tested. A consistent and proper coding style is adopted from the beginning. The style standard used is one chosen by professionals in the C++ community.

Pascal is a language of roughly the same size and utility as C. This book is self-contained and trains the Pascal programmer to be a C++ programmer. For the Pascal programmer who wants additional material on C, this book can be supplemented by *A Book on C,* Second Edition, by Al Kelley and Ira Pohl (Benjamin/Cummings, 1990). As a package, the two books offer an integrated treatment of the C and C++ programming languages and their use that is unavailable elsewhere.

The book incorporates:

An Evolutionary Approach. The Pascal programmer is introduced to equivalent concepts in the C programming language. By showing how individual elements of a Pascal program translate into C, the Pascal programmer can immediately gain a facility with the C programming language. Chapters 1 and 2 transform the Pascal programmer into a C programmer. Chapter 3 provides an overview of the C++ language and the OOP paradigm. The middle chapters show how classes work. Classes are the basis for abstract data types and object-oriented programming. The later chapters give advanced details of the use of inheritance and stream I/O. Chapter 10 describes important additions to C++ that are found in C++ version 2.0 compilers. At any point in the text the programmer can stop and use the new material.

Teaching by Example. The book is a tutorial that stresses examples of working code. Right from the start, the student is introduced to full working programs. An interactive environment is assumed. Exercises are integrated with the examples to encourage experimentation. Excessive detail is avoided in explaining the larger elements of writing working code. Each chapter has several important example programs, major elements of which are explained by the method of dissection.

Object-Oriented Programming (OOP). The reader is led gradually to the object-oriented style. Chapter 0 discusses how the Pascal programmer can benefit in important ways from a switch to C++ and object-oriented programming. The terminology of object-oriented concepts is defined, and the way in which these concepts are supported by C++ is introduced. Chapter 5 introduces classes. This is the basic mechanism for producing modular programs and implementing abstract data types. Class variables are the *objects* being manipulated. Chapter 8 develops inheritance and virtual functions, two key elements in this paradigm. Chapter 10 integrates all the previous techniques, showing how to properly write multicomponent programs in an object-oriented style.

Chapter 10 describes the OOP design process as an exercise in *Platonism*. These views give new insight into the extra steps required and the added benefits derived from OOP. The book leads the student or professional programmer to OOP's profound but subtle changes to program development.

Data Structures in C++. The text emphasizes many of the standard data structures from computer science. Stacks, safe arrays, dynamically allocated multidimensional arrays, lists, trees, and strings are all implemented. Exercises extend the student's understanding of how to implement and use these structures. Implementation is consistent with an abstract data type approach to software.

Each chapter has:

Dissections. A program particularly illustrative of the themes of that chapter is analyzed by dissection. Dissection is similar to a structured walk-through of the code. Its intention is to explain to the reader newly encountered programming elements and idioms.

Summary. A succinct list of points covered in the chapter is re-iterated as helpful review.

Exercises. The exercises test the student's knowledge of the language. Many exercises are intended to be done interactively while reading the text. This encourages self-paced instruction by the reader. The exercises also frequently extend the reader's knowledge into advanced areas.

Acknowledgments

My special thanks go to my wife, Debra Dolsberry, who encouraged me throughout this project. She acted as technical editor and implemented and tested all major pieces of code. Her careful implementations of the code and exercises often led to important improvements. Many students contributed to the writing of this text by acting as a critical audience. Daniel Edelson's comments and suggestions were especially useful; our work together on evaluating the C++ language design has been especially important. Others who provided helpful suggestions include: Al Conrad, UCSC; Samuel Druker, Zortech Limited; Robert Durling, UCSC; Gene Fisher, UCD; Paul Fleck; Robert Hansen, Lattice, Incorporated; John Hardin, HP; Al Kelley, UCSC; John McGregor, Clemson; George Vassilakis, USC; and Mike Walker. In addition, my editors Alan Apt, Jean Foltz, and Mark McCormick were very supportive. Much appreciation to Niklaus Wirth for inventing Pascal and many ideas in the structured programming paradigm. Finally, I thank Bjarne Stroustrup for inventing such an elegant language and encouraging others to help develop and teach it.

Ira Pohl
University of California, Santa Cruz

CONTENTS

CHAPTER 0

From Pascal to Object-Oriented Programming in C++

Pascal is a useful starting point for C++ because many key ideas in C++ are extensions of related ideas in Pascal. Pascal was created by Niklaus Wirth in 1970 with the goal of being a small language for teaching good programming practice. It had strong typing, a useful set of derived types, and a mechanism for building user-defined types.

C++ was created by Bjarne Stroustrup in the early 1980s. Stroustrup had two main goals: (1) C++ was to be compatible with ordinary C, and (2) it was to extend C using the class construct of Simula 67. The class construct is an extension of the C struct. The language, in an early form, is described in B. Stroustrup, *The C++ Programming Language* [1]. Important additions to the current language are described in B. Stroustrup, *The Evolution of C++ : 1985 to 1987* [2].

This book teaches C++ to programmers already familiar with Pascal. It can also be used by programmers familiar with C [3]. It does this by building from Pascal to C to C++. Two aspects of C++ as a successor language to C are stressed. The first is C++'s superiority to Pascal or C as a general-purpose programming language because of its new features. The second is the success of C++ as an *object-oriented*

1

programming language. In the next section we define what this new concept means.

Pascal teaches programmers structured programming habits. In the small, this involves writing larger programs as a series of procedure calls on properly structured data. Pascal has a limited form of data abstraction. The Pascal `type` declaration allows the programmer to extend the named types available to the program. This improves on strong typing and provides user-defined aggregates with understandable names. The C++ `class` declaration is a powerful extension of these concepts. As we shall see, it provides strong typing, data hiding (see Chapter 5), and code reuse through inheritance (see Chapter 8). Also, C++ allows programming teams to program in the large using file encapsulation, function encapsulation, and class encapsulation techniques. As a consequence, C++ can be used to teach modular programming habits within the object-oriented paradigm.

0.1 OBJECT-ORIENTED PROGRAMMING

We will be using the terms *abstract data type (ADT)* and *object-oriented programming (OOP)* to refer to a powerful new programming approach. An ADT is a user-defined extension to the existing types available in the language. It consists of a set of values and a collection of operations that can act on those values. For example, Pascal and C do not have a complex number type. In Pascal, one can use the `type` declaration to define complex as a record type. But it could not be used with the arithmetic operators. C++ provides the class construct to add such a type and integrate it with existing types and operators. *Objects* are class variables. Object-oriented programming allows ADTs to be easily created and used. OOP uses the mechanism of *inheritance* to conveniently derive a new type from an existing user-defined type. It allows the programmer to model the objects found in the problem domain by programming their content and behavior with a class.

The class construct in C++ provides the *encapsulation* mechanism to implement ADTs. Encapsulation packages both the internal implementation details of the type and the externally available operations and functions that can act on objects of that type. The implementation details can be made inaccessible to client code that uses the type. For example, stack might be implemented as a fixed-length array, while the publicly available operations would include push and pop. Changing the internal implementation to a linked list should not affect how push and pop are used externally. The implementation of stack is hidden from its clients. The details of how to provide data hiding in classes are touched on in Chapter 3 and developed thoroughly in Chapters 5 and 8.

0.2 WHY C++ IS BETTER THAN PASCAL

Pascal is a small language invented to teach structured programming to students. It is a great success. It has been used not only at many colleges to introduce programming but has been used in industry as well, and been the basis for very successful extensions, such as Modula 2 and Ada. The extensions reflect certain limits that Pascal has as a program language. After teaching Pascal in first courses, many colleges switch to C or other languages for their advanced courses in systems, graphics, and data structures. Why? Because Pascal cannot capture modern software practice and needs. Pascal restricts the beginner in order to promote a disciplined style. In doing so, Pascal hampers the professional.

Pascal does not support modules and independent compilation. This is necessary for team projects and medium-to-large software development. Pascal does not have an adequate associated standard library with which to write systems applications. Modern languages rely on highly standardized libraries for different applications areas. Pascal typing is too rigid and restricts the programmer's ability to write generic or reusable code.

C++ as a language retains many of Pascal's advantages without its limitations. C++, like Pascal, is a very strongly typed language. This is important for program reliability. The lack of strong typing was often criticized in C [4]. C++ improves on C in significant ways, but especially in supporting strong typing. The function prototype syntax, as now required by ANSI C [3][5], is a C++ innovation. C++ allows for highly efficient translation. Almost all of its constructs are readily translated into native machine code. C++ allows type extension, but goes far beyond Pascal type definitions. C++, in its essence, is a small language. It has very little redundancy as it is a minimal extension to an existing small language, C. C++ is highly portable, and translators for it exist on many different machines and systems. To sum up, C++ and Pascal share these characteristics: strong typing, type extensibility, efficient compilation, portability, and small size.

C++ has many advantages over Pascal, especially for large-scale or reusable software development. C++ provides a complete set of OOP language features. Unlike other object-oriented languages, such as Smalltalk, C++ is an extension of an existing language in wide use on many machines. If C++ is viewed as an object-oriented language alternative to Smalltalk, it is a relatively inexpensive alternative. Programming in C++ does not require a graphics environment, nor do C++ programs incur run-time expense from type checking or garbage collection.

C++ is a marriage of the low level with the high level. As a consequence, unlike Pascal, it is readily used as a systems language. C++ compilers are highly compatible with existing C programs because maintaining such compatibility was a design objective. To paraphrase Stroustrup [1], "C is at the machine level, while C++ is at the problem domain level." The user can write code at the level appropriate to the problem, while still maintaining contact with the machine-level implementation details. Pascal keeps its distance from the machine, and resides in an intermediate level of abstraction between machine and problem domain.

C++ allows the programmer to create an abstraction that directly reflects the problem domain. Abstract data types are implemented in C++ through the `class` mechanism. Classes allow a programmer to control the visibility of the underlying implementation. What is public is accessible and what is private is hidden. Data hiding is one component of object-oriented programming. Classes have member functions, including those that overload operators. Member functions allow the programmer to code the appropriate functionality for the ADT. Classes can be defined through an inheritance mechanism that allows for improved code sharing and library development. Inheritance is another hallmark of object-oriented programming.

In C++, operators can be given new definitions based on the types of their arguments. This operator overloading supports the implementation of new types that may be operated upon transparently. Normal functions, like operators, may be overloaded. Conversions between types are allowed, provided they are well defined. In fact, the language allows the programmer to create conversion functions between arbitrary types.

Parameter passing in C is unchecked with regard to type or number of actual parameters. This leads to bugs that the compiler cannot catch. In C++, function prototypes allow functions to be fully checked as to count and type. Functions taking variable types or numbers of arguments are also supported. The addition of function prototypes is an aid to the programmer, bringing to the compiler argument type-checking capability, which is similar to that found in Pascal.

The Pascal array model is tied to individual array bounds. This hampers the writing of generic array code. Development and use of dynamic arrays is not supported in Pascal. C++ classes, however, provide a satisfactory means of transparently implementing general arrays. Multidimensional, dynamic, and bounds-checked arrays can be implemented in libraries. C++ has major advantages over Pascal: data hiding, full type extensibility, standard extensive libraries, machine level access, independent compilation, and OOP features, such as inheritance, that will be explained later.

0.3 WHY SWITCH TO C++?

C++ supports the object-oriented programming style. This is a major advance over the structured programming style of Pascal. A chief cost of this advance, however, is the increased complexity of the language. Pascal has 35 keywords, 16 operators, a simple syntax, simple built-in I/O, and a simple semantics. It is an excellent teaching language. Its drawbacks include inflexibility, lack of adequate terminal and file I/O, inability to access the machine address space, and lack of separate compilation.

C is a more complex language, but better suited to developing large software projects. Its semantics are closer to the machine level. It has a complicated syntax, it provides for file inclusion and separate compilation, and it relies on sophisticated standard libraries to do I/O. C, like Pascal, is a procedural, imperative language. Such languages have a small set of built-in types (integers, floats, characters, and so on) and allow array and record structuring. This restricts their usefulness in domains that are not simply constructed and manipulated from the built-in types.

C++ remedies these limitations by allowing arbitrary user-defined types. The price for this, as noted, is increased complexity. The complexity that C++ adds to the C language is one of its biggest drawbacks. C++ has 47 keywords, an increase of 60 percent over traditional C's 29. This increase partly reflects the large number of new ideas incorporated, but makes mastery more difficult. To overcome this problem, this book approaches the learning process by gradually transforming the Pascal programmer into a practiced C++ programmer. Each chapter extends from the previous chapter the range of ideas the programmer may use. At any point, the reader can stop and still be partly proficient in C++. In effect, the reader evolves into an object-oriented C++ programmer.

C++ is a language for the future. It is supported by AT&T and several major computer firms, as well as many universities, are committed to its increased use.

C++ is a better C. There is increased convenience in writing code and increased security in the code. Features such as // for single line comments, `const` and `inline`, `new` and `delete` for storage management, and call-by-reference parameters simplify the coding process from that of C. Unlike C programmers, Pascal programmers have a familiarity with and used these concepts to their advantage. Stronger typing in general, and function prototypes in particular, enhance security and facilitate software methodology. C++ is considerably more powerful than Pascal. C++ enhances type extensibility, abstraction, and reuse far beyond either Pascal or C.

0.4 REFERENCES

1. B. Stroustrup, *The C++ Programming Language*, Addison-Wesley, Reading, Mass., 1986.
   The de facto language reference manual.
2. B. Stroustrup, *The Evolution of C++: 1985 to 1987*, appears in 1987 USENIX C++ Papers, Santa Fe, N.M., 1987, pp. 1–21.
   Brings his book up-to-date with version 2 language changes.
3. A. Kelley and I. Pohl, *A Book on C*, Second Edition, Benjamin/Cummings, Redwood City, Calif., 1990.
   A comprehensive text on the ANSI C programming language.
4. I. Pohl and D. Edelson, *A-Z: C Language Shortcomings*, in *Computer Languages*, vol. 13, no. 2, 1988, pp. 51–64.
   A brief paper criticizing 26 defects in the original C language.
5. A. Kelly and I. Pohl, *Turbo C*, Benjamin/Cummings, Redwood City, Calif., 1988.
   A tutorial introduction to a popular ANSI C compiler.

CHAPTER 1

C for Pascal Programmers: Data and Statements

This chapter, together with Chapter 2, will provide the parallels between programming in C and programming in Pascal. The two languages are approximately the same in size, and both are derived from the Algol 60 and FORTRAN tradition of conventional imperative languages. Most Pascal programs can be converted in a straightforward manner to C programs. Many of the differences are superficial syntactic differences. The intent of this chapter and the next is to give the experienced Pascal programmer the ability to program in that subset of C++ that corresponds to C. This chapter focuses on basic data types and statements.

1.1. PASCAL AS A STARTING POINT

Pascal is an effective starting point for C++ because Pascal is strongly typed and provides a limited form of type extensibility through its type declarations. The Pascal programmer understands that a properly modular program is a better program. This modularity is created by defining small procedures that encapsulate the functionality the programmer intends to capture. Modularity is also enhanced by Pascal being block structured. Some Pascal systems, such as Turbo Pascal, allow file level modularity, which is found also in C. In addition, Pascal programmers have access to well-supported libraries, such as graphics packages and numerical packages, that extend the benefits of the language by allowing code reuse and enhanced portability.

A major premise of OOP is that a program needs to be designed around appropriate ADTs. An ADT, such as a stack, has a data repesentation and associated operations. How this is implemented are details that users or clients of this ADT need not be concerned with. The Pascal language allows ADTs to be built using record and array aggregates. For example, a stack in Pascal can be constructed as follows:

```
const
    SIZE = 100;                    {implementation detail}
type
    stackIndex = 0..SIZE;
    stack = record         {stack definition}
                s:    array[stackIndex] of integer;
                top: stackIndex
            end;
var
    stk   : stack;         {an instance of a stack}
```

Operations on stacks would be expressed as function or procedure calls. For example, a program that detects whether a stack is full would be implemented as

```
function full( stk : stack): boolean;
begin
    full := (stk.top = SIZE);
end; {full}
```

1.2. PROGRAM STRUCTURE

The program structure in standard Pascal is shown in the following program, which computes the greatest common denominator of two integers:

```
{  Greatest common divisor program.     }

program GcdProgram (input, output);
   var
      x, y : integer;

   function Gcd (m, n : integer) : integer;
      var
         r : integer;   {remainder}
   begin
      while n <> 0 do
         begin
            r := m mod n;
            m := n;
            n := r
         end;
      Gcd := m   {returned result}
   end;

begin {GcdProgram}
   writeln('PROGRAM GcdProgram');
   while true do   {infinite loop - exit by an interrupt}
      begin
         write('Enter two integers: ');
         readln(x, y);
         writeln('GCD(', x:4, ',', y:4, ') = ', (Gcd (x, y)):4)
      end
end.  {GcdProgram}
```

In standard Pascal, a program is considered monolithic. It starts with the keyword program followed by an identifier naming the program. It may contain a series of declarations whose order must be: (1) labels, (2) constants, (3) types, (4) variables, and (5) procedures and functions. The procedures and functions have a structure similar to the program and may nest. The declarations are followed by the keyword begin, a series of executable statements, and finally a matching keyword end followed by a period.

The corresponding program in C follows:

```c
/*  Greatest common divisor program.     */
#include <stdio.h>

int  gcd (int m, int n)
{
   int r;   /* remainder */

   while (n != 0) {
      r = m % n;
      m = n;
      n = r;
   }
   return(m);
}

int main()
{
   int x, y;

   printf("PROGRAM GcdProgram\n");
   while (1) {   /* infinite loop - exit by an interrupt */
      printf("Enter two integers: ");
      scanf("%d%d", &x, &y);
      printf("GCD(%4d,%4d) = %4d\n", x, y, gcd(x, y));
   }
}
```

Some minor differences are easily seen in these two versions of the greatest common divisor program.

- The assignment symbol is = in C.
- The not equal symbol is != in C.
- The comment symbols are /* and */.
- The Pascal keywords begin and end are replaced by { and }.
- The Pascal keyword do is omitted in the C while statement.
- The Pascal keyword function is omitted in the C function declaration. The return type of a function is specified as part of the declaration before the function's name.
- A function's value is returned using the return statement.

As can be seen, C is considerably terser than Pascal.

Some major differences involve program organization.

- C relies on an external standard library to provide input/output. The information the program needs to use this library resides in the file *stdio.h*.

- C uses a preprocessor to handle a set of directives, such as the `include` directive, to convert the program from its preprocessing form to pure C syntax. These directives are introduced by the symbol *#*.

- A C program consists of declarations in possibly different files. Each function is on the external or global level and may not be declared in a nested manner. The files act as modules and may be compiled separately.

- The function `main()` is used as the starting point for execution of the program. It obeys the C rules for function declaration.

C compilers can compile multifile programs. Large C programs are prepared as separate files. Each file is conceptually a module that contains related program declarations and definitions. On many systems C source files have the suffix *.c*. So,

```
cc module1.c module2.c my_main.c
```

is the Unix C compile command *cc*, acting on the three files *module1.c*, *module2.c*, and *my_main.c*. If compilation shows no errors, then an executable *a.out* is produced. The AT&T C++ translator command is *CC*.

1.3. SIMPLE DATA

The four simple types in Pascal are `real`, `integer`, `char`, and `boolean`. Except for the `boolean` type, the equivalent C types are `double`, `int`, and `char`. The Pascal and C types are for most practical purposes equivalent, and usually each has a set of values and representation that is tied to the underlying machine architecture on which the compiler is running. Although C has no built-in `boolean` type, it uses the value zero to mean *false* and nonzero values to mean *true*. This usage is important in understanding the semantics of iterative and conditional statements. Enumeration types in C or C++ (see Section 4.3) can be used to add a boolean type explicitly.

Two important differences exist between C simple types and Pascal simple types.

1. C simple types can be modified by the keywords short, long, signed, and unsigned to yield further simple types.

2. C allows a far wider range of automatic conversions when types are mixed.

For example, there are three basic floating point types in C. In order of significance, these are float, double, and long double. An implementation must guarantee that a larger type has at least the significance of a smaller type. If these types are mixed in a single expression, the smaller types are converted automatically to the largest type in the expression. For example, adding an int and a double results in a double. This is also true for char and other integral types. The type char can be considered a small integer.

The following table lists these types shortest to longest. Automatic conversions occur in an expression with mixed types, resulting in a final expression whose value is that of the longest occurring type.

Fundamental data types		
char	signed char	unsigned char
short	int	long
unsigned short	unsigned	unsigned long
float	double	long double

Thus the type unsigned char is a longer type than char. And an unsigned long is the longest possible integral type. On a 16-bit machine, a char might be stored in a byte, an int in two bytes, and a long in four bytes.

The next program converts miles to kilometers. Miles will be kept as an integer value and kilometers will be computed in floating point.

```
{ Miles are converted to kilometers. }

program MilesToKM(input, output);
    const
        M_TO_K = 1.609;
    var
        miles: integer;
    function Convert(mi: integer): real;
        begin
            Convert := mi * M_TO_K
        end;  {Convert}

begin
    repeat
        write('Input distance in miles. ');
        read(miles);
        writeln('This distance is ', Convert(miles), 'km.');
    until (miles <= 0);
end.  {MilesToKM}
```

This program uses the type `integer` and the type `real`. The mixed type expression

```
Convert := mi * M_TO_K
```

is automatically promoted to `real`.

In C this program can be written as follows:

```
/* Miles are converted to kilometers. */

#include <stdio.h>
#define  M_TO_K  1.609
#define  CONVERT(MI)  ((MI) * (M_TO_K))

main()
{
    int miles;

    do {
        printf("Input distance in miles. ");
        scanf("%d", &miles);
        printf("\nThis distance is %f km.\n",  CONVERT(miles));
    } while (miles > 0);
}
```

Notice that the preprocessor directive define is used first to produce a symbolic constant and second to produce a macro. Where the identifier M_TO_K appears, the preprocessor substitutes 1.609. Where the macro CONVERT () appears, it is replaced by the code defining it with appropriate substitutions for its argument MI. Thus

CONVERT(miles)   *is replaced by*   ((miles) * (1.609))

Macros are used to avoid function call overhead by replacing a function call with in-line code. In Section 3.2, we have the same example program written in C++ using the keywords inline and const to avoid the pre-processor define directive.

1.4. EXPRESSIONS

C has a greater variety of operators (see Appendix B) and expression forms than Pascal. For example, assignment is an expression. The following is legal C:

```
a = b + (c = d + 3);
```

The equivalent Pascal code would be

```
c := d + 3;
a := b + c;
```

Arithmetic expressions are similar in both languages. One important difference is that in Pascal the division operator / is a real operation always yielding a real result, while in C its result depends on its argument types.

```
a = 3 / 2;      Pascal equivalent is      a := 3 div 2;
a = 3 / 2.0;    Pascal equivalent is      a := 3 / 2.0;
```

A second important difference is that C has a more tolerant attitude about mixing types and automatic conversions. In general, Pascal allows arithmetic type promotion. For example, real is a wider type than integer, so expressions that mix these two types are promoted to real and may be assigned to a real variable. This is also true in C, but C also allows assignment conversions that narrow type, so a `double` may be assigned to an `int` or even a `char`.

```
a = b / c;         Pascal equivalent is    a := b / c;
i = b / 2.0;       Pascal equivalent is    i := trunc(b / 2.0);
ch = 'A' + 1.0;    not allowed in Pascal
```

The more liberal attitude taken in C invites bad programming practice and should not be encouraged. Narrowing conversions and mixing types can affect program correctness and should be used carefully.

In Pascal, boolean expressions are used to effect flow of control in various statement types. In C, the values zero and nonzero are used instead of boolean values. The following table contains the C and Pascal operators that are most often used to affect flow of control.

Relational, Equality, and Logical Operators	C	Pascal
Relational operators: less than:	<	<
greater than:	>	>
less than or equal:	<=	<=
greater than or equal:	>=	>=
Equality operators: equal:	==	=
not equal:	!=	<>
Logical operators: (unary) negation:	!	not
logical and:	&&	and
logical or:	||	or

Just as with other operators, the relational, equality, and logical operators have rules of precedence and associativity that determine precisely how expressions involving these operators are evaluated (see Appendix B). These rules are different from Pascal. The negation operator ! is unary. All the other relational, equality, and logical operators are binary. They operate on expressions and yield either the `int` value 0 or the `int` value 1. The value for *false* can be either 0 or 0.0, and the value for *true* can be any value other than 0 or 0.0.

One pitfall in C is that the equality operator and the assignment operator,

```
a == b      and      a = b
```

are *visually* similar. The expression a == b is a test for equality, whereas a = b is an assignment expression. One of the more common C programming mistakes is to code something like

```
if (i = 1)
    . . . . .              /* do something */
```

intending

```
if (i == 1)
    . . . . .              /* do something */
```

The first if statement assigns 1 to i and evaluates to 1, so it is always *true*. This error can be very difficult to find.

The logical operators !, &&, and || when applied to expressions yield either the int value 0 or the int value 1. Logical negation can be applied to an arbitrary expression. If an expression has value 0 or 0.0, then its negation will yield the int value 1. If the expression has a nonzero value, then its negation will yield the int value 0.

While logical negation is a very simple operator, there is one subtlety. The operator ! in C is unlike the *not* operator in mathematics. If *s* is a mathematical statement, then

not (not s) = s,

whereas in C the value of !!5, for example, is 1.

The precedence of && is higher than ||, but both operators are of lower precedence than all unary, arithmetic, and relational operators. Their associativity is "left to right." Pascal has and at the precedence level of the multiplicative operators and or at the precedence level of the additive operators. Both are of higher precedence than the relational operators.

In the evaluation of expressions that are the operands of && and ||, the evaluation process stops as soon as the outcome *true* or *false* is known. This is called *short-circuit* evaluation. Suppose that *expr1* and *expr2* are expressions. If *expr1* has zero value, then in

   expr1 && *expr2*

expr2 will not be evaluated because the value of the logical expression is already determined to be 0. Similarly, if *expr1* has nonzero value, then in

   expr1 | | *expr2*

expr2 will not be evaluated because the value of the logical expression is already determined to be 1.

Some examples in C and Pascal are

```
a + 5 && b      Pascal equivalent is    (a + 5 <> 0)  and  (b <> 0)
! (a < b) && c  Pascal equivalent is    not (a < b)  and  (c <> 0)
1 | | ( a != 7) Pascal equivalent is    true
```

Of all the operators in C the comma operator has the lowest precedence. It is a binary operator with expressions as operands. In a comma expression of the form

   expr1 , *expr2*

expr1 is evaluated first, and then *expr2*. The comma expression as a whole has the value and type of its right operand. An example would be

```
sum = 0,  i = 1
```

If i has been declared an int, then this comma expression has value 1 and type int. The comma operator sometimes is used typically in the control expression part of an iterative statement, when more than one action is required. The comma operator associates from left to right.

The conditional operator ? : is unusual in that it is a ternary operator. It takes as operands three expressions. In a construct such as

   expr1 ? *expr2* : *expr3*

expr1 is evaluated first. If it is nonzero (*true*), then *expr2* is evaluated and that is the value of the conditional expression as a whole. If *expr1* is zero (*false*), then *expr3* is evaluated and that is the value of the conditional expression as a whole. The following example uses a conditional operator to assign the smaller of two values to the variable x:

```
x = (y < z) ? y : z;
```

The parentheses are not necessary because the conditional operator has precedence greater than the assignment operator. However, parentheses are good style because they clarify what is being tested for.

The type of the conditional expression

expr1 ? *expr2* : *expr3*

is determined by *expr2* and *expr3*. If they are different types, then the usual conversion rules apply. The conditional expression's type cannot depend on which of the two expressions *expr2* or *expr3* is evaluated. The conditional operator ?: associates right to left.

C provides bit manipulation operators. They operate on the machine-dependent bit representation of integral operands.

Bitwise Operators	Meaning
~	unary one's complement
<<	left shift
>>	right shift
&	and
^	exclusive or
|	or

In some cases, bit manipulation can be used to represent Pascal sets.

C uses the cast operator to perform explicit type conversion. Its form is

(*type*) *expression*

C++ has a lot to say about conversions and allows a functional notation for type conversion (see Section 7.2).

C considers function call () and indexing [] to be operators. It also has an address & operation and an indirection * operation. The address operator is a unary operator that yields the address or location where an object is stored. The indirection operator is a unary operator that is applied to an object of type pointer. It retrieves the value from the location being pointed at. This is also known as dereferencing (see Section 4.4).

C also has the `sizeof` operator. This is used to determine the number of bytes a particular object or type requires for storage. It is important for obtaining an appropriate amount of storage for dynamically allocated objects.

1.5. STATEMENTS

C and Pascal have assignment statements, procedure statements, transfer statements, empty statements, compound statements, conditional statements, selection statements, and iterative statements. Two important differences are

1. C uses the semicolon as a statement terminator; Pascal uses it as a statement separator.
2. C is more of an expression-oriented language.

For example, the assignment statement and the procedure statement in C are syntactically an *expression* followed by a semicolon. This means that they may be written any place in a program that an expression can legally appear.

Assignment and Expressions

In C, assignment occurs as part of an assignment expression. We wish to consider several forms of assignment expression. An ordinary assignment is much the same as in Pascal.

    a = b + 1;   *is equivalent to*   a := b + 1;

The effect is to evaluate the right-hand side of the assignment and convert it to a value compatible with the left-hand side variable. More generally, the left-hand side must be an *lvalue*. An lvalue is a location (in memory) where a value can be stored or retrieved. Simple variables are lvalues. As we shall see, C has wider latitude than Pascal in what constitutes an lvalue.

C compilers are more flexible than Pascal compilers in the order in which they evaluate expressions; Pascal compilers usually follow strict precedence and associativity rules. In practice, the order of evaluation of C expressions can be guaranteed by using either the comma operator or statement termination. Both forms require that expressions be evaluated sequentially.

```
a = b() + e() * f();   /* can be reordered */
a = b(), t = e(), t = t * f(), a = a + t;   /* fixed ordering */
a = b(); t = e(); t = t * f(); a = a + t;   /* fixed ordering */
```

C allows multiple assignment in a single statement.

```
a = b + (c = 3);     is equivalent to     c := 3; a := b + c;
```

C provides assignment operators that combine an assignment and some other operator.

```
a += b;      is equivalent to     a := a + b;
a *= a + b;  is equivalent to     a := a * (a + b);
```

C also provides autoincrement ++ and autodecrement -- operators in both prefix and postfix form. In prefix form, the autoincrement operator adds 1 to the value stored at the lvalue it acts upon. Similarly, the autodecrement operator subtracts 1 from the value stored at the lvalue it acts upon.

```
++i;     is equivalent to     i := i + 1;
--x;     is equivalent to     x := x - 1;
```

The postfix form behaves differently than the prefix form by changing the affected lvalue after the rest of the expression is evaluated.

```
j = ++i;   is equivalent to     i := i + 1; j := i;
j = i++;   is equivalent to     j := i; i := i + 1;
i = ++i + i++; /* poor practice that is system dependent */
```

The null statement is written as a single semicolon. It causes no action to take place. Usually a null statement is used where a statement is required syntactically, but no action is desired. This situation some-times occurs in statements that affect the flow of control.

The Compound Statement

A compound statement in C is a series of statements surrounded by the braces { and }. The chief use of the compound statement is to group statements into an executable unit. The body of a C function is always a compound statement. When declarations come at the beginning of a compound statement, the statement is called a block. In C, wherever it is possible to place a statement, it is also possible to place a compound statement. This is equivalent to using begin *statement list* end in Pascal.

The if and the if-else Statements

The general form of an if statement is

if (*expression*)
   statement

If *expression* is nonzero (*true*), then *statement* is executed; otherwise *statement* is skipped. After the if statement has been executed, control passes to the next statement. In the example

```
if (temperature >= 32)
    printf("Above Freezing!\n");
printf("Fahrenheit is %d.\n", temperature);
```

is equivalent to

```
if (temperature >= 32) then
    writeln('Above Freezing!');
writeln('Fahrenheit is ', temperature, '.');
```

"Above Freezing" is printed only when temperature is greater than or equal to 32. The second printf() statement is always executed. Usually the expression in an if statement is a relational or equality or logical expression. Note that in C the Pascal keyword then is not part of this syntax. The C expression must be parenthesized.

Closely related to the if statement is the if-else statement. It has the general form

```
if (expression)
    statement1
else
    statement2
```

If *expression* is nonzero, then *statement1* is executed and *statement2* is skipped; if *expression* is zero, then *statement1* is skipped and *statement2* is executed. After the if-else statement has been executed, control passes to the next statement. Consider the following code:

```
if (x < y)
    min = x;
else
    min = y;
printf ("min = %d\n", min);
```

is equivalent to

```
if (x < y) then
    min := x
else
    min := y;
writeln ('min = ', min);
```

If x < y is *true*, then min will be assigned the value of x, and if it is *false*, then min will be assigned the value of y. After the if-else statement is executed, the printf () statement is executed, causing the value of min to be printed.

The while Statement

The general form of a while statement is

```
while (expression)
    statement
```

First *expression* is evaluated. If it is nonzero (*true*), then *statement* is executed and control passes back to the beginning of the while loop. The effect of this is that the body of the while loop, namely *statement*, is executed repeatedly until *expression* is zero (*false*). At that point control passes to the next statement. The effect of this is that *statement* can be executed zero or more times. Note that in C the Pascal keyword do is not part of this syntax. The C expression must be parenthesized.

An example of a while statement is the following:

```
while (i <= 10) {
    sum += i;
    ++i;
}
```

> *is equivalent to*

```
while (i <= 10) do
    begin
        sum : =  sum + i;
        i := i + 1
    end
```

Assume that just before this loop the value of i is 1 and the value of sum is 0. Then the effect of the loop is to repeatedly increment the value of sum by the current value of i and then to increment i by 1. After the body of the loop has been executed 10 times, the value of i is 11 and the value of the expression i <= 10 is 0 (*false*). Thus the body of the loop is not executed and control passes to the next statement. When the while loop is exited, the value of sum is 55.

The for **Statement**

The for statement is an iterative statement typically used with a variable that is incremented or decremented. As an example, the following code uses a for statement to sum the integers from 1 to 10:

```
sum = 0;
for (i = 1; i <= 10; ++i)
    sum += i;
```

> *is equivalent to*

```
sum := 0;
for i := 1 to 10 do
    sum :=  sum + i;
```

The C `while` statement that is equivalent to this is

```
sum = 0;
i = 1;
while (i <= 10) {
    sum += i;
    ++i;
}
```

More generally, for C the construction

for (*expression1*; *expression2*; *expression3*)
    statement
next statement

is equivalent in C to

expression1;
while (*expression2*) {
    statement
    expression3;
}
next statement

provided that *expression2* is nonempty, and provided that a `continue` statement is not in the body of the `for` loop. From our understanding of the `while` statement, we can deduce the semantics of the `for` statement. First *expression1* is evaluated. Typically, *expression1* is used to initialize a variable used in the loop. Then *expression2* is evaluated. If it is nonzero (*true*), then *statement* is executed, *expression3* is evaluated, and control passes back to the beginning of the `for` loop again, except that evaluation of *expression1* is skipped. This iteration continues until *expression2* is zero (*false*), at which point control passes to *next statement*. An example is the following:

```
for (factorial = n, i = n - 1; i >= 1; --i)
    factorial *= i;
```

   is equivalent to

```
factorial := n;
for i := - 1 downto 1 do
    factorial := factorial * i;
```

Any or all of the expressions in a `for` statement can be missing, but the two semicolons must remain. If *expression1* is missing, then no initialization step is performed as part of the `for` loop. The code

```
i = 1;
sum = 0;
for ( ; i <= 10; ++i)
    sum += i;
```

will compute the sum of the integers from 1 to 10.

The special rule for when *expression2* is missing is that the test is always *true*. Thus the `for` loop in the code

```
for (i = 1, sum = 0 ; ; sum += i++ )
    printf("%d\n", sum);
```

is an infinite loop.

The `do` **Statement**

The `do` statement can be considered a variant of the `while` statement. However, instead of making its test at the top of the loop, it makes it at the bottom. An example is the following:

```
do {
    sum += i;
    scanf("%d", &i);
} while (i > 0);
```

> *is equivalent to*

```
repeat
    sum := sum + i;
    read(i)
until (i <= 0)
```

Consider a construction of the form

```
do
    statement
while (expression);
next statement
```

First *statement* is executed, and then *expression* is evaluated. If it is nonzero (*true*), then control passes back to the beginning of the do statement and the process repeats itself. When the value of *expression* is zero (*false*), then control passes to *next statement*. As an example, suppose we want to read in a positive integer, and we want to insist that the integer is positive. The following code will accomplish this:

```
do {
    printf ("Input a positive integer:   ");
    scanf ("%d", &n);
} while (n <= 0);
```

The user will be prompted for a positive integer. A negative or zero value will cause the loop to be executed again, asking for another value. Control will exit the loop only after a positive integer has been entered.

Transfer Statements

C has several statements that transfer flow of control. C and Pascal share the goto statement. The break and continue statements are used to interrupt ordinary iterative flow of control in loops. In addition, the break statement is used within a switch statement. A switch statement can select among several different cases. Its Pascal equivalent is the case statement. The return statement is a transfer statement that exits a function call. It is discussed in the next section as it is contextually dependent on function call semantics.

The break **and** continue **Statements**

To interrupt normal flow of control within a loop, the programmer can use the two special statements

  break; and continue;

The break statement, in addition to its use in loops, can also be used in a switch statement. It causes an exit from the innermost enclosing loop or switch statement.

 The following example illustrates the use of a break statement. A test for a negative value is made, and if the test is *true*, the break statement causes the while loop to be exited. Program control jumps to the statement immediately following the loop.

```
while (scanf ("%lf", &x) == 1) {
    if (x < 0.0) {
        printf ("All done - bye.\n");
        break;        /* exit loop if value is negative */
    }
    printf ("%f\n", sqrt (x));
}
/* break jumps to here */
.  .  .  .  .
```

This is a typical use of a break statement. When a special condition is met, an appropriate action is taken and the loop is exited.

The continue statement causes the current iteration of a loop to stop and causes the next iteration of the loop to begin immediately. The following code processes all characters except digits:

```
while ((c = getchar ()) != EOF) {
    if (isdigit (c))
        continue;
        .  .  .  .  .    /* process other characters */
/* continue jumps to here*/
}
```

In this example, all characters except digits are processed. When the continue statement is executed, control jumps to just before the closing brace, causing the loop to begin execution at the top again. Notice that the continue statement ends the current iteration, whereas a break statement would end the loop.

A break statement can occur only inside the body of a for, while, do, or switch statement. The continue statement can occur only inside the body of a for, while, or do statement.

The switch **Statement**

The switch statement is a multiway conditional statement generalizing the if-else statement. Its general form is given by

switch (*expression*)
    statement

where *statement* is typically a compound statement containing case labels and optionally a default label. Typically, a switch is composed of many cases, and the expression in parentheses following the keyword switch determines which, if any, of the cases get executed.

The following switch statement and its Pascal equivalent count the number of test scores by category:

```
switch (score){
case 9: case 10:
    ++a_grades; break;
case 8:
    ++b_grades; break;
case 7:
    ++c_grades; break;
default:
    ++fails;
}
```

is equivalent to

```
case score of
   9, 10: aGrades := aGrades + 1;
   8: bGrades := bGrades + 1;
   7: cGrades := cGrades + 1;
   0, 1, 2, 3, 4, 5, 6 : fails := fails + 1
end {case}
```

A case label is of the form

case *constant integral expression*:

In a switch statement, the case labels must all be unique. Typically, the action taken after each case label ends with a break statement. If there is no break statement, then execution "falls through" to the next statement in the succeeding case or default (see exercise 12).

If no case label is selected, then control passes to the default label, if there is one. A default label is not required. If no case label is selected, and there is no default label, then the switch statement is exited. To detect errors, programmers frequently include a default even when all the expected cases have been accounted for.

The keywords `case` and `default` cannot occur outside of a `switch`.

The effect of a switch

1. Evaluate the integral expression in the parentheses following `switch`.

2. Execute the `case` label having a constant value that matches the value of the expression found in step 1, or, if a match is not found, execute the `default` label, or, if there is no `default` label, terminate the `switch`.

3. Terminate the `switch` when a `break` statement is encountered, or terminate the `switch` by "falling off the end."

The `goto` Statement

The `goto` statement is the most primitive method of interrupting ordinary control flow. It is an unconditional branch to an arbitrary labeled statement in the function. The `goto` statement is considered a harmful construct in most accounts of modern programming methodology. Thus it can undermine all the useful structure provided by other flow of control mechanisms (`for`, `while`, `do`, `if`, `switch`).

A label is an identifier. By executing a `goto` statement of the form

```
goto label;
```

control is unconditionally transferred to a labeled statement. An example would be

```
if (d == 0.0)
   goto error;
else
   ratio = n / d;
 .  .  .  .  .
error:  printf("ERROR:  division by zero\n");
```

Both the `goto` statement and its corresponding labeled statement must be in the body of the same function. In general the `goto` should be avoided.

1.6. Summary

1. A C program consists of declarations in possibly different files. Each function is on the external or global level and may not be declared in a nested manner. The files act as modules and may be separately compiled.

2. The function `main ()` is used as the starting point for execution of the program. It obeys the C rules for function declaration.

3. C uses a preprocessor to handle a set of directives, such as the `include` directive, to convert the program from its preprocessing form to pure C syntax. These directives are introduced by the symbol `#`.

4. C relies on an external standard library to provide input/output. The information the program needs to use this library resides in the file *stdio.h*.

5. The four required simple types in Pascal are `real`, `integer`, `char`, and `boolean`. Except for the `boolean` type, the equivalent C types are `double`, `int`, and `char`. Although C has no built-in `boolean` type, it uses the value zero to mean *false* and nonzero values to mean *true*. This usage is important in understanding the semantics of iterative and conditional statements.

6. C and Pascal have assignment statements, procedure statements, transfer statements, empty statements, compound statements, conditional statements, selection statements, and iterative statements. Two important differences are that C uses the semicolon as a statement terminator; C is an expression-oriented language.

7. The general form of an `if` statement is

   `if` (*expression*)
      statement

   If *expression* is nonzero (*true*), then *statement* is executed; otherwise *statement* is skipped. After the `if` statement has been executed, control passes to the next statement.

8. The general form of a `while` statement is

   `while` (*expression*)
      statement

First *expression* is evaluated. If it is nonzero (*true*), then *statement* is executed and control passes back to the beginning of the while loop. The effect of this is that the body of the while loop, namely *statement*, is executed repeatedly until *expression* is zero (*false*). At that point control passes to the next statement.

9. To interrupt normal flow of control within a loop, the programmer can use the two special statements

```
break;  and    continue;
```

The break statement, in addition to its use in loops, can also be used in a switch statement. It causes an exit from the innermost enclosing loop or switch statement.

10. The goto statement is the most primitive method of interrupting ordinary control flow. It is an unconditional branch to an arbitrary labeled statement in the function. The goto statement is considered a harmful construct in most accounts of modern programming methodology and should be avoided.

1.7. Exercises

1. C++ introduces a one-line comment symbol // (see Sections 3.1, 4.1). Its effect is to comment out the rest of the line. Rewrite the *Gcd Program* with this style of comment.

2. Rewrite the *Gcd Program* with a for loop replacing the while loop. Have the program exit after computing five greatest common divisors.

3. Rewrite the *Gcd Program* to read a value for how_many greatest common divisors will be computed. The variable how_many will be used to exit the for loop.

4. On most systems, input can be *redirected* from a file. Assume that the *Gcd Program* has been compiled into an executable called *gcd*. The command

   gcd < gcd.dat

will take its input from the file *gcd.dat* and write the answers to the screen. Test this with a file containing:

```
4   4 6   6 21   8 20   15 20
```

On most systems, output can be redirected to a file. The command

$$gcd > gcd.ans$$

will place its output in the file *gcd.ans*, taking its input from the keyboard. Enter the same data as above and check the file *gcd.ans* to see that it has the four correct answers. The two redirections can be combined as follows:

$$gcd < gcd.dat > gcd.ans$$

5. The following `while` loop will print the letters *A to Z*:

```
ch = 'A'
while (ch <= 'Z'){
    printf("%c   is ASCII   %d\n", ch, ch);
    ch++;
}
```

Write a program that will print both uppercase and lowercase. Rewrite your program using `for` loops.

6. Short-circuit evaluation is an important feature. The following code illustrates the importance of the feature in a typical situation:

```
/* compute roots of a quadratic a * x * x + b * x + c   */
scanf("%d%d%d", &a, &b, &c);
discr = b * b - 4 * a * c;
if ((discr > 0) && (sq_disc = sqrt(discr))) {
    root1 = (-b + sq_disc) / (2 * a);
    root2 = (-b - sq_disc) / (2 * a);
}
else if (!discr) {
    /*   complex roots */
    . . .
}
else
    root1 = root2 = -b / (2 * a);
```

The `sqrt()` function would fail on negative values and short-circuit evaluation protects the program from this error. Complete this program by having it compute roots and print them out for the following values:

```
a = 1.0, b = 4.0, c = 3.0
a = 1.0, b = 2.0, c = 1.0
a = 1.0, b = 1.0, c = 1.0
a = 1.0, b = 1.0, c = 1.0
```

7. What will the following program print?

```
#include    <stdio.h>

main()
{
    char     c = 'A';
    int      i = 3, j = 1, k = -2, m = 0;
    enum boolean { false, true } p = false, q = true;

    printf("%c    %d\n", c, !c);
    printf("%d    %d\n", i, !i);
    printf("%d    %d    %d    %d\n", !!i, !j, !k, !m);
    printf("%d    %d\n", p, q);
    printf("%d    %d\n", !p, !q);
    printf("%d    %d\n", !(i + j) || m, !m && k);
    printf("%d    %d\n", q || (j / m), !m && k);
    printf("%d    %d\n", (j / m) || q,  k && !m);
}
```

8. The following Pascal program tests a simple conjecture on the integers:

```
program CheckConjecture (input, output);
    label 1, 2;
    var
        i, n : integer;
        A, SUMA, SUMASQ : array [1 .. 100] of real;
    begin
        writeln('PROGRAM CHECKCONJECTURE');
        write('How many values do you want to read in? (up to 100) ');
        read(n); {size of array n <= 100 for test}
        writeln('Read in values: ');
        for i := 1 to n do
            read(A[i]);
        SUMA[1] := A[1];
        SUMASQ[1] := A[1] * A[1];
        for i := 2 to n do
```

```
            begin
                SUMA[i] := A[i] + SUMA[i-1];
                SUMASQ[i] := A[i] * A[i] + SUMASQ[i-1];
                if SUMASQ[i] > SUMA[i] * SUMA[i]
                    then goto 1 {fail}
            end;
            writeln('Sum of (the values squared) =', SUMA[i] * SUMA[i]);
            writeln('(Sum of the values) squared =', SUMASQ[i]);
            writeln('conjecture true');
            goto 2 {finish};
            1 {fail} :
            writeln('Sum of (the values squared) =', SUMA[i] * SUMA[i]);
            writeln('(Sum of the values) squared =', SUMASQ[i]);
            writeln('conjecture false');
            2 {finish} :
    end.  {CheckConjecture}
```

Write this program in C, avoiding the use of goto statements. Several simple ways exist to avoid goto's in C. You might wish to add the test for failure to the head of the C for loop or you might use the break statement inside the for loop.

9. Redo exercise 8 by using a C function to test the conjecture.

```
    int check_conject(int a[], int n);
    /* returns 1 if the conjecture is true and 0 if false */
```

10. The following C program counts various characters found in a file. Write the program in file *count.c*. Compile the program and test it using redirection on the file *count.c*.

```
    /* Count blanks, digits, letters, newlines, and others. */

    #include    <stdio.h>

    main()
    {
        int    blank_cnt = 0, c, digit_cnt = 0,
               letter_cnt = 0, nl_cnt = 0, other_cnt = 0;
```

```
    while ((c = getchar()) != EOF)
       if (c == ' ')
          ++blank_cnt;
       else if (c >= '0' && c <= '9')
          ++digit_cnt;
       else if (c >= 'a' && c <= 'z' || c >= 'A' && c <= 'Z')
          ++letter_cnt;
       else if (c == '\n')
          ++nl_cnt;
       else
          ++other_cnt;

    printf("%10s%10s%10s%10s%10s%10s\n\n",
       "blanks", "digits", "letters", "lines", "others", "total");
    printf("%10d%10d%10d%10d%10d%10d\n\n",
       blank_cnt, digit_cnt, letter_cnt, nl_cnt, other_cnt,
       blank_cnt + digit_cnt + letter_cnt + nl_cnt + other_cnt);
}
```

The getchar() function reads in one character value from standard input. Note that on most systems the constant EOF has value −1. It is the system value read in when an end of file is encountered.

11. Change the above code to use a switch statement.

12. The switch statement, unlike the Pascal case statement, allows two or more cases to be executed for the same value by allowing the code to "fall through."

```
switch (i) {
case 0: case 1:
   ++hopeless;        /* fall through */
case 2: case 3:
   ++weak;
case 4: case 5:
   ++fails; break;
case 6: case 7:
   ++c_grades; break;
case 8:
   ++b_grades; break;
case 9:
   ++a_grades; break;
default:
   printf("incorrect grade  %d\n", i);
}
```

Hand simulate this statement for i equals 1. Write the equivalent Pascal case statement.

CHAPTER 2

C for Pascal Programmers: Functions and Complex Data

This chapter continues the discussion of the analogs between Pascal and C, focusing on functions and aggregate data. In C, the primary unit for structuring a program is the function. Aggregate data in C are either arrays or structures. In both cases, C uses a pointer type as a mechanism for accessing such data. These types are analogous to the Pascal array, record, and pointer. Key differences exist because the C pointer can be used in a more unrestricted way to store a machine address. As a consequence, C can be used more flexibly and efficiently than Pascal.

2.1. FUNCTIONS

A problem in C or Pascal is decomposed into small subproblems, which can be coded directly. This is the method of *stepwise refinement*. The function construct in C is used to write code for these directly solvable subproblems. These functions are combined into other functions and ultimately used in `main()` to solve the original problem. The function mechanism is provided in C to perform distinct programming tasks. Some functions, such as `printf()` and `scanf()`, are provided by the system. Others can be written by the programmer.

Function Invocation

A C program is made up of one or more functions, one of which is `main()`. Program execution always begins with `main()`. When program control encounters a function name, the function is called, or invoked. This means that program control passes to the function. After the function does its work, program control is passed back to the calling environment, which then continues with its work. As a simple example, consider the following program *ring*, which rings a bell:

```
/* ring my bell using '\007' ASCII for the bell. */

#include <stdio.h>
#define BELL '\007'

void ring()
{
    printf("%c%c%c", BELL, BELL, BELL);
}

main()
{
    ring();
}
```

Function Definition

The C code that describes what a function does is called the function definition. Its form is

function header
{
    declarations
    statements
}

The function header has two syntactic variations. There is an older form and a newer ANSI form. The older form is

type name(parameter list)
parameter declarations

The newer form is

type name(parameter declaration list)

Everything before the first brace comprises the *header* of the function definition, and everything between the braces comprises the *body* of the function definition. The ANSI form provides for stronger type checking than the earlier form and is considered the preferable style (see Section 4.6).

In the function definition for `ring()` above, the parameter list is empty, so there are no declarations of parameters. The body of the function consists of a `printf()` statement. Since the function does not return a value, the type of the function was `void`.

The *type* of a function depends on the type of the value that the function returns, if any. If an `int` value is returned, the type of the function can be omitted since `int` is implicit. The `return` mechanism is explained below.

Parameters are syntactically identifiers, and they can be used within the body of the function. Sometimes the parameters in a function definition are called *formal parameters* to emphasize their role as place holders for actual values that are passed to the function when it is called. Upon function invocation, the value of the argument corresponding to a formal parameter is used within the body of the executing function. Parameters in C are *call-by-value*. C++ provides a *call-by-reference* mechanism (see Section 4.7).

To illustrate these ideas, let us rewrite the above program so that `ring()` has a formal parameter. The parameter will be used to specify how many times the bell is rung.

```
/* Repeated bell ringing. */

#include <stdio.h>
#define BELL '\007'
```

```
void ring(int k)
{
    int    i;

    for (i = 0; i < k; ++i)
        printf("%c%c%c", BELL, BELL, BELL);
}

main()
{
    int    n;

    printf("Input a small positive integer:  ");
    scanf("%d", &n);
    ring(n);
}
```

The pre-ANSI style as used in traditional C was

```
void ring(k)
int    k;   /* old style */
{
      . . .
```

This style is considered archaic and need not be supported by a C++ compiler.

The return Statement

The return statement is used for two purposes. When a return statement is executed, program control is immediately passed back to the calling environment. In addition, if an expression follows the keyword return, then the value of the expression is returned to the calling environment as well. This value must agree in type with the function definition header. If no type is explicitly declared, the type is implicitly int. A return statement has one of the following two forms:

```
return;
return expression;
```

Some examples are

```
return (3);

return (a + b);
```

Although it is not necessary, it is considered good programming practice to enclose in parentheses the expression being returned so that it is more clearly visible.

As an example, let us write a program that computes the minimum of two integers.

```c
/* minimum finding. */

#include <stdio.h>

int min(int x, int y)
{
    if (x < y)
        return (x);
    else
        return (y);
}

main()
{
    int    j, k, m;

    printf("Input two integers:   ");
    scanf("%d%d", &j, &k);
    m = min(j, k);
    printf("\n%d is the minimum of %d and %d\n\n", m, j, k);
}
```

The equivalent Pascal program is

```pascal
program Minimum(input, output);
    var
        j, k, m : integer;

    function min(x, y : integer) : integer;
        begin
            if (x < y) then
                min := x
            else
                min := y
        end; {min}

    begin
        writeln('Input two integers:   ');
        read(j, k);
        m := min(j, k);
        writeln(m, ' is the minimum of ', j, ' and   ', k)
    end. {Minimum}
```

We have designed `min()` to work with integer values. Suppose instead that we want to work with values of type `double`. We will rewrite `min()` to use `double`.

```
double min(double x, double y)
{
    if (x < y)
        return (x);
    else
        return (y);
}
```

Function Prototypes

In the traditional style, a function can be used before it is defined. It can be defined later in the file or can come from a library or a user-specified file. In traditional style, the type and number of arguments of a function can be unknown. This leads to error-prone code (see exercise 10).

A function prototype (see Section 4.6) remedies this by providing the type and number of arguments explicitly. It has the following general form:

type name(argument-declaration-list);

The *argument-declaration-list* is typically a comma-separated list of types. If a function has no parameters, then the keyword `void` may be used. In C++, the preferred style for an empty parameter list is *function_name()*. This list can include the argument identifiers. This information allows the compiler to enforce type compatibility. Arguments are converted to these types as if they were following rules of assignment.

In the following, we recode `main()` taken from the program *ring* to introduce the function prototype for `ring()`:

```
main()
{
    int     n;
    void    ring(int);

    printf("Input a small positive integer:   ");
    scanf("%d", &n);
    ring(n);
}
```

The declaration of the function prototype informs the compiler that `ring()` must be used with a single integer argument, and that it does not return a value when called.

In the last section, we used in the *minimum* program the function `min()`. Its prototype in `main()` would be

```
int min(int, int);
```

Both the function type and the argument list types are explicitly mentioned. The definition of `min()` that occurs in the file must match this declaration. The function prototype can also include the identifier names of the arguments. In the case of `min()` this would be

```
int min(int x, int y);
```

2.2. DERIVED TYPES

C and Pascal both have arrays and records as derived types. In C terminology, a record is a *structure* and its fields are called *members*. C and Pascal both use pointers to reference structures and records, respectively. However, C makes much more extensive use of pointers. C pointers are used to reference simple variables and machine addresses. They are intimately tied to array and string processing. And finally, they give to standard C the equivalent of Pascal's variable parameters.

Pointers

Pointers are used in programs to access memory and manipulate addresses. We have already seen the use of addresses as arguments to `scanf()`. A function call such as `scanf("%d", &v)` causes an appropriate value to be stored at a particular address in memory.

If `v` is a variable, then `&v` is the address, or location, in memory of its stored value. The address operator `&` is unary and has the same precedence and right to left associativity as the other unary operators. Pointer variables can be declared in programs and then used to take addresses as values. The declaration

```
int    *p;
```

declares p to be of type "pointer to int." The legal range of values for any pointer always includes the special address 0, also defined as NULL in <stdio.h>, and a set of positive integers that are interpreted as machine addresses on a particular C system. Some examples of assignment to the pointer p are

```
p = &i;
p = NULL;              /* equivalent to  p = 0; */
p = (int *) 1507;      /* an absolute address in memory */
```

In the first example, we think of p as "referring to i" or "pointing to i" or "containing the address of i." The compiler decides what address to assign the variable i. This will vary from machine to machine and may even be different for different executions on the same machine. The second example is the assignment of the special value 0 to the pointer p. This value is typically used to indicate the end of a pointer chain. In the third example, the cast is necessary to avoid a compiler warning. In this example an actual memory address is used.

Addressing and Dereferencing

We have already seen that addresses are passed as arguments to scanf(). We want to show how a pointer can be used instead. Suppose we declare

```
int    i, *p;
```

Then the statements

```
p = &i;
scanf("%d", p);
```

cause the next value from the standard input stream to be stored at p. But since p points to i, this is equivalent to storing the value at the address of i.

The dereferencing or indirection operator * is unary and has the same precedence and right to left associativity as the other unary operators. If p is a pointer, then *p is the value of the variable that p points to. The direct value of p is a memory location, whereas *p is the indirect value of p, namely the value at the memory location stored in p. In a certain sense, * is the inverse operator to &.

Call-by-Reference

Whenever variables are passed as arguments to a function, their values are copied to the corresponding function parameters, and the variables themselves are not changed in the calling environment. This call-by-value mechanism is strictly adhered to in C. In this section, we describe how the *addresses* of variables can be used as arguments to functions so the stored values of the variables can be modified in the calling environment.

For a function to effect call-by-reference, pointers must be used in the parameter list in the function definition. Then, when the function is called, addresses of variables must be passed as arguments. As an example of this, let us write a simple program that orders the values of two variables.

```
main()
{
    int    i = 7, j = 3;
    void   order(int*, int*);

    printf("%d  %d\n", i, j);      /* 7   3 is printed */
    order(&i, &j);
    printf("%d  %d\n", i, j);      /* 3   7 is printed */
}
```

Most of the work of this program is carried out by the function call to order(). Notice that the addresses of i and j are passed as arguments. As we shall see, this allows the function call to change the values of i and j in the calling environment.

```
void order(int *p, int *q)
{
    int    temp;

    if (*p > *q) {
        temp = *p;
        *p = *q;
        *q = temp;
    }
}
```

■ DISSECTION OF THE order () FUNCTION

```
void order(int *p, int *q)
{
    int    temp;
```

- The parameters p and q are both of type pointer to int. The variable temp is local to this function and is of type int.

```
if (*p > *q) {
    temp = *p;
    *p = *q;
    *q = temp;
}
```

- If the value of what is pointed to by p is greater than the value of what is pointed to by q, then the following is done. First, temp is assigned the value of what is pointed to by p; second, what is pointed to by p is assigned the value of what is pointed to by q; and third, what is pointed to by q is assigned the value of temp. This has the effect of interchanging in the calling environment the stored values of whatever p and q are pointing to.

■

Call-by-reference is accomplished by
1. declaring a function parameter to be a pointer
2. using the dereferenced pointer in the function body
3. passing an address as an argument when the function is called

C++ introduces reference declarations (see Section 4.7). These declarations can be used for call-by-reference arguments. This feature is **not** available in standard C. However, the feature is similar to Pascal variable parameters, and thus it allows the Pascal programmer a simpler transition to coding C functions.

The function `order()` using this mechanism is recoded as:

```
void order(int &p, int &q)
{
    int    temp;

    if (p > q) {
        temp = p;
        p = q;
        q = temp;
    }
}
```

is equivalent to

```
procedure order(var p, q : integer);
    var temp : integer;
begin
    if (p > q) then
        begin
            temp := p;
            p := q;
            q := temp
        end
end; {order}
```

It would be prototyped and invoked in `main()` as follows:

```
main()
{
    void   order(int&, int&);
    . . .
    order(i, j);
    . . .
}
```

Arrays and Pointers

Arrays are a data type that is used to represent a large number of homogeneous values. The elements of an array are accessed by the use of subscripts. Arrays of all types are possible, including arrays of arrays. Strings are just arrays of characters. A typical array declaration allocates memory starting from a base address. In C, an array name is in effect a pointer constant to this base address.

To illustrate some of these ideas, let us write a small program that fills an array, prints out values, and sums the elements of the array.

```
#include <stdio.h>
#define    SIZE    5

main()
{
    int    a[SIZE];         /* space for a[0], ..., a[4] is allocated *
    int    i, sum = 0;

    for (i = 0; i < SIZE; ++i){
        a[i] = i * i;
        printf("a[%d] = %d      ", i, a[i]);
        sum += a[i];
    }
    printf("\nsum = %d\n", sum);
}
```

The output of this program is

```
a[0] = 0     a[1] = 1     a[2] = 4     a[3] = 9     a[4] = 16
sum = 30
```

This array required memory to store five integer values. Thus, if a[0] is stored at location 1000, then on a system needing four bytes for an int, the remaining array elements are successively stored at locations 1004, 1008, 1012, and 1016. It is considered good programming practice to define the size of an array as a symbolic constant. Since much of the code may depend on this value, it is convenient to be able to change a single #define line to process different size arrays. Notice how the various parts of the for statement are neatly tailored to provide a terse notation for dealing with array computations.

The equivalent Pascal program is

```
program arrayPrint(input, output);
    const
        UB = 4;
    var
        i, sum : integer;
        a : array[0 .. UB] of integer;
```

```
    begin
       sum := 0;
       for i := 0 to UB do
          begin
             a[i] := i * i;
             write('a[', i:1, '] = ', a[i]:2, '   ');
             sum := sum + a[i]
          end;
       writeln;
       writeln('sum = ', sum:3)
end. {arrayPrint}
```

Subscripting

Assume that a declaration of the form

```
int i, a[size];
```

has been made. Then we can write a[i] to access an element of the array. More generally, we may write a[expr], where *expr* is an integral expression, to access an element of the array. We call *expr* a subscript, or index, of a. The value of a C subscript should lie in the range 0 to *size* − 1. An array subscript value outside this range often causes a run-time error. When this happens, the condition is called "overrunning the bounds of the array" or "subscript out of bounds." It is a common programming error. The effect of the error in a C program is system-dependent and can be quite confusing. One frequent result is that the value of some unrelated variable will be returned or modified. Thus the programmer must ensure that all subscripts stay within bounds.

The Relationship Between Arrays and Pointers

An array name by itself is an address, or pointer value, and pointers and arrays are almost identical in terms of how they are used to access memory. However, there are differences, and these differences are subtle and important. A pointer is a variable that takes addresses as values. An array name is a particular fixed address that can be thought of as a constant pointer. When an array is declared, the compiler must allocate a base address and a sufficient amount of storage to contain all the elements of the array. The base address of the array is the initial location in memory where the array is stored; it is the address of the first element (index 0) of the array. Suppose that we write the declaration

```
#define    N    100

long    a[N],  *p;
```

and that the system causes memory bytes numbered 300, 304, 308, . . . , 696 to be the addresses of a[0], a[1], a[2], . . . , a[99], respectively, with location 300 being the base address of a. We are assuming that each byte is addressable and that four bytes are used to store a long. The two statements

```
p = a;      and      p = &a[0];
```

are equivalent and would assign 300 to p. Pointer arithmetic provides an alternative to array indexing. The two statements

```
p = a + 1;      and      p = &a[1];
```

are equivalent and would assign 304 to p. Assuming that the elements of a have been assigned values, we can use the following code to sum the array:

```
sum = 0;
for (p = a; p < &a[N];  ++p)
    sum += *p;
```

In this loop, the pointer variable p is initialized to the base address of the array a. Then the successive values of p are equivalent to &a[0], &a[1], ..., &a[N 1]. In general, if i is a variable of type int, then p + i is the ith offset from the address p. In a similar manner, a + i is the ith offset from the base address of the array a. Here is another way of summing the array:

```
sum = 0;
for (i = 0;  i < N;  ++i)
    sum += *(a + i);
```

Just as the expression *(a + i) is equivalent to a[i], so is the expression *(p + i) equivalent to p[i]. Although it is obscure and poor practice, the expression i[a] is legal and is equivalent to a[i].

In many ways arrays and pointers can be treated alike, but there is one essential difference. Because the array a is a constant pointer and not a variable, expressions such as

```
a = p          ++a          a += 2
```

are illegal. We cannot change the address of a.

Passing Arrays to Functions

In a function definition, a formal parameter that is declared as an array is actually a pointer. When an array is being passed, its base address is passed call-by-value. The array elements themselves are not copied. As a notational convenience, the compiler allows array bracket notation to be used in declaring pointers as parameters. This notation reminds the programmer and other readers of the code that the function should be called with an array. To illustrate this, we write a function that sums the elements of an array of type int.

```
int sum(int a[], int n)      /* n is the size of a[] */
{
   int    i, s = 0;

   for(i = 0; i < n; ++i)
      s += a[i];
   return(s);
}
```

As part of the header of a function definition the declaration

```
int a[];
```
is equivalent to
```
int *a;
```

However, as declarations within the body of a function, they are *not* equivalent. The first will create a constant pointer (and no storage), whereas the second will create a pointer variable.

Suppose that v has been declared to be an array with 100 elements of type int. After the elements have been assigned values, we can use the above function sum() to add various of the elements of v. The following table illustrates some of the possibilities.

Various ways that sum() might be called	
Invocation	What gets computed and returned
sum(v, 100)	v[0] + v[1] + ⋯ + v[99]
sum(v, 88)	v[0] + v[1] + ⋯ + v[87]
sum(v + 7, k)	v[7] + v[8] + ⋯ + v[k+6]

The last function call illustrates again the use of pointer arithmetic. The base address of v is offset by 7, and sum() initializes the local pointer variable a to this address. This causes all address calculations inside the function call to be similarly offset.

In C, a function with a formal array parameter can be called with an actual array argument of any size provided the array has the right base type. This is **not** possible in Pascal. Pascal treats array as a type defined in part by its bounds. Therefore, arrays of different bounds must be treated as different types.

Multidimensional Arrays

The C language allows arrays of any type, including arrays of arrays. With two bracket pairs we obtain a two-dimensional array. This idea can be iterated to obtain arrays of higher dimension. With each bracket pair we add another array dimension.

Examples of declarations of arrays	Remarks
int a[100];	a one-dimensional array
int b[3] [5];	a two-dimensional array
int c[7] [9] [2];	a three-dimensional array

A k-dimensional array has a size for each of its k dimensions. If we let s_i represent the size of its ith dimension, then the declaration of the array will allocate space for $s_1 \times s_2 \times \cdots \times s_k$ elements. In the above table, b has 3×5 elements, and c has $7 \times 9 \times 2$ elements. Starting at the base address of the array, all the array elements are stored contiguously in memory.

The Aggregate Type `struct`

In analogy to the Pascal type `record`, C has the aggregate type `struct`. In Chapter 5, we review the C type `struct` and show how it is extended to the C++ type `class`. We will not repeat this treatment here, but will show how `struct` in traditional C can be used to define a singly linked list.

2.3. AN EXAMPLE: LINKED LIST

In this section, we define structures with pointer members that refer to the structure type containing them. These are called *self-referential* structures. Self-referential structures often require storage management routines to explicitly obtain and release memory.

Let us define a structure with a member field that points at the same structure type. We wish to do this in order to have an unspecified number of such structures linked together.

```
struct list {
    char        data;
    struct list *next;
};
```

   is equivalent to

```
type
    listPointer = ^list;
    list = record
                data : char;
                next : listPointer
            end;
```

Each variable of type `struct list` has two members `data` and `next`. The pointer variable `next` is called a *link*. Each structure is linked to a succeeding structure by way of the member `next`.

The pointer variable `next` contains an address of either the location in memory of the successor `struct list` element or the special value NULL, which is usually defined in *stdio.h* as a symbolic constant with value 0.

The Use of typedef

C provides a number of fundamental types, such as char and int, and other types that are derived from these, such as arrays, pointers, and structures. In addition, the language provides the typedef facility, which allows a type to be explicitly associated with an identifier. An example of this is

```
typedef    char    DATA;
```

The identifier DATA can now be used to declare variables and functions in the same way that ordinary types are used. For example,

```
DATA    a, b, c;
```

declares the variables a, b, and c to be of type DATA, which is equivalent to char.

Notice that although DATA is simply the type char, conceptually it could be a more complicated type, such as an array or a structure.

A *linear linked list* is like a clothesline on which the data structures hang sequentially. A head pointer addresses the first element of the list, and each element points at a successor element, with the last element having a link value NULL. Typically, a linked list is created dynamically. In this section, we will show how this is done. Also, we will show how the typedef facility can be used to create a new name for a type. In practice, the typedef facility is often used to rename a structure type.

Let us begin by creating a header file that will be included with the list processing functions that we will write in the sections that follow. This header file includes the file *stdio.h* because that is where NULL is defined.

In file list.h:

```
#include    <stdio.h>
#include    <stdlib.h>    /* has malloc() and free() prototypes */

typedef    char    DATA;      /* we will use char in examples */

struct linked_list {
   DATA                    d;
   struct linked_list    *next;
};

typedef    struct linked_list    ELEMENT;
typedef    ELEMENT *              LINK;
```

Dynamic Storage Allocation

The declaration of `struct linked_list` in *list.h* does not allocate storage. It acts as a template for the storage that the system will allocate later when variables and arrays of this type are declared. We used the `typedef` facility to rename the type as ELEMENT, because we wish to think of it as an element in our list. What makes self-referential structure types such as ELEMENT especially useful is that utility functions exist to allocate storage dynamically. The function `malloc()` is provided in the standard library and prototyped in *list.h*. A function call of the form

```
malloc(size)
```

returns a pointer to enough storage for an object of *size* bytes. The function `malloc()` takes a single argument of type `unsigned` and returns a pointer to `void` that points to the base address of the storage allocated by the function. A value of type pointer to `void` is used because it matches any other pointer type. If `head` is a variable of type LINK, then

```
head = (LINK) malloc(sizeof(ELEMENT));
```

obtains a piece of memory from the system adequate to store an ELEMENT and assigns its base address to the pointer `head`. As in the above example, a function call to `malloc()` is often used with a cast and the `sizeof` operator. Without the cast, a nonportability warning would occur. The cast guarantees a correct conversion of the generic pointer value returned by `malloc`. The `sizeof` operator calculates the required number of bytes for the particular data structure.

In Pascal, free store is obtained using the `new()` procedure. The argument to `new()` is a pointer. An appropriate amount of memory is allocated from the free store. In C++, the `malloc()` function can be replaced with the C++ operator `new` (see Section 4.10). The following Pascal code allocates a list:

```
{ ABC Linked List}

program List(input, output);

type
    listPointer = ^list;
    list = record
                data : char;
                next : listPointer
            end;

  var
    a, p : listPointer;
```

```pascal
begin
   new(p);
   a := p;
   p^.data := 'A';
   new(p^.next);
   p := p^.next;
   p^.data := 'B';
   new(p^.next);
   p := p^.next;
   p^.data := 'C';
   p^.next := nil;
   p := a;
   while (p <> nil) do
      begin
         write('-->  ', p^.data);
         p := p^.next
      end;
      writeln('-->  NIL');
end. {List}
```

The output of this program is

```
-->  A-->  B-->  C-->  NIL
```

The equivalent C program using the definitions in *list.h* is

```c
/*  ABC Linked List */

#include "list.h"

main()
{
   LINK a, p;

   p = (LINK) malloc(sizeof(ELEMENT));
   a = p;
   p -> d = 'A';       /* equivalent is (*p).d = 'A'; */
   p -> next = (LINK) malloc(sizeof(ELEMENT));
   p = p -> next;
   p -> d = 'B';
   p -> next = (LINK) malloc(sizeof(ELEMENT));
   p = p -> next;
   p -> d = 'C';
   p -> next = NULL;
   p = a;
   while (p) {
         printf("-->  %c", p -> d);
         p = p -> next;
   }
   printf("-->  NIL");
}
```

The C program uses the arrow for a structure pointer operator (see Section 5.2). The Pascal notation *pointer`.record field* is equivalent to the C notation *pointer->member_name* or the C notation (* *pointer*). *member_name*.

List Operations

Some of the basic operations on linear linked lists include:

1. creating a list
2. counting the elements
3. looking up an element
4. inserting an element
5. deleting an element

We will demonstrate the techniques for programming such operations on lists. The use of recursive functions is natural, since lists are a recursively defined construct. Each routine will require the specifications in the header file *list.h*. Observe that d in these examples could be redefined as a more complicated data structure.

As a first example we will write a function that will produce a list from a string. The function will return a pointer to the head of the resulting list. The heart of the function creates a list element by allocating storage and assigning member values.

```
/* List creation by recursion. */

#include    "list.h"

LINK string_to_list(char s[])
{
    LINK    head;

    if (s[0] == '\0')      /* base case */
        return (NULL);
    else {
        head = (LINK) malloc(sizeof(ELEMENT));
        head -> d = s[0];
        head -> next = string_to_list(s + 1);
        return (head);
    }
}
```

■ DISSECTION OF THE string_to_list() FUNCTION

```
LINK string_to_list(char s[])
{
    LINK    head;
```

● When a string is passed as an argument, a linked list of the characters in the string is created. Since a pointer to the head of the list will be returned, the type specifier in the header to this function definition is LINK.

```
if (s[0] == '\0')      /* base case */
    return (NULL);
```

● When the end-of-string sentinel is detected, NULL is returned, and, as we will see, the recursion terminates. The value NULL is used to mark the end of the linked list.

```
else {
    head = (LINK) malloc(sizeof(ELEMENT));
```

● If the string s[ ] is not the null string, then malloc() is used to retrieve enough bytes to store an object of type ELEMENT. The cast is necessary to avoid a warning in the assignment. The pointer variable `head` now points at the block of storage provided by `malloc()`.

```
head -> d = s[0]
```

- The member `d` of the allocated ELEMENT is assigned the first character in the string `s[]`.

```
head -> next = string_to_list(s + 1);
```

- The pointer expression `s + 1` points to the remainder of the string. The function is called recursively with `s + 1` as an argument. The pointer member `next` is assigned the pointer value that is returned by `string_to_list(s + 1)`. This recursive call returns as its value a LINK, or, equivalently, a pointer to ELEMENT, that points to the remaining sublist.

```
return (head);
```

- The function exits with the address of the head of the list.

Counting and Lookup

In this section, we will write two more recursive functions that perform list operations. The first function is `count()`. It can be used to count the elements in a list. It involves moving recursively down the list and terminating when the NULL pointer is found. If the list is empty, the value 0 is returned; otherwise the number of elements in the list is returned.

```
/* Count a list recursively. */

#include    "list.h"

int count(LINK head)
{
    if (head == NULL)
        return (0);
    else
        return (1 + count(head -> next));
}
```

The next function searches a list for a particular element. If the element is found, a pointer to that element is returned; otherwise the NULL pointer is returned.

```
/* Lookup c in the list pointed to by head. */

#include    "list.h"

LINK lookup (DATA c, LINK head)
{
    if (head == NULL)
        return (NULL);
    else if (c == head -> d)
        return (head);
    else
        return (lookup (c, head -> next));
}
```

2.4. KEY DIFFERENCES

C allows a program to be multifile. It uses a preprocessor and separate compilation techniques to manage large programs. Conventionally, Pascal is monolithic.

C uses pointers in many contexts. For example, pointers can be used as an array access method; they can provide a form of call-by-reference; and they can access absolute addresses.

C does not bind array types to their array bounds. General generic array routines can readily be written in C.

C does not have built-in I/O but uses standard libraries. Besides *stdio.h*, there are standard libraries supporting key applications such as string handling, file I/O, complex arithmetic, exception handling, graphics, sorting, and many others.

C has automatic, static, external, and register storage classes. The default for variables declared inside a block is automatic. This is similar to Pascal variables. The keyword static when used in a declaration means that a variable retains its value even when it is out of scope. Upon reentering a block in which a static variable is declared, its last value is retained (see exercise 11). The keyword register when used in a declaration means that a variable is automatic and is to be stored in a high speed register, if possible. All functions are external or global. They may not be nested as in Pascal. Variables declared outside of functions have external scope. The keyword `extern` when used in a declaration means that a variable is defined in an external context. Finally, it is possible to declare global identifiers as `static`. This creates a form of file privacy and restricts the use of that identifier to the file in which it is found. The same identifier in another file can be declared independently of any static external declarations.

C allows initialization of variables within their declarations. For example,

```
int  i = 5;   /* i is initially 5 */
int  a[3] = { 5, 6, -9}; /* a[0] = 5, a[1] = 6, a[2] = -9 */
struct int_char{ int j; char c} iandc = { 90, 'Z'};
```

For aggregate types, a comma-separated set of values enclosed in braces is used.

C is operator-oriented. There are large numbers of operators and many levels of precedence. For example, in C, assignment and array indexing are operators.

Despite the many differences, it is fairly easy to translate Pascal code into C (C to Pascal can be much harder). C++ extends C in ways that make it much more powerful than either language. C++ by allowing general type extensibility allows an even easier translation from Pascal code.

2.5. Summary

1. The C code that describes what a function does is called the function definition. Its form is

   function header
   {
       declarations
       statements
   }

   Whenever variables are passed as arguments to a function, their values are copied to the corresponding function parameters, and the variables themselves are not changed in the calling environment. This call-by-value mechanism is strictly adhered to in C. For a function to effect call-by-reference, pointers must be used in the parameter list in the function definition. Then, when the function is called, addresses of variables must be passed as arguments.

2. In traditional C, a function can be used before it is defined. It can be defined later in the file or can come from a library or a user-specified file. In traditional style, the type and number of arguments of a function can be unknown. A function prototype remedies this by providing the type and number of arguments explicitly. It has the following general form:

   type name(argument-declaration-list);

   The *argument-declaration-list* is typically a comma-separated list of types. This list can include the argument identifiers. The information allows the compiler to enforce type compatibility.

3. Pointer variables can be declared in programs and then used to take addresses as values. The declaration

   ```
   int    *p;
   ```

   declares p to be of type "pointer to int." The legal range of values for any pointer always includes the special address 0, also defined as NULL in <stdio.h>.

4. Arrays are a data type that is used to represent a large number of homogeneous values. The elements of an array are accessed by the use of subscripts. Arrays of all types are possible, including arrays of arrays. Strings are just arrays of characters. Conventionally, strings are terminated with the character value '\0'. A typical array declaration allocates memory starting from a base address. In C, an array name is in effect a pointer constant to this base address.

5. In analogy to the Pascal type record, C has the aggregate type struct. In Chapter 5, we review the C type struct and show how it is extended to the C++ type class. Structures with pointer members that refer to the structure type containing them are called *self-referential* structures.

2.6. Exercises

1. The following Pascal code computes a Boolean truth table:

```
{ Print a table of values for some boolean functions. }

program Bool(output);
    var
        b : array [1 .. 5] of boolean;
        cnt : integer;

    begin
        writeln;
        writeln('Count    b1    b2    b3    b4    b5    f1    f2    maj')
        writeln;

        for cnt := 1 to 32 do
            begin
                b[1] := (cnt mod 2 = 0);
                b[2] := ((cnt div 2) mod 2 = 0);
                b[3] := ((cnt div 4) mod 2 = 0);
                b[4] := ((cnt div 8) mod 2 = 0);
                b[5] := ((cnt div 16) mod 2 = 0);
                writeln( cnt:6, b[1]:6, b[2]:6, b[3]:6,
                    b[4]:6, b[5]:6,
                    b[1] or b[3] or b[5]:6,
                    b[1] and b[2] or b[4] and b[5]:6,
                    ord(b[1]) + ord(b[2]) + ord(b[3]) + ord(b[4])
                        + ord(b[5]) >= 3)
            end;
        writeln
    end. {Bool}
```

Recode into C.

2. C strings are by convention terminated with the value 0. The following function implements a string equality test. Note its use of pointer arithmetic. The construct *s1++ means dereference the pointer s1, and after using this value in the expression, add 1 to its pointer value.

```
int streq(char* s1, char* s2)
{
    while ( *s1 != 0 && *s2 != 0)
        if ( *s1++ != *s2++)
            return(0);
    if (*s1 == *s2)
        return(1);
    else
        return(0);
}
```

Write and test a function

```
int strneq(char* s1, char* s2, int n);
```

that returns 1 if the first n characters of the two strings are the same and otherwise returns 0.

3. Reimplement the above functions using array notation.

```
int streq(char s1[], char s2[])
{
    int    i = 0;
    while ( s1[i] != 0 && s2[i] != 0)
        if ( s1[i++] != s2[i])
            . . .
}
```

4. The standard header file *string.h* contains the prototypes for a number of useful string functions found in the standard library. Among them is

```
int strlen(char* s);
```

which returns the length of a string. Write this function as a recursion.

5. Code the `string_to_list()` function as an iterative loop.

6. Write a C function to insert an element into an ordered list.

7. Write a C function to delete an element from a list.

8. The following is Pascal for a recursive greatest common divisor function:

```
function Gcd (m, n : integer) : integer;
   var
      r : integer;   {remainder}
begin
   r := m mod n;
   if r = 0 then
      Gcd := m
   else
      Gcd := Gcd(r, m)
end; {Gcd}
```

Rewrite this as a C function.

9. In the Pascal function for Gcd, we wish to count the number of times function call is used. We can modify the program using a global variable fcnCalls as follows:

```
function Gcd (m, n : integer) : integer;
   var
      r : integer;   {remainder}
begin
   fcnCalls := fcnCalls + 1;
   r := m mod n;
   if r = 0 then
      begin
         writeln('No. of calls = ', fcnCalls);
         Gcd := m
      end
   else
      Gcd := Gcd(r, m)
end; {Gcd}
```

It is generally bad practice to use globals inside functions. In C++, we can use a local static variable instead of a global.

```
int gcd(int m, int n)
{
    static int fcn_calls = 1;   //happens once
    int r;

    fcn_calls++;
    r = m % n;
    . . .
}
```

Complete and test this C++ version.

10. The following C program uses traditional C function style:

```
/* Compute a table of cubes. */

#define  N     15
#define  MAX   3.5

main()
{
    int     i;
    double  x, cube();

    printf("\n\nINTEGERS\n");
    for (i = 1; i <= N; ++i)
        printf("cube(%d) = %d\n", i, cube(i));
    printf("\n\nREALS\n");
    for (x = 1; x <= MAX; x += 0.3)
        printf("cube(%f) = %f\n", x, cube(x));
}

double cube(x)
double  x;
{
    return(x * x * x);
}
```

It gives the wrong answers for the integer arguments, and it does so because integer arguments are passed as if their bit representation were double. It is unacceptable as C++ code. Recode as a proper function prototype and run using a C++ or ANSI C compiler. These compilers enforce type compatibility on function argument values. Therefore the integer values are properly promoted to double values. Pascal programmers are unfamiliar with this type of pitfall since it has always been a strongly typed language.

11. Pascal has no equivalent to the C static storage class. Predict what the following program prints:

```
#include <stdio.h>

int foo(int n)
{
    static  int  ct = 0;
    ++ct;
    if ( n <= 1){
        printf("%d\n", ct);
        return(n);
    }
    else
        foo(n / 3);
}

main()
{
    foo(21);
    foo(27);
    foo(243);
}
```

What would be printed if the declaration of ct were changed to

```
register  ct = 0;
```

12. Pascal has no equivalent to the C static extern storage class. This storage class is useful in multifile compilation. Predict what the following program prints:

```
/*  file A.c  */

static int foo(int i)
{
    return(i * 3);
}

int  goo(int i)
{
    return( i * foo(i));
}


/*  file B.c */
#include <stdio.h>

int foo(int i)
{
    return(i * 5);
}

int  goo(int i);  /* imported from file A.c */
```

```
main ()
{
    printf ("foo (%d)  =  %d\n",  5,  foo (5));
    printf ("goo (%d)  =  %d\n",  5,  goo (5));
}
```

The program is compiled as follows: *CC A.c B.c.*
A function is always extern. The foo() in file *A.c* is private to that
file, but goo() is not. Thus redefining foo() in file *B.c* does not
cause an error. Try this again, this time dropping static, to see what
error message your compiler gives.

13. C has a string library *string.h*. Among the functions found there is
a function for computing string length.

```
// iterative string length
int strlen (char *s)
{
    int len = 0;

    while (*s != '\0') { // string terminator
        ++len;      // increment length
        ++s;        // advance pointer
    }
    return (len);
}
```

This algorithm marches the pointer s down the string looking
for the termination character. External to the function, the
pointer value has not been changed because it is called by
value. Write a recursive version of this function.

14. C provides a method to pass command line arguments into the function main(). The following code prints its command line arguments:

```
// Print command line arguments rightmost first.
#include <stdio.h>

main (int argc, char **argv)
{
    for (  ; argc >= 0; --argc)
        printf ("%s\n", argv [argc]);
}
```

Compile this into an executable called *echo*. Run it with the following command line arguments:

echo She is nearly He

The argument `argc` is passed the number of command line arguments. Each argument is a string placed in the two-dimensional array `argv`.

15. Modify the previous program to print the command line arguments from left to right, and to number each of them.

CHAPTER 3

An Overview of C++ and Object-Oriented Programming

This chapter gives an overview of the C++ programming language. It also provides an introduction to C++'s use as an object-oriented programming language. In the chapter, a series of programs is presented, and the elements of each program are carefully explained. The programs increase in complexity, and the examples in the later sections illustrate some of the concepts of object-oriented programming. This approach should give the student a sense of how the language works.

Each feature of C++ is explained briefly. Later chapters will explain each new concept in detail. The examples in this chapter give simple, immediate hands-on experience with key features of the C++ language. The chapter introduces the reader to stream I/O, operator and function overloading, reference parameters, classes, constructors, destructors, and inheritance.

Object-oriented programming is implemented in the class construct. The class construct in C++ is an extension of struct in C. The Pascal record is similar to the C struct. C++, like Pascal, is a strongly typed language. It improves on Pascal by having better modularity constructs, and by having user-type extensibility that goes beyond Pascal type declarations. The later examples in this chapter illustrate how C++ implements OOP concepts, such as data hiding, ADTs, inheritance, and type hierarchies.

3.1. OUTPUT

Programs must communicate to be useful. Our first example is a program that prints on the screen the phrase "C++ is an improved C." The complete program is

```
//A first C++ program illustrating output.

#include <stream.h>

main()
{
    cout << "C++ is an improved C.\n";
}
```

The program prints on the screen

```
C++ is an improved C.
```

■ DISSECTION OF THE *advert* PROGRAM

```
//A first C++ program illustrating output.
```

- The double slash // is a new comment symbol. The comment runs to the end of the line. The old C bracketing comment symbols /* */ are still available for multiline comments.

```
#include <stream.h>
```

- The *stream.h* header introduces I/O facilities for C++.

```
cout << "C++ is an improved C.\n";
```

- This statement prints to the screen. The identifier `cout` is the name of the standard output stream. The operator `<<` passes the string `"C++ is an improved C.\n"` to standard out. Used in this way the *output operator* `<<` is referred to as the *put to* or *insertion* operator.

■
_____

We can rewrite our first program as follows:

```
//A first C++ program illustrating output.

#include <stream.h>

main()
{
    cout << "C++ is an improved C." << "\n";
}
```

Although it is different from the first version, it produces the same output. Each time the `<<` is used with `cout`, printing continues from the position where it previously left off. In this case the newline character is output after a second use of the put to operator.

3.2. INPUT

We will write a program to convert to kilometers the distance in miles from the earth to the moon. In miles this distance is, on average, 238,857 miles. This number is an integer. To convert miles to kilometers, we multiply by the conversion factor 1.609, a real number.

Our conversion program will use variables capable of storing integer values and real values. In C++, all variables must be declared before their use, but unlike in C, they need not be at the head of a block. Declarations may be mixed in with executable statements. Their scope, however, is still the block within which they are declared. Identifiers should be chosen to reflect their use in the program. In this way, they serve as documentation, making the program more readable.

```
//The distance to the moon converted to kilometers.

#include <stream.h>

main()
{
    const int moon = 238857;
    cout << "The moon's distance from Earth is " << moon;
    cout << " miles.\n";

    int moon_kilo;
    moon_kilo = moon * 1.609;
    cout << "In kilometers this is " << moon_kilo;
    cout << " km.\n";
}
```

The output of the program is

```
The moon's distance from Earth is 238857 miles.
In kilometers this is 384320 km.
```

These programs assume a 4-byte int, but on some machines these integer types should be declared long.

■ DISSECTION OF THE *moon* PROGRAM

```
const int moon = 238857;
```

- The keyword const is new in C++. It replaces some uses of the preprocessor command define to create named literals. Using this type modifier informs the compiler that the initialized value of moon cannot be changed.

```
cout << "The moon's distance from Earth is " << moon;
```

- The stream I/O in C++ can discriminate among a variety of simple values without needing additional formatting information. Here the value of moon will be printed as an integer.

```
int moon_kilo;
moon_kilo = moon * 1.609;
```

- Declarations can occur after executable statements. This allows declarations of variables to be nearer to their use.

Let us write a program that will convert a series of values from miles to kilometers. The program will be interactive. The user will type in a value in miles, and the program will convert this value to kilometers and print it out.

```
//Miles are converted to kilometers.

#include <stream.h>
const float m_to_k = 1.609;
inline int convert(int mi) { return (mi * m_to_k); }

main()
{
    int miles;

    do {
        cout << "Input distance in miles: ";
        cin >> miles;
        cout << "\nDistance is " << convert(miles) << " km.\n";
    } while (miles > 0);
}
```

This program uses the input stream variable cin, which is normally standard input. The *input operator* >> is called the *get from* or *extraction* operator; it assigns values from the input stream to a variable. This program illustrates both input and output.

■ DISSECTION OF THE *mi_km* PROGRAM

```
const float m_to_k = 1.609;
inline int convert(int mi) { return (mi * m_to_k); }
```

- C++ reduces C's traditional reliance on the preprocessor. For example, instead of having to use define, special constants, such as the conversion factor 1.609, are simply assigned to variables specified as constants. The new keyword inline specifies that a function is to be compiled, if possible as a macro. As a rule, inline should be done sparingly and only on short functions. Also note how the parameter mi is declared within the function parentheses. C++ uses *function prototypes* to define and declare functions. This will be explained in the next section.

```
do {
    cout << "Input distance in miles: ";
    cin >> miles;
    cout << "\nDistance is " << convert(miles) << " km.\n";
} while (miles > 0);
```

- The program repeatedly prompts the user for a distance in miles. The program is terminated by a zero or negative value. The value placed in the standard input stream is automatically converted to an integer value assigned to miles.

■

Pascal uses built-in functions read() and write() for basic I/O. C++ uses libraries. This is a more powerful and flexible approach. Libraries are readily customized to new machines and easily extended to new applications. Some C++ users will use the C header file *stdio.h*, which contains printf() and scanf(). Our text will use the C++ header file *stream.h*, which overloads the operators << and >> to act as I/O functions. We shall also use (in exercises) the C++ header file *iostream.h*, which extends the stream I/O scheme and is largely compatible with the older scheme defined in *stream.h*.

3.3. FUNCTION PROTOTYPES

The syntax of functions in C++ inspired the new function prototype
syntax found in ANSI C compilers. Basically, the types of parameters
are listed inside the header parentheses. By explicitly listing the type
and number of arguments, strong type checking and assignment-compatible conversions are possible in C++. Weak type checking in traditional C kept it from being widely taught at an introductory level.
C++, like Pascal, insists on strong typing. The following example illustrates these points:

```
//A program illustrating function prototypes.

#include <stream.h>

main()
{
    int    add3(int, int, int);
    float average(int);
    int    score_1, score_2, score_3, sum;

    cout << "\nEnter 3 scores: ";
    cin >> score_1 >> score_2 >> score_3;
    sum = add3(score_1, score_2, score_3);
    cout << "\nTheir sum is " << sum << ".\n";
    cout << "\nTheir average is " << average(sum) << ".\n";
    sum = add3(1.5 * score_1, score_2, score_3);
    cout << "\nThe weighted sum is " << sum << ".\n";
    cout << "\nTheir average is " << average(sum) << ".\n";
}

int add3(int a, int b, int c)
{
    return (a + b + c);
}

float average(int s)
{
    return (s / 3.0);
}
```

■ DISSECTION OF THE *add3* PROGRAM

```
int    add3(int, int, int);
float average(int);
```

- These declarations at the head of main are function prototypes. They inform the compiler of the type and number
  of arguments to expect for each externally specified function. The list of arguments can optionally include variable
  names. So,

```
    int add3(int a, int b, int c);
```

is also possible.

```
sum = add3(1.5 * score_1, score_2, score_3);
```

- This would not be correct in traditional C. In traditional
  C, the first argument 1.5 * score_1 is promoted to double
  and passed unconverted to a local place holder that is
  expecting an integer. In C++, this expression is converted
  to an integer value as per the function prototype specification. This single change markedly improves C++ program reliability over traditional C.

```
int add3(int a, int b, int c)
{
    return (a + b + c);
}
```

- Here is the actual function definition. It could just as well
  have been imported from another file. It is compatible with
  the function prototype declaration in main.

In Pascal, the function average() would be written as follows:

```
function average (s : integer) : real;
begin
   average := s / 3.0;
end; {average}
```

Notice that C and C++ do not have keywords distinguishing between function and procedure. The distinction depends on a C function returning a value. The return construct is a flexible flow of control construct unavailable in Pascal. C++ functions can be recursive, but unlike Pascal cannot nest.

3.4. CLASSES AND ABSTRACT DATA TYPES

What is truly novel about C++ is its aggregate type class, which the language introduces. A class is an extension of the idea of struct in traditional C. This is similar to a Pascal record type. A class provides the means for implementing a user-defined data type and associated functions and operators. Therefore a class is an implementation of an abstract data type (ADT). Let us write a class called string that will implement a restricted form of string.

```
//An elementary implementation of type string.

#include <string.h>
#include <stream.h>

const int max_len = 255;

class string {
   char s[max_len];
   int  len;
public:
   void assign(char* st) { strcpy(s, st); len = strlen(st); }
   int  length() { return (len); }
   void print() { cout << s << "\nLength: " << len << "\n"; }
};
```

Two important additions to the structure concept of traditional C are found in this example: (1) It has members that are functions, such as assign, and (2) it has both public and private members. The keyword `public` indicates the visibility of the members that follow it. Without this keyword the members are private to the class. Private members are available for use only by other member functions of the class. Public members are available to any function within the scope of the class declaration. Privacy allows part of the implementation of a class type to be "hidden." This restriction prevents unanticipated modifications to the data structure. Restricted access or *data hiding* is a feature of object-oriented programming.

The declaration of member functions allows the ADT to have particular functions act on its private representation. For example, the member function `length` returns the length of the string defined to be the number of characters up to but excluding the first zero value character. The member function `print` outputs both the string and its length. The member function `assign` stores a character string into the hidden variable `s` and computes and stores its length in the hidden variable `len`.

We can now use this data type `string` as if it were a basic type of the language. It obeys the standard block structure scope rules of C. Other code that uses this type is a *client*. The client can use the public members only to act on objects of type `string`.

```
//Test of the class string.
main()
{
    string   one, two;
    char three[40] = {"My name is Charles Babbage."};

    one.assign("My name is Alan Turing.");
    two.assign(three);
    cout << three;
    cout << "\nLength: " << strlen(three) << "\n";
    //Print shorter of one and two.
    if (one.length() <= two.length())
       one.print();
    else
       two.print();
}
```

The variables `one` and `two` are of type `string`. The variable `three` is of type pointer to `char` and is not compatible with `string`. The member functions are called using the dot operator or "structure member operator." This is analogous to the Pascal use of the period as a "field designator." The Pascal name for member is "field." The structure member operator is explained in detail in Section 5.1. As is seen from their definitions, these member functions act on the hidden private member fields of the named variables. One cannot write inside `main` the expression `one.len` expecting to access this member. The output of this example program is

```
My name is Charles Babbage.
Length: 27
My name is Alan Turing.
Length: 23
```

3.5. OVERLOADING

The term *overloading* refers to the practice of giving several meanings to an operator or a function. The meaning selected depends on the types of the arguments used by the operator or function. Let us overload the function `print` in the previous example. This will be a second definition of the `print` function.

```
void print(char* c)
{
    cout << c << "\nLength is " << strlen(c) << "\n";
}
```

This version of `print` takes a single argument of type pointer to `char`. Unlike the original version, however, it is not a member function. We can modify `main` by deleting the two lines

```
cout << three;
cout << "\nLength: " << strlen(three) << "\n";
```

from the previous example and replacing them with a call to `print`:

```
print(three);
```

It is also possible to overload most of the standard C operators. For example, let us overload + to mean concatenate two strings. To do this, we need to introduce two new keywords: `friend` and `operator`. The keyword `operator` introduces the operator token and replaces what would otherwise be a function name in a function declaration. The keyword `friend` gives a function access to the private members of a class variable. A `friend` function is not a member of the class, but has the privileges of a member function in the class in which it is declared.

```
//Overloading the function print and the operator + .

#include <string.h>
#include <stream.h>

const int max_len = 255;

class string {
    char s[max_len];
    int  len;
public:
    void assign(char* st) { strcpy(s, st); len = strlen(st); }
    int  length() { return (len); }
    void print() { cout << s << "\nLength: " << len << "\n"; }
    friend string operator +(string& a, string& b);
};

string operator +(string& a, string& b)    //overload +
{
    string temp;

    temp.assign(a.s);
    temp.len = a.len + b.len;
    if (temp.len < max_len)
        strcat(temp.s, b.s);
    else
        cerr << "Max length exceeded in concatenation.\n";
    return (temp);
}

void print(char* c)
{
    cout << c << "\nLength: " << strlen(c) << "\n";
}
```

```
main()
{
    string      one, two, both;
    char three[40] = {"My name is Charles Babbage. "};

    one.assign("My name is Alan Turing. ");
    two.assign(three);
    print(three);            //one form of print
    //Print shorter of one and two.
    if (one.length() <= two.length())
        one.print();          //member function form of print
    else
        two.print();
    both = one + two;        //plus overloaded to be concatenate
    both.print();
}
```

■ DISSECTION OF THE *operator* + FUNCTION

```
string operator +(string& a, string& b)
```

- Plus is overloaded. The two arguments it will take are both strings. The arguments are called by reference. The declaration *type& identifier* declares the identifier to be a reference variable. This extension to traditional C allows call-by-reference as found in languages such as Pascal.

```
string temp;
```

- The function needs to return a value of type `string`. This local variable will be used to store and return the concatenated string value.

```
temp.assign(a.s);
temp.len = a.len + b.len;
if (temp.len < max_len)
    strcat(temp.s, b.s);
```

- The string `a.s` is copied into `temp.s` by calling the `strcpy` library function. The length of the resulting concatenated string is tested to see that it does not exceed the maximum length for strings. If the length is acceptable, the standard library function `strcat` is called with the hidden string members `temp.s` and `b.s`. The references to `temp.s`, `a.s`, and `b.s` are allowed because this function is a `friend` of class `string`.

```
cerr << "Max length exceeded in concatenation.\n";
```

- The standard error stream `cerr` is used to print an error message, and no concatenation takes place. Only the first string will be returned.

```
return (temp);
```

- The operator was given a return type of `string`, and `temp` has been assigned the appropriate concatenated string.

■

3.6. CONSTRUCTORS AND DESTRUCTORS

A constructor is a member function whose job is to initialize a variable of its class. Such a variable is an *object*. In many cases, this involves dynamic storage allocation. Constructors are invoked anytime an object of its associated class is created, typically when a variable is declared. A destructor is a member function whose job is to deallocate a variable of its class. Where an object has been allocated dynamically, its associated memory can be deallocated (returned to free store) by a destructor. This is done by implicitly invoking the destructor upon block exit for any class variables declared inside the block.

Let us change our `string` example by dynamically allocating store for each `string` variable. We will replace the private array variable by a pointer. The remodeled class will use a constructor to allocate an appropriate amount of storage dynamically using the `new` operator.

```
//An implementation of dynamically allocated strings.

class string {
   char* s;
   int   len;
public:
   string(int n) { s = new char[n + 1]; len = n; }
   void assign(char* st) { strcpy(s, st); len = strlen(st); }
   int  length() { return (len); }
   void print() { cout << s << "\nLength: " << len << "\n"; }
   friend string operator + (string& a, string& b);
};
```

A constructor is a member function whose name is the same as the class name. The keyword new is an addition to the C language. It is a unary operator that takes as an argument a data type that can include an array size. It allocates from free store the appropriate amount of memory to store this type and returns the pointer value that addresses this memory. In the preceding example, n + 1 bytes would be allocated from free store. Thus the declaration

```
string a(40), b(100);
```

would allocate 41 bytes for the variable a, pointed at by a.s, and 101 bytes for the variable b, pointed at by b.s. We add one byte for the end-of-string value 0. Storage obtained by new is persistent and is not automatically returned on block exit. When storage return is desired, a destructor function must be included in the class. A destructor is written as an ordinary member function whose name is the same as the class name and is preceded by the tilde symbol ~. Typically, a destructor uses the unary operator delete, another addition to the language, to automatically deallocate storage associated with a pointer expression.

```
//Add as a member function to class string.
~string() { delete s; } //destructor
```

It is usual to overload the constructor, writing a variety of such functions to accommodate more than one style of initialization. Consider wanting to initialize a string with a pointer to char value. Such a constructor is

```
string(char* p)
{
    len = strlen(p);
    s = new char[len + 1];
    strcpy(s, p);
}
```

A typical declaration invoking this version of the constructor is

```
char*   str = "I came on foot.";
string  a("I came by bus."), b(str);
```

It would also be desirable to have a constructor of no arguments:

```
string() { len = 255; s = new char[255]; }
```

This would be invoked by declarations without parenthesized arguments and would, by default, allocate 255 bytes of memory. Now all three constructors would be invoked in the following declaration:

```
string  a,  b(10),  c("I came by horse.");
```

The overloaded constructor is selected by the form of each declaration. The variable a has no parameters and so is allocated 255 bytes. The variable b has an integer parameter and so is allocated 11 bytes. The variable c has a pointer parameter to the literal string "I came by horse." and so is allocated 17 bytes, with this literal string copied into its private s member.

3.7. OBJECT-ORIENTED PROGRAMMING AND INHERITANCE

The central element of OOP is the encapsulation of an appropriate set of data types and their operations. The class construct with its member functions and data members provides an appropriate coding tool. Class variables are the *objects* to be manipulated.

Classes also provide data hiding. Access privileges can be managed and limited to whatever group of functions needs access to implementation details. This promotes modularity and robustness.

Another important concept in OOP is the promotion of code reuse through the *inheritance* mechanism. This is the mechanism by which a new class is *derived* from an existing one called the *base* class. The base class can be added to or altered to create the derived class. In this way a hierarchy of related data types that share code can be created.

Many useful data structures are variants of one another, and it is frequently tedious to produce the same code for each. A derived class inherits the description of the base class. It can then be altered by adding additional members, overloading existing member functions, and modifying access privileges. Without this reuse mechanism, each minor variation would require code replication.

We will imagine that a stockbroker gets in a series of orders that are transactions. There will be different types of transactions. One type will be to buy or sell a stock. A second type will be to buy or sell a call on a stock. A call is an agreement that allows its holder to purchase a stock at an agreed to *strike-price* for a fixed length of time.

In this example, we will code a base class transact. This class will have information common to subtypes that are derived from it called stock and call. These types inherit the public members of the base class. In OOP, the types the user defines correspond to natural parts of the problem domain.

In transact there is a virtual function profit_loss. This function is overloaded in the derived class stock. These functions allow for dynamic or run-time typing. A pointer to the base class can also point at objects of the derived classes. When such a pointer is used to point at the overloaded virtual function, it dynamically selects which version of the member function to call. This is a difficult point that will be explained in detail in Chapter 8.

```
//Manipulating transactions using inheritance

#include <stream.h>

struct transact {          //base class for stock and call
    char      security[20];
    int       p_buy;
    int       p_sell;
    virtual int profit_loss() { return (p_sell - p_buy); }
};

//derived classes
class stock : public transact {
public:
    int   dividend;
    int   profit_loss() { return (dividend + p_sell - p_buy); }
};

class call : public transact {
public:
    int   strike_price;
    int   month;
};
```

```
main()
{
    transact* t[2];         //pointers to the base class
    stock     s;
    call      c;

    s.p_buy = 10;
    s.p_sell = 11;
    s.dividend = 2;
    c.p_buy = 10;
    c.p_sell = 11;

    t[0] = &s;              //a base class pointer can
    t[1] = &c;              //point at a derived class

    //the version of profit_loss selected corresponds
    //to the type of the object pointed at
    cout << t[0] -> profit_loss() << "\n";
    cout << t[1] -> profit_loss() << "\n";
}
```

Code reuse is achieved through inheritance. The derived classes stock and call have their own data members security[20], p_buy, and p_sell inherited from transact. It is easy to extend this code modularly to other transaction categories, such as bonds and puts. Inheritance creates a type hierarchy that can be used dynamically with virtual functions.

The OOP programming task is frequently more difficult than normal procedural programming as found in C. There is at least one extra design step before one gets to the coding of algorithms. This involves the hierarchy of types that is useful for the problem at hand—frequently one is solving the problem more generally than is strictly necessary.

The belief is that this will pay dividends in several ways. The solution will be more encapsulated and thus more robust and easier to maintain and change. Also, the solution will be more reusable. For example, where the code needs a stack, that stack is easily borrowed from existing code. In an ordinary procedural language, such a data structure is frequently "wired into" the algorithm and cannot be exported.

All these benefits are especially important for large coding projects that require coordination among many programmers. Here the ability to have header files specify general interfaces for different classes allows each programmer to work on individual code segments with a high degree of independence and integrity.

3.8. Summary

1. The double slash // is a new comment symbol. The comment runs to the end of the line. The old C bracketing comment symbols /* */ are still available for multiline comments.

2. The *stream.h* header introduces I/O facilities for C++. The identifier cout is the name of the standard output stream. The operator << passes its argument to standard out. Used in this way, the << is referred to as the *put to* operator.

3. The identifier cin is the name of the standard input stream. The operator >> is the input operator, called *get from*, that assigns values from the input stream to a variable.

4. C++ reduces C's traditional reliance on the preprocessor. Instead of using define, special constants are assigned to variables specified as const. The new keyword inline specifies that a function is to be compiled, if possible as a macro. As a rule, this should be done sparingly and only on short functions.

5. The syntax of functions in C++ inspired the new function prototype syntax found in ANSI C compilers. Basically, the types of parameters are listed inside the header parentheses—for example, int add3(int, int, int). By explicitly listing the type and number of arguments, strong type checking and assignment-compatible conversions are possible in C++.

6. What is truly novel about C++ is the aggregate type class, which is introduced by the language. A class is an extension of the idea of struct in traditional C. Its use is a way of implementing a data type and associated functions and operators. Therefore a class is an implementation of an abstract data type (ADT). There are two important additions to the structure concept: (1) It includes members that are functions and (2) it employs a new keyword, public. This keyword indicates the visibility of the members that follow it. Without this keyword, the members are private to the class. Private members are available for use only by other member functions of the class. Public members are available to any function within the scope of the class declaration. Privacy allows part of the implementation of a class type to be "hidden."

7. The term *overloading* refers to the practice of giving several meanings to an operator or a function. The meaning selected will depend on the types of the arguments used by the operator or function.

8. The keyword `operator` introduces the operator token and replaces what would otherwise be a function name in a function declaration. The keyword `friend` gives a function access to the private members of a class variable. A `friend` function is not a member of the class, but has the privileges of a member function in the class in which it is declared.

9. A constructor is a member function whose job is to initialize a variable of its class. In many cases this involves dynamic storage allocation. Constructors are invoked anytime an object of its associated class is created, typically when a variable is declared.

10. A destructor is a member function whose job is to deallocate a variable of its class. Where an object has been allocated dynamically, its associated memory can be deallocated (returned to free store) by a destructor. This is done by implicitly invoking the destructor upon block exit for any class variables declared inside the block.

11. The central element of object-oriented programming (OOP) is the encapsulation of an appropriate set of data types and their operations. These user-defined types are ADTs. The class construct with its member functions and data members provides an appropriate coding tool. Class variables are the *objects* to be manipulated.

12. Another important concept in OOP is the promotion of code reuse through the *inheritance* mechanism. This is the mechanism by which a new class is *derived* from an existing one called the *base* class. The base class can be added to or altered to create the derived class. In this way, a hierarchy of related data types can be created that share code. This typing hierarchy can be used dynamically by `virtual` functions. Virtual member functions in a base class are overloaded in a derived class. These functions allow for dynamic or runtime typing. A pointer to the base class can also point at objects of the derived classes. When such a pointer is used to point at the overloaded virtual function, it dynamically selects which version of the member function to call.

3.9. Exercises

1. Using stream I/O, write on the screen the words

   ```
   she sells sea shells by the seashore
   ```

   (a) all on one line, (b) on three lines, (c) inside a box.

2. Write a program that will convert distances measured in yards to distances measured in meters. The relationship is 1 meter equals 1.0936 yards. Write the program to use `cin` to read in distances. The program should be a loop that does this calculation until it receives a zero or negative number for input.

3. Most systems allow *redirection* of input/output. In redirection, the symbol < means that input is redirected from the named file, and the symbol > means that output is redirected to the named file. Compile the previous program into an executable *mitok* and execute

   mitok < data > answers

   The file data should contain the numbers

   ```
   1 5 10 26 0
   ```

   Print the contents of file *answers* to check the results.

4. Take a working program, omit each line in turn, and run it through the compiler. Record the error messages each such deletion causes. For example, use the following code:

   ```cpp
   #include <stream.h>

   main()
   {
       int  m, n, k;
       cout << "\nEnter two integers: ";
       cin  >> m >> n;
       k = m + n;
       cout << "\nTheir sum is " << k << ".\n";
   }
   ```

5. Convert the following Pascal program to C++:

```
{ Print the minimum and maximum of a series of reals. }
program minmax (input, output);
    var
        x, min, max : real;
    begin
        read(min);
        max := min;
        while not eoln do
            begin
                read(x);
                if x < min then
                    min := x
                else if x > max then
                    max := x
            end;
        writeln(' Minimum = ', min, '   Maximum = ', max)
end. {minmax}
```

6. Write a program that asks interactively for your *name* and *age* and responds with

    Hello *name*, next year you will be *next_age*.

    where *next_age* is *age* + 1.

7. Stream I/O also allows formatted output using the function form(). The function prototype is

    ```
    char* form(const char* format, ...);
    //... denotes a variable number of arguments
    ```

    Here are some examples of its use:

    ```
    cout << form("\nThe value of i = %d\n", i);
    cout << form("%f %f %f", x, y, z);
    cout << form("%10.4f %4d %5c", x, i, 'c');
    ```

    It mimics printf() in traditional C, and it respects the same format symbols and conversion characters.

Write a program using `form()` to print out a table whose entries are

```
i       i * i       square root      i * i * i
-------------------------------------------------
1          1       1.00000                     1
. . .
```

Note that the C function `sqrt()` to compute real square roots is prototyped in *math.h* and that some compilers require a special linkage flag for the math library—for example,

CC prttab.c -lm

The newer library *iostream.h* does not have `form()`. See Appendix C for its description. One reason for abandoning `form()` is that it is not type checked. If this feature is available on your system, redo this exercise using the following file inclusions:

```
#include <iostream.h>
#include <iomanip.h>
```

You will need to read the library header to understand the member function `setprecision()`, which allows you to control the formatting of floating values.

8. The traditional C swapping function is

```
void swap(int* i, int* j)
{
    int  temp;

    temp = *i;
    *i = *j;
    *j = temp;
}
```

C++ and Pascal have call-by-reference. Rewrite this using C++ reference parameters and test it.

```
void swap(int& i, int& j)
. . .
```

9. In C++, the following code reads character data until an end-of-file is found:

```
#include <stream.h>

main()
{
    char   c;

    while (cin.get(c))       // read a character until eof
        if (c == '\n')       //test for new line
            cout << "\n\n";   //double space output
        else
            cout.put(c);     //output character
}
```

Change this program to capitalize all alphabetic characters. *Hint:* It is useful to study the macros in *ctype.h*.

10. Add to the class string a member function reverse. This function reverses the underlying representation of the character sequence stored in the private member s.

11. Add to the class string a member function void print(int k). This function overloads print() and is meant to print the first k characters of the string.

12. Overload the operator * in class string. Its member declaration will be

```
string operator *(string& a, int n);
```

The string represented by a should be copied back into a n times. Check that this does not overrun storage.

13. Test your compiler on character output by running

```
#include <stream.h>

main()
{
    char   c = 'C';
    int    i = c;
    while ( c != 'P') {
        cout << c << " : " << chr(c) << " : "
                << dec(c, 6) << " : "
                << form("%c", c) << "\n";
        i = ++c;
    }
}
```

On some systems the first value printed will be 67. The special format functions chr and dec force the integer-valued expression to be printed as char and int, respectively.

On systems with *iostream.h* try running

```
#include <iostream.h>

main()
{
    char   c = 'C';
    int    i = c;

    while ( c != 'P') {
        cout    << c << " : "
                << dec << i << " : "
                << hex << i << " : "
                << oct << i << endl;
        i = ++c;
    }
}
```

The endl *manipulator* flushes the output and emits a newline. The format states dec, hex, and oct change the default output style for integers to decimal, hexadecimal, and octal, respectively. For a more extensive discussion of this topic see Chapter 9.

14. Write the beginnings of a simple Pascal to C++ translator. It should read in each character of the Pascal program and make the following changes:

a. Change the comment symbols { } to /* and */.

b. Change begin to { and end to }

c. After an if, place a parenthesis (and replace then by).

CHAPTER 4

C++ as a Better C

C++ extends the C programming language in a number of important ways. C and Pascal are traditional imperative languages. Chapters 1 and 2 taught the Pascal programmer how to program in C. C++ has features that extend traditional C, making it more reliable and easier to use than traditional C. Many of these features are independent of the additions connected to the class construct. This chapter describes these improvements. Its theme is that C++ can be used as an improved and better C.

Some of the changes described are minor though useful. Among these is the new comment style. Some of the changes are major, such as function prototypes, which have been adopted into the ANSI C standard. The type compatibility rules are much stronger in C++ than in traditional C, and are similar to the checking that is found in strongly typed languages, such as Pascal.

Several features of C++ affect type declarations. These include the use of void, void*, enum, and const, all unavailable in traditional C, but adopted in more recent compilers and in the ANSI C standard. They also include the use of the keyword inline for function declarations and the use of & to mean the declaration is reference to. All these changes will be explained with examples.

In this chapter, then, we discuss the new comment style, the use of the keywords const and inline, the uses of the void and void* type, the function prototype construct, the use of reference declarations, the overloading of functions, and the use of the free store operators new and delete.

4.1. COMMENT STYLE

Programs must be documented to be useful. C++ introduces a one-line comment symbol //. This is in addition to the bracket pair comment symbols /* */ of traditional C. Everything on a single line after the symbol // is treated as a comment. This is the case even when the symbol appears in a string, which is not true for bracket pair comments. The one-line comment symbol is the preferred C++ style. In general it is less error prone—bracket pair symbols can cause problems, for example, when one of the pair is omitted.

```
//The computation of circumference and area of circles.
//              by
//          Geometrics Inc.
//          Version 2.2

#include <stream.h>

const  float pi = 3.14159;    //pi accurate to six places
const  int true = 1;          //mnemonic identifier

inline float circum(float rad) { return (pi * 2 * rad); }
inline float area(float rad) { return (pi * rad * rad); }
```

```
main()
{
   float  r;

   while (true) {                       //exit with control-C
      cout << "\nEnter radius: ";    //prompt for input
      cin >> r;
      cout << "\nArea is " << area(r);
      cout << "\nCircumference is " << circum(r) << "\n";
   }
}
```

4.2. AVOIDING THE PREPROCESSOR: inline AND const

In the previous example and in examples in Chapter 3, the new keywords inline and const are used to avoid the use of the preprocessor define. Using the preprocessor to define macros has a clear drawback: namely, the preprocessor does not understand C syntax. For example:

```
#define SQ(X)    X * X
```

expands the code

```
SQ(a + b)
```

to

```
a + b * a + b
```

This problem is avoided by fully parenthesizing the original macro. However, the solution does not protect against improper types being used. This latter defect is remedied by using inline.

```
inline int SQ(int x) { return (x * x); }
```

The keyword inline is a request to the compiler that the function be compiled as a macro. The compiler may choose to ignore this suggestion, but either way the semantics are identical. Only very short functions, where function call overhead is an issue, should use this function specifier.

The const keyword is a type specifier. When used alone in a declaration, the base type is implicitly int. A variable declared as const cannot have its value changed. Thus a const variable cannot be used on the left-hand side of an assignment. A non-const variable can have its value changed. It is a modifiable *lvalue*. Recall that an lvalue is an expression that refers to an object, typically a reference to a variable. A const variable should also be initialized. As in the previous program, it is used to create named constants, an important documentation aid. Some examples are

```
const   false = 0;            //implicit type is int
const   double e = 2.71828;   //natural logarithm base
const   int M_size = 100;     //used in an array declaration
const*  p = &M_size;          //a pointer to a constant int
char*   const s = "abcde";    //a constant pointer to char
```

Some care needs to be taken with respect to constant declarations of pointer types. The distinction is between the form

const *type* identifier*

which declares the *identifier* as a pointer whose pointed at value is constant, and the form

type* const *identifier*

which declares the *identifier* as a pointer constant. So,

```
const int* const cp = &M_size;
```

declares cp to be a constant pointer whose pointed at value is constant.

The Pascal use of const declarations is akin to the C preprocessor use of #define.

```
{Pascal Constants}
const
    pi = 3.14159;
    N  = 100;
```

is equivalent to

```
#define  pi   3.14159
#define  N    100
```

Both are methods of naming literals. The const modifier in C++ is a more general mechanism.

4.3. DECLARATIONS

This section describes changes to declarations in C++. It discusses the meaning of `enum` and illustrates the fact that declarations can be inter-mixed with executable statements. It also explains that the `struct` tag name and `enum` tag name are types. The Pascal enumerated type is similar to the C++ `enum` declaration.

We will write a card shuffling program to illustrate these points. First, we define a card as a `struct`.

```
enum suit {clubs, diamonds, hearts, spades};

struct card {
   suit   s;
   int    pips;
};

card deck[52];    //a declaration using card as the type
```

In Pascal these declarations would be as follows:

```
type
   suit = {clubs, diamonds, hearts, spades};
   card = record
              s   : suit;
              pips: integer
          end;
var
    array [0 .. 51] of card;   {a declaration using card}
```

In traditional C, the identifiers `card` and `suit` are tag names. Traditional C declarations would have to be

```
enum suit {clubs, diamonds, hearts, spades};

struct card {
   enum suit   s;
   int         pips;
};

struct card deck[52];
```

In C++, the tag names are types.

Enumerated types were added to C compilers in the early 1980s. Frequently they were implemented with a variety of underlying semantics. C++ treats enumerated types as distinct integral types. When listed without initialized values, the identifiers in the enumerated lists are implicitly initialized consecutively starting with 0. These identifiers are named integer constants and may not be changed. So, the two declarations

```
enum suit {clubs, diamonds, hearts, spades};
enum suit {clubs = 0, diamonds = 1, hearts = 2, spades = 3};
```

are equivalent, as are

```
enum suit {clubs = 5, diamonds, hearts, spades = 3};
enum suit {clubs = 5, diamonds = 6, hearts = 7, spades = 3};
```

Pascal enumeration constants have strict ordinal values 0, 1, 2, . . . , which cannot be otherwise defined or changed.

As we saw in Chapter 3, C++ allows declarations to be intermixed with executable statements. Consider a function that initializes a deck of cards to the normal 52 card values.

```
void init_deck(card d[])
{
    for (int i = 0; i < 52; ++i) {
        d[i].s = (suit)(i/13);
        d[i].pips = 1 + i % 13;
    }
}
```

In this function, the declaration int i occurs inside the for statement parentheses. The scope of the declaration is the innermost block within which it is found, and the identifier is visible starting at the point at which it is declared. Otherwise the scope rules are the same as in C, which means that declarations can be readily placed near their use. Both Pascal and C are block-structured languages. They allow blocks to be nested and inner block identifier declarations to hide outer block declarations.

The program for deck shuffling follows:

```
//  Shuffling a card deck

#include  <stream.h>

int  random(void);              // standard library function

enum suit {clubs, diamonds, hearts, spades};

struct card {
   suit   s;
   int    pips;
};

void pr_card(card cd)
{
   switch (cd.pips)  {
      case 1 :   cout << "A"; break;
      case 11:   cout << "J"; break;
      case 12:   cout << "Q"; break;
      case 13:   cout << "K"; break;
      default:   cout << cd.pips;
   }
   switch (cd.s)  {
      case clubs:     cout << "C"; break;
      case diamonds:  cout << "D"; break;
      case hearts:    cout << "H"; break;
      case spades:    cout << "S"; break;
      default :       cerr << "suit error\n"; exit(1);
   }
   cout << "  ";
}


void init_deck(card d[])
{
   for (int i = 0; i < 52; ++i) {
      d[i].s = (suit)(i/13);
      d[i].pips = 1 + i % 13;
   }
}
```

```
void shuffle(card d[])
{
   for (int i = 0; i < 52; ++i) {
      int k = random() % 52;        //choose a random card
      card t = d[i];                //swap two cards
      d[i] = d[k];
      d[k] = t;
   }
}

void pr_deck(card d[])
{
   for (int i = 0; i < 52; ++i) {
      if (i % 13 == 0)
         cout << "\n";
      pr_card(d[i]);
   }
   cout << "\n\n";
}

main()
{
   card deck[52];

   init_deck(deck);
   pr_deck(deck);                   //print unshuffled deck
   shuffle(deck);
   pr_deck(deck);                   //print shuffled deck
}
```

■ DISSECTION OF THE *shuffle* PROGRAM

```
int random(void);                 // standard library function
```

- We use the prototype (see Section 4.6) for this library function. More standard is the pseudorandom number generator rand; however, its statistical properties are not as good as random. The use of void here indicates that the function has no arguments. This style is an alternative to leaving the list empty.

```
void shuffle(card d[])
```

- A function returning no value is of type void. The parameter d is of type pointer to card.

```
for (int i = 0; i < 52; ++i) {
    int k = random() % 52;      //choose a random card
    card t = d[i];              //swap two cards
    d[i] = d[k];
    d[k] = t;
}
```

- Again, there is a mixing of executable statements and declarations. Note how the code is more readable than if the declarations were at the head of the function block.

4.4. THE USES OF void

The type void was introduced in some C compilers in the early 1980s. It is standard in ANSI C. In the previous section, we saw two of the normal uses of the keyword void. The keyword void is used both as the return type of a function not returning a value, and to indicate an empty argument list to a function. Two additional uses are as a cast and as part of the type pointer to void.

As the type within the cast operator, it informs the compiler that the expression's computed value is to be discarded.

```
//Simple use of void.

#include <stream.h>

int foo(int i)
{
    cout << "i is " << i;
    return (i);
}

main()
{
    int k = 5;

    (void)foo(k);   //throw away the int return value
}
```

Most interesting, however, is the use of void* as a generic pointer type. This type is also in the ANSI C standard. A pointer declared as type pointer to void, as in void* gp, can be assigned a pointer value of any underlying base type. But it may not be dereferenced. Dereferencing is the operation * acting on a pointer value to obtain what is pointed at. It would not make sense to dereference a pointer to a void value. Therefore

```
void* gp;        //generic pointer
int*  ip;        //int pointer
char* cp;        //char pointer

gp = ip;         //legal conversion
ip = (int*)gp;   //legal conversion
cp = ip;         //illegal conversion
*ip = 15;        //legal dereferencing of a pointer to int
*ip = *gp;       //illegal dereferencing of a generic pointer
```

A key use for this type is as a formal parameter. For example, the library function memcpy is declared in string.h as

```
void* memcpy(void* s1, const void* s2, unsigned int n);
```

This function copies n characters from the object based at s2 into the object based at s1. It works with any two pointer types as actual arguments.

Pascal programmers have procedures and functions—for example:

```
procedure p(i : integer);
   begin
      writeln(' i is ', i)
   end; {procedure p}

function q(i : integer) : integer;
   begin
      writeln(' i is ', i);
      q := i * i
   end; {function q}
```

C++ makes this distinction using the void type:

```
void p(int i)
{
   cout << "i is " << i << "\n";
}

int q(int i)
{
   cout << "i is " << i << "\n";
   return(i * i);
}
```

4.5. SCOPE RESOLUTION OPERATOR : :

C is a block-structured language. C++ inherits the same notions of block and scope. As in Pascal, the same identifier can be used to mean different objects. A use in an inner block *hides* the outer block or external use of the same name. C++ introduces the operator : : called the scope resolution operator. When used in the form : : *variable*, it allows access to the externally named variable. As in the following example, it is assumed that this uncovers an otherwise hidden object. Beware! Because it breaks the modularity of the code, its use is a dangerous practice that is rarely justified.

```
//  ::  scope resolution operator

int i = 1;                 //external i

#include   <stream.h>

main()
{
   int   i = 2;             //redeclares i locally

   {
      cout << "enter inner block\n";
      int  n = i;           //the global i is still visible
      int  i = 3;           //hides the global i

      //print the local i and the external i
      cout << i  << "  i <> ::i  " << ::i << "\n";
      cout << "n = " << n << "\n";
   }
   cout << "enter outer block\n";
   cout << i  << "  i <> ::i  " << ::i << "\n";
}
```

The output of this code is

```
enter inner block
3   i <> ::i   1
n = 2
enter outer block
2   i <> ::i   1
```

The major uses of this notation are important for classes. They will be discussed in the next chapters.

4.6. FUNCTION PROTOTYPES

The single feature in C++ that most accounts for its greater reliability over traditional C is its use of function prototypes. Pascal is noted for strong typing. By explicitly listing the type and number of arguments, strong type checking and assignment-compatible conversions are possible in C++. As a consequence, C++ is a strongly typed language and is no longer disadvantaged in this regard when compared to Pascal.

In traditional C, a function may be declared before it is defined, with the form

type name () ;

This declaration announces that the function is defined elsewhere with the given `return` type. However, the compiler makes no assumptions about type and number of arguments. Therefore, in traditional C, when a function is invoked with an actual argument, the explicit value of that argument is passed as is, without being converted to the defined function's corresponding argument type. A most common error occurs when functions such as `sqrt()` are passed `int`-valued expressions.

```
printf("%f is sqrt of 4\n", sqrt(4));
```

This prints 0 on many traditional C systems. The function `sqrt()` expects a `double`, and the bit configuration for the `int` constant 4, when interpreted as `double`, passes `sqrt()` an argument whose value is 0.

In C++, the prototype form is

type name (argument-declaration-list) ;

Examples are:

```
double sqrt(double x);
void    pr_int(char*, int);
void    ring_bell();                     //function of no arguments
int     printf(char* format, ...);   //variable number of args.
```

With the above `sqrt()` prototype definition, the call to

```
sqrt(4)
```

causes a conversion from `int` value 4 to `double` value 4.0 to occur before
the function call is executed. The argument-declaration-list can either
have named arguments or omit them. These names are intended as possible documentation. It is not necessary, but it is good style for names
in prototype declarations to match names used in the actual definition.
The prototype for the `stdio.h` function `printf` has an ellipsis "..." that
is used to specify that the function argument list has unknown length
and type.
The following example illustrates these points.

```
//Compute the average of a set of int values.

#include <stream.h>

int data[10] = {99, 87, 67, 90, 66, 43, 89, 88, 97, 76};

main()
{
    void    pr_arr(char*, int*, int);
    void    pr_dbl(char* name, double x);
    double  avg_arr(int a[], int size);

    pr_arr("data", data, 10);
    pr_dbl("average", avg_arr(data, 10));
}

void pr_int(char* name, int k)
{
    cout << form("%s = ", name) << k << "\n";
}

void pr_dbl(char* name, double x)
{
    cout << form("%s = ", name) << x << "\n";
}
```

```
void pr_arr(char* name, int a[], int size)
{
    cout << name ;
    pr_int(" array, size ", size);
    for (int i = 0; i < size; ++i)
        cout << a[i] << "\t";
    cout << "\n";
}

double avg_arr(int a[], int size)    //compute average
{
    int  sum = 0;

    for (int i = 0; i < size; ++i)
        sum += a[i];
    return ((double) sum / size);
}
```

The output from this program is

```
data array, size  = 10
99    87    67    90    66    43    89    88    97    76
average = 80.2
```

The program uses the *stream.h* library function form to provide formatted output. This function is described in detail in Section 9.2.

4.7. CALL-BY-REFERENCE AND REFERENCE DECLARATIONS

Call-by-reference is available in Pascal but not in C. C++ allows *reference to* declarations. These are typically of the form

type& identifier = object

Such declarations declare the identifier to be an alternative name for an object specified in an initialization of the reference. Some examples are

```
int    n;
int&   nn = n;           //nn is an alternative name for n
double a[10];
double& last = a[9];    //last is an alias for a[9]
char&  new_line = '\n';
```

In these examples, the names n and nn are aliases for each other; that is, they refer to the same object. Modifying nn is equivalent to modifying n and vice versa. The name last is an alternative to the single array element a[9]. These names, once initialized, cannot be changed. Also, it is possible to initialize a reference to a literal. In the examples, new_line is initialized to the char constant \n, which creates a reference to the otherwise unknown location where the literal is stored.

One use of reference declarations is in formal parameter lists. This usage allows C++ to have *call-by-reference* arguments directly. As explained in Chapter 2, this is similar to var parameters in Pascal. Reference declaration is unavailable in C. Let us use this mechanism to write a function greater that exchanges two values if the first is greater than the second. First, we write it in Pascal:

```
function greater(var a, b : integer) : boolean;
   var   temp : integer;
   begin
      if a > b then
         begin
            temp := a; a := b; b := temp;
            greater := true
         end
      else
         greater := false;
   end; {greater}
```

The same function coded in C++ is

```
int greater(int& a, int& b)
{
   if (a > b) {               //exchange
      int temp = a;
      a = b;
      b = temp;
      return (1);
   }
   else
      return (0);
}
```

Now, if i and j are two int variables, then

```
greater(i, j)
```

will use the reference to i and the reference to j to exchange, if necessary, their two values. In traditional C, this operation must be accomplished using pointers and dereferencing.

4.8. DEFAULT ARGUMENTS

A formal parameter can be given a default argument. This is usually a constant that occurs frequently when the function is called. Use of a default argument saves writing in this default value at each invocation. The following function illustrates the point:

```
int mult(int n, int k = 2)            //k = 2 is default
{
   if (k == 2)
      return (n * n);
   else
      return (mult(n, k - 1) * n);
}
```

We assume that most of the time the function is used to return the value of n squared.

```
mult(i + 5)                    //computes (i + 5) * (i + 5)
mult(i + 5, 3)                 //computes (i + 5) cubed
```

Only the trailing parameters of a function can have default values. Some examples are

```
void foo(int i, int j = 7);                 //legal
void goo(int i = 3, int j);                 //illegal
void hoo(int i, int j = 3, int k = 7);      //legal
void moo(int i = 1, int j = 2, int k = 3);  //legal
void noo(int i, int j = 2, int k);          //illegal
```

4.9. OVERLOADING FUNCTIONS

The term *overloading* refers to using the same name for multiple meanings of an operator or a function. The meaning selected depends on the type and number of arguments used in calling the operator or function. Here we will restrict our discussion to function overloading and leave operator overloading to later chapters, as the latter is chiefly used with classes.

The usual reason for picking a function name is to indicate the function's chief purpose. Readable programs generally have a diverse and literate choice of identifiers. Sometimes different functions are used for the same purpose. For example, consider a function that averages the values in an array of double versus one that averages the values in an array of int. Both are conveniently named avg_arr, as in a previous example. The two functions are defined with different argument lists, sometimes called their *signature* because it is the basis for distinguishing the two meanings.

```
double avg_arr(double a[], int size);
double avg_arr(int a[], int size);

double avg_arr(int a[], int size)
{
    int   sum = 0;

    for (int i = 0; i < size; ++i)
        sum += a[i];                 //performs int arithmetic
    return ((double) sum / size);
}

double avg_arr(double a[], int size)
{
    double  sum = 0.0;

    for (int i = 0; i < size; ++i)
        sum += a[i];                 //performs double arithmetic
    return (sum / size);
}
```

The following code shows how each is invoked:

```
main()
{
    int    w[5] = {1, 2, 3, 4, 5};
    double x[5] = {1.1, 2.2, 3.3, 4.4, 5.5};

    cout << avg_arr(w, 5) << "  int array average\n";
    cout << avg_arr(x, 5) << "  double array average\n";
}
```

The compiler chooses the function with matching types and arguments. Note that older systems need the keyword overload. With these compilers add the line:

```
overload avg_arr;   //an anachronism compatible with older systems
```

4.10. FREE STORE OPERATORS new AND delete

The unary operators new and delete are available to manipulate *free store*. They are analogous to Pascal's new() and dispose() procedures. Free store is a system-provided memory pool for objects whose lifetime is directly managed by the programmer. The programmer creates the object by using new and destroys the object by using delete. This is important for dynamic data structures such as lists and trees.

The operator new is used in the following forms:

```
new type-name
new type-name initializer
new (type-name)
```

In each case, there are at least two effects. First, an appropriate amount of store is allocated from free store to contain the named type. Second, the base address of the object is returned as the value of the new expression. The expression is a pointer value and can be assigned to that pointer type variable. The use of the operator with initializer, which applies to its use with classes, is not discussed here.

The following example uses new:

```
int* i;
i = new int;
*i = 5;
```

In this code, the pointer to int variable i is assigned the address of the store obtained in allocating an object of type int. The pointer is dereferenced and assigned the value 5. This use is not usual for a simple type such as int in that it is far more convenient and natural to automatically allocate an integer variable on the stack or to do so globally.

The operator delete destroys an object created by new, in effect returning its allocated storage to free store for reuse. The following example uses these constructs to dynamically allocate an array:

```
//Use of new operator to dynamically allocate an array.

#include <stream.h>

main()
{
    int*  data;
    int   size;

    cout << "\nEnter array size: ";
    cin >> size;

    data = new int[size];
    for (int j = 0; j < size; ++j)
        cout << (data[j] = j) << "\t";
    cout << "\n\n";

    delete data;
    data = new int[size];
    for (j = 0; j < size; ++j)
        cout << data[j] << "\t";
}
```

■ DISSECTION OF THE *dynamic* PROGRAM

```
int*  data;
int   size;

cout << "\nEnter array size: ";
cin >> size;

data = new int[size];
```

● The pointer variable data is used as the base address of a dynamically allocated array whose number of elements is the value of size. The user is prompted for the integer-valued size. The new operator is used to allocate sufficient storage from free store for an object of type int[size]. On a system where integers take four bytes, this would allocate 4 * size bytes. At this point data is assigned the base address of this store.

```
for (int j = 0; j < size; ++j)
    cout << (data[j] = j) << "\t";
```

- This statement initializes the values of the data array and prints them.

```
delete data;
```

- The operator delete returns to free store the storage associated with the pointer variable data. This can be done only with objects allocated by new.

```
data = new int[size];
for (j = 0; j < size; ++j)
    cout << data[j] << "\t";
```

- We access free store again, but this time do not initialize the data array. On a typical system, the same memory just returned to free store is used, with the old values reappearing. However, there are no guarantees on what values will appear in objects allocated from free store. Test this on your system. The programmer is responsible for properly initializing such objects.

■ ───────────────────────────────────

The operator delete is used in the following forms:

```
delete expression
delete [ expression ] expression
```

The first form is the most common. The expression is typically a pointer variable used in a previous new expression. The second form is occasionally used when returning store that was allocated as an array type. The bracketed expression gives the number of elements of the array. The operator delete does not return a value. Equivalently, one can say its return type is void.

4.11. ODDS AND ENDS

Several other features of C++ that do not appear in traditional C are relatively minor. They do not have direct analogs in Pascal. Among these are the use of `signed`, the treatment of `float`, and the use of anonymous unions and anonymous enumerations. We will treat these matters briefly.

The ANSI C standard introduces the keyword `signed`, which is analogous to the keyword `unsigned`. The keywords `signed` and `unsigned` are type specifiers for the integral types. The `unsigned` type does not allow negative values while the `signed` type does.

The type `float` in traditional C was always promoted to `double` when used in expressions. C++, however, reserves the right to do arithmetic in single precision `float`. Actual usage must be checked, though, as this is system-dependent.

An anonymous `enum` is an `enum` declared without a tag name. C++ allows the enumerator names of such enumerations to be used directly, but they must be distinct from other identifiers defined within the same scope. Such an enumeration is a convenient grouping of related named integer constants.

An anonymous `union` is a `union` declared without a tag name. C++ allows the member names of such unions to be used directly, but they must be distinct from other identifiers defined within the same scope. A global anonymous union has storage class `static`. An example is

```
//Anonymous unions and anonymous enumerations.

#include <stream.h>

static union {     //file scope anon. union requires static
    int     i;
    char    c[4];
};

enum {TOLOW = 32, UPPER = 65, LOWER = 97};   //ASCII alphabet

main()
{
    i = 65;
    cout << form("%c is ASCII %d\n", c[3], i);
    if (i < LOWER) {
        i += TOLOW;
        cout << form("%c is ASCII %d\n", c[3], i);
    }
}
```

What gets printed is:

```
A is ASCII 65
a is ASCII 97
```

The low-order byte that is used by the integer member i to store the value 65 is accessed by the indexed character member c[3]. In a union, the member declarations share the same storage. This technique is used to conserve storage and avoid unnecessary type conversions.

4.12. Summary

1. Programs must be documented to be useful. C++ introduces a one-line comment symbol //. This is in addition to the bracket pair comment symbols /* */ of traditional C. Everything on a single line after the symbol // is treated as a comment.

2. The keyword inline is a request to the compiler that the function be compiled as a macro. Only very short functions, where function call overhead is an issue, should use this function specifier. The const keyword is a type specifier. When used alone in a declaration, the base type is implicitly int. A variable declared as const cannot have its value changed. It can be used in places that otherwise would require a literal, such as an array size.

3. Enumerated types were added to C compilers in the early 1980s. C++ treats them as distinct integral types. When listed without initialized values, the identifiers in the enumerated lists are implicitly initialized consecutively starting with 0. These *enumerators* are named integer constants and may not be changed.

4. The tag names of both enumerated and structure types can be used as type names. Declarations may be intermixed with executable statements.

5. The type void was introduced in some C compilers in the early 1980s. It is standard in ANSI C. It improves both documentation and type checking over traditional C. The keyword void is used as the return type of a function not returning a value as well as to indicate an empty argument list. Two further uses are as a cast, and as part of the type pointer to void.

6. C++ introduces the operator :: called the scope resolution operator. When used in the form :: *variable*, it allows access to the externally named variable.

7. The single feature in C++ that most accounts for its greater reliability over traditional C is its use of function prototypes. By explicitly listing the type and number of arguments, strong type checking and assignment-compatible conversions are possible in C++. In C++, the prototype form is

   type name (argument-declaration-list) ;

Examples are:

```
double sqrt (double x) ;
void    pr_int (char*, int) ;
void    ring_bell () ;                      //function of no arguments
int     printf (char* format, ... ) ;   //variable number of args.
```

8. C++ allows *reference to* declarations. These are typically of the form

   type & identifier = object

   They declare the identifier to be an alternative name for an object specified in an initialization of the reference. The chief use of reference declarations is in formal parameter lists. This allows C++ to have *call-by-reference* arguments.

9. A formal parameter can be given a default argument. This is usually a constant that occurs frequently when the function is called. Use of the default argument saves writing in this default value at each invocation.

10. The term *overloading* refers to using the same name for various meanings of an operator or a function. The meaning selected depends on the types of the arguments used by the operator or function. A C++ anachronism is the keyword overload to indicate that a particular name will be so used.

11. The unary operators new and delete are available to manipulate *free store*. Free store is a system-provided memory pool for objects whose lifetime is directly managed by the programmer. The pro-

grammer creates the object by using new and destroys the object by using delete. The operator new is used in the following forms:

new *type-name*
new *type-name initializer*
new (*type-name*)

The operator delete is used in the following forms:

delete *expression*
delete [*expression*] *expression*

The expression is typically a pointer variable used in a previous new expression.

4.13. Exercises

1. C++ style follows C style in layout. Generally, a tab stop of three to five blank spaces is used to indent sections of code to reflect flow of control. Proper commenting and choice of identifier names are important to readable code. Try to understand the following code and rewrite it in good style:

```
#include <stream.h>
const float f = 3.14159;
inline float v(float b) {return 4*f*b*b*b/3.0; }
main() {float b; while (1) { cout << "enter b"; cin >> b;
cout << form("\nVolume is %f \n", v(b)); }}
```

2. Can you have the following as comments in C and C++?

```
//one liner
/*one liner
/*    old style   */
/*    is nesting /* allowed */ on your system? */
//what happens if we repeat // on this line
a /*p; where p is a pointer
"/* within a string */"
"// within a string"
//   /* within a one liner */
/*   //okay I give up   */
```

3. Recode the following `#define` preprocessor lines using `const` and `inline` declarations:

```
#define TRUE          1
#define c             299792.4562  //light speed in km/sec
#define EOF           (-1)
#define LARGER (X, Y) ((X > Y) ? (X) : (Y))
#define CUBE (X)      (X) * (X) * (X)
```

4. Using the declaration of `card deck[52]` as found in this chapter, write code that will deal out and print six 5-card hands. A hand should be stored in a two-dimensional array.

```
const int players = 6;
const int nc      = 5;
card   hand[players] [nc];
```

5. Continuing with exercise 4, write code that checks if a hand is a flush. A flush is a hand that contains five or more cards of the same suit. It can be tested by summing for each suit the number of cards of that suit that occur. You will write the function

```
int is_flush(card h[]);   //returns 1 if a flush else 0
```

Generate 1000 deals at random and print out the probability of getting a flush.

6. On most C compilers the following program runs:

```
char strg[5] = "ABCD";

main()
{
    int  i = 7, *p = &i;
    char* c;

    c = *p;
    c = strg + 1;
    *c = 'X';
}
```

On C++ compilers, the program gives a syntax error. Discuss these differences. Which is preferred?

7. The following program uses pointer types and modifies a string:

```
#include <stream.h>

main()
{
    char*          c;
    static char*   const strg = "ABCD";

    cout << "\nstrg is " << strg;
    c = strg + 1;
    *c = 'X';
    cout << "\n strg is " <<   strg;
}
```

What is wrong with changing the `strg` declaration to

```
static const char*   const strg = "ABCD";
```

8. Given the following declarations:

```
int    i = 5;
int*   pi = &i;
char   c = 'C';
char*  pc = &c;
void*  pv;
char   s[100];
```

what do the following expressions mean? Are any illegal under C++ typing?

```
*pi = i + c;
*pc = s + 10;
pc  = s + 10;
pv  = pi;
pv  = s + 1;
pv  = ++s;
pc  = pv;
*pc = *pv;
*pc = (char)*pv;
```

9. Use the library function `memcpy` to copy a string into another character array. Also copy an integer array into another integer array. Finally, copy a character array into an integer array. On most systems the header `string.h` has `memcpy`.

10. Implement your own version of `memcpy` to conform to the function prototype found in Section 4.4.

11. What gets printed by the following code?

```
//  ::   scope resolution operator

double x = 1.23;

#include   <stream.h>

main()
{
   double   x = 2.34;

   {
      double  y = x;
      double  x = 3.45;
      cout << x  << "   x <> ::x  " << ::x << "\n";
      cout << "y = " << y << "\n";
   }
   cout << x  << "   x <> ::x  " << ::x << "\n";
}
```

12. The following traditional C function uses pointer variables and de-referencing to implement a circular shift:

```
void shift(pc1, pc2, pc3, pc4)
char*  pc1;
char*  pc2;
char*  pc3;
char*  pc4;
{
   char   temp;

   temp = *pc1;
   *pc1 = *pc2;
   *pc2 = *pc3;
   *pc3 = *pc4;
   *pc4 = temp;
}
```

Convert it to a function in C++ using call-by-reference.

```
void shift(char& c1,  char& c2,  char& c3,  char& c4)
```

Write a test program that prints the before and after values using shift.

13. The following function computes the minimum and maximum values found in an array:

```
//Find both the minimum and maximum values of an array.

void minmax(int data[], int size, int* min, int* max)
{
    *min = *max = data[0];
    for (int i = 1; i < size; ++i)
        if (*min > data[i])
            *min = data[i];
        else if (*max < data[i])
            *max = data[i];
}
```

Convert it to a function that uses call-by-reference. Write a program to test it.

14. A more efficient method for finding minimum and maximum is as follows. Compare a pair of elements and use the smaller element for finding the minimum and the larger element for finding the maximum. With this method, rewrite the function used in exercise 13. How many comparisons are saved over the previous method? A description of this method is found in "A Sorting Method and Its Complexity" (*Communications of the ACM*, Vol. 15, No. 6, 1972) by Ira Pohl.

15. Change the solution to exercise 13 to use a default `size` parameter. Let the default value be 10. (*Reminder:* The argument `size` must now be at the end of the argument list.)

16. Write three overloaded functions that each print an array. One will print an array of `int`, the second an array of `float`, and the third an array of `char`.

```
void print(int data[], int size = 20);     //int version
void print(float data[], int size = 20);   //float version
void print(char data[], int size = 20);    //char version
```

Note that each declaration has a default value for `size`. Use stream I/O when writing each function.

17. First, write a function that creates a vector of a user-keyed `size` and that reads in, using `cin`, its size and initial values.

```
void create_vec(int* &v, int& size);
//get array size from cin
//use new to create v[size]
//and then use a for loop to assign values from cin
```

Next write a function that will add two vectors. If the vectors are not the same size, add them for the lesser of the two sizes.

```
void add_vec(int* v1, int* v2, int* sum, int size);
//add_vec  returns vector sum   sum[i] = v1[i] + v2[i]
```

Finally, print out the resulting array.

```
void print_vec (int* v, int size);
```

18. The following code uses `new` to allocate a two-dimensional array:

```
//Dynamically allocated two-dimensional arrays

#include <stream.h>

main()
{
    int**   data;
    int     sz1, sz2;

    cout << "\nEnter two sizes: ";
    cin >> sz1 >> sz2;
    data = new int* [sz1];              //an array of pointers
    for (int i = 0; i < sz1; ++i)
        data[i] = new int[sz2];         //each row is allocated
    cout << "\nEnter " << sz1 << " by " << sz2 << " ints\n";
    for (i = 0; i < sz1; ++i)
        for (int j = 0; j < sz2; ++j)
            cin >> data[i][j];
    for (i = 0; i < sz1; ++i)
        for (j = 0; j < sz2; ++j)
            cout << data[i][j] << "\t";
    cout << "\n";
}
```

Notice that you must do the allocation in two stages. This is because C has a simple linear interpretation of an array. Use the ideas found in this code to write the two-dimensional routines `create_matrix` and `add_matrix`. These are analogous to the functions written in exercise 17.

19. Anonymous unions must be used carefully, as they are machine-dependent. Let us use them to check on conversion between the types `int` and `float`. Fill in the *Prints* column in the following table.

Declarations and assignments		

`//in main()`
`union {`
`    int j;`
`    float y;`
`};`
`int i = 1024;`
`float x = 1.0;`		

Expression	**Output expression**	**Prints**
`j = i`	`cout << j`	1024
`j = i`	`cout << y`	
`y = x`	`cout << j`	
`j = 2 * x`	`cout << y`	

20. Convert the following Pascal program to C++ using enumerated types:

```pascal
{ Go into work program. }
program workDay(input, output);
    type
        day = (mond, tues, weds, thur, frid, satu, sund);
    var
        today : day;

    function work(d : day) : boolean;
        begin
            if ord(d) < ord(satu) then
                work := true
            else
                work := false
        end; {work}
```

```
procedure readDay(var d : day);
   var   i : integer;
   begin
      read(i);
      case i of
         1 : d := mond; 2 : d := tues; 3 : d := weds;
         4 : d := thur; 5 : d := frid; 6 : d := satu;
         7 : d := sund;
      end
   end; {readDay}

begin
   writeln('Enter day with monday = 1, ..., sunday = 7   : ');
   readDay(today);
   writeln;
   if work(today) then
      writeln('Go to work lazy bones!')
   else
      writeln('Enjoy yourself!')
end. {workDay}
```

CHAPTER 5

Classes

This chapter introduces the reader to struct and class. The original name given by Stroustrup to his language was "C with classes." A class is an extension of the idea of struct found in traditional C. It is a way of implementing a data type and associated functions and operators. User-defined data types, such as stack, complex numbers, and card decks, are examples of ADT implementation. Each of these types is coded in C++ and used in a major example.

We will explain here the new concept of class by first reviewing how traditional C structures work. In C++, structures may have member functions. Structures also can have parts of their description private.

129

Both of these extensions will be described. These extensions lead naturally to the `class` concept that, in effect, is a `struct` with a default visibility of `private`.

Allowing private and public visibility for members gives the programmer control over what parts of the data structure are modifiable. The private parts are hidden from client code while the public parts are available. It is possible to change the hidden representation but not change the public access or functionality. If done properly, client code need not change when the hidden representation is modified. A large part of the OOP design process involves thinking up the appropriate ADTs for a problem. Good ADTs not only model key features of the problem but are frequently reusable in other code.

5.1. The Aggregate Type `struct`

The structure type allows the programmer to aggregate components into a single, named variable. A structure has components, called *members,* that are individually named. Since the members of a structure can be of various types, the programmer can create aggregates that are suitable for describing complicated data.

As a simple example, let us define a structure that will describe a playing card. The spots on a card that represent its numeric value are called *pips*. A playing card, such as the three of spades, has a pip value, 3, and a suit value, spades. As in Chapter 4, we can declare the structure type

```
enum suit {clubs, diamonds, hearts, spades};

struct card {
    suit   s;
    int    pips;
};
```

In traditional C, the declaration of `card` would be illegal. It would have to be

```
struct card {
    enum suit   s;
    int         pips;
};
```

As we described in Chapter 4, in C++, the tag names are types. Our examples will use this C++ innovation. In this declaration, `struct` is a keyword, `card` is the structure tag name, and the variables `pips` and `suit` are members of the structure. The variable `pips` will take values from 1 to 13, representing ace to king.

This declaration creates the derived data type `struct card`, or in C++ the type `card`. The declaration can be thought of as a template; it creates the type, but no storage is allocated. The declaration

```
card    c1, c2;
```

allocates storage for the identifiers `c1` and `c2`, which are of type `card`. To access the members of `c1` and `c2`, we use the structure member operator " . ". Suppose we want to assign to `c1` the values representing the five of diamonds and to `c2` the values representing the queen of spades. To do this we can write

```
c1.pips = 5;
c1.suit = diamonds;
c2.pips = 12;
c2.suit = spades;
```

A construct of the form

structure_variable . member_name

is used as a variable in the same way a simple variable or an element of an array is used. The member name must be unique within the specified structure. Since the member must always be prefaced or accessed through a unique structure variable identifier, there is no confusion between two members having the same name in different structures. An example is

```
struct fruit {
    char    name[15];
    int     calories;
};

struct vegetable {
    char    name[15];
    int     calories;
};

fruit        a;      //struct fruit     a; in traditional C
vegetable    b;      //struct vegetable b; in traditional C
```

Having made these declarations, we can access a.calories and b.calories without ambiguity.

5.2. Structure Pointer Operator

We have already seen the use of the member operator " . " in accessing members. In this section we introduce the structure pointer operator ->.

   C provides the structure pointer operator -> to access the members of a structure via a pointer. This operator is typed on the keyboard as a minus sign followed by a greater than sign. If a pointer variable is assigned the address of a structure, then a member of the structure can be accessed by a construct of the form

   pointer_to_structure -> member_name

An equivalent construct is given by

   (**pointer_to_structure*). *member_name*

The operators -> and " . ", along with () and [], have the highest precedence, and they associate *left to right*. In complicated situations the two accessing modes can be combined. The following table illustrates their use in a straightforward manner.

Declarations and assignments		

card cd, *p = &cd;
 card deck[52];
 	
 cd.pips = 5;
 cd.suit = spades;
 deck[0] = cd;		

Expression	Equivalent expression	Value
cd.pips	p -> pips	5
cd.suit	p -> suit	spades
deck[0].pips	deck -> pips	5
(*p).suit	p -> suit	spades

5.3. An Example: Stack

The stack is one of the most useful standard data structures. A stack is a data structure that allows insertion and deletion of data to occur only at a single restricted element, the top of the stack. This is the last-in-first-out discipline (LIFO). Conceptually, it behaves like a pile of trays that pops up or is pushed down when trays are removed or added. Typically, a stack allows as operations *push*, *pop*, *top*, *empty*, and *full*. The push operator places a value on the stack. The pop operator retrieves and deletes a value off the stack. The top operator returns the top value from the stack. The empty operator tests if the stack is empty. The full operator tests if the stack is full. The stack is a typical ADT.

We wish to implement a stack as a C++ data type using struct in its traditional form. An implementation choice will be to use a fixed-length char array to store the contents of the stack. The top of the stack will be an integer-valued member named top. The various stack operations will be implemented as functions, each of whose argument lists includes a pointer to stack parameter. This will avoid copying a potentially large stack to perform a simple operation.

```
//A traditional C implementation of type stack.

const int max_len = 1000;
enum boolean {false, true};
enum {EMPTY = -1, FULL = max_len - 1};

struct stack {
    char s[max_len];
    int  top;
};

void reset(stack* stk)
{
    stk -> top = EMPTY;
}

void push(char c, stack* stk)
{
    stk -> top++;
    stk -> s[stk -> top] = c;
}
```

```
char pop(stack* stk)
{
   return (stk -> s[stk -> top--]);
}

char top(stack* stk)
{
   return (stk -> s[stk -> top]);
}

boolean empty(stack* stk)
{
   return (stk -> top == EMPTY);
}

boolean full(stack* stk)
{
   return (stk -> top == FULL);
}
```

■ DISSECTION OF THE *stack* FUNCTIONS

```
const int max_len = 1000;
enum boolean {false, true};
enum {EMPTY = -1, FULL = max_len - 1};

struct stack {
   char s[max_len];
   int  top;
};
```

- We declare a new type boolean. In C++ the tag name of an enum type is a new type. The constant false is initialized to 0 and the constant true is initialized to 1. The struct declaration creates the new type stack. It has two members, the array member s and the int member top.

```
void reset(stack* stk)
{
   stk -> top = EMPTY;
}
```

- This function is used for initialization. The member `top` is assigned the value EMPTY. The stack starts out as empty. The particular stack that this works on is an argument passed in as an address.

```
void push(char c, stack* stk)
{
    stk -> top++;
    stk -> s[stk -> top] = c;
}

char pop(stack* stk)
{
    return (stk -> s[stk -> top--]);
}
```

- The operation *push* is implemented as a function of two arguments. The member `top` is incremented. The value of `c` is shoved onto the top of the stack. This function assumes that the stack is not full. The operation *pop* is implemented in a like fashion. It assumes the stack is not empty. The value of the top of the stack is returned, and the member `top` is decremented.

```
boolean empty(stack* stk)
{
    return (stk -> top == EMPTY);
}

boolean full(stack* stk)
{
    return (stk -> top == FULL);
}
```

- These functions return an enumerated type `boolean` value. Each tests the `stack` member `top` for an appropriate condition. In all functions the stack argument is passed in as address and the structure pointer operator `->` is used to access members.

Given that these declarations reside in the file stack.h, we can test these operations with the following program, which enters the characters of a string onto a stack and pops them, printing each character out in reverse order:

```
//Test of stack implementation by reversing a string.

#include <stream.h>
#include "stack.h"        //stack implementation imported

main()
{
    stack       s;
    static char str[40] = {"My name is Betty Dolsberry!"};
    int         i = 0;

    cout << str << "\n";        //print the string
    reset(&s);
    while (str[i])              //push onto stack
        if (!full(&s))
            push(str[i++], &s);
    while (!empty(&s))          //print the reverse
        cout << pop(&s);
    cout << "\n";
}
```

The output from this test program is

```
My name is Betty Dolsberry!
!yrrebsloD ytteB si eman yM
```

Note that one of the actual arguments to each function is &s, the address of the stack variable declared in main. This argument is given because each function expects an address of a stack variable.

5.4. Member Functions

The concept of struct is augmented in C++ to allow functions to be members. The function declaration is included in the structure declaration and is invoked by using access methods for structure members. The idea is that the functionality required by the `struct` data type should be directly included in the `struct` declaration. This construct improves the encapsulation of the ADT stack operations by packaging it directly with its data representation.

Let us rewrite our stack example by declaring as member functions, the various functions associated with the stack.

```
struct stack {
    //data representation

    char  s[max_len];
    int   top;
    enum {EMPTY = -1, FULL = max_len - 1};

    //operations represented as member functions

    void    reset() { top = EMPTY; }
    void    push(char c) { top++; s[top] = c; }
    char    pop() { return (s[top--]); }
    char    top_of() { return (s[top]); }
    boolean empty() { return (top == EMPTY); }
    boolean full() { return (top == FULL); }
};
```

The member functions are written much as other functions. One difference is that they can use the data member names as is. Thus the member functions in `stack` use `top` and `s` in an unqualified manner. When invoked on a particular object of type `stack`, they act on the specified member in that object.

The following example illustrates these ideas. If two `stack` variables

```
stack data, operands;
```

are declared, then

```
data.reset();
operands.reset();
```

invoke the member function `reset`, which has the effect of setting both `data.top` and `operands.top` to EMPTY. If a pointer to `stack`

```
stack* ptr_operands = &operands;
```

is declared, then

```
ptr_operands -> push('A');
```

invokes the member function push, which has the effect of incrementing operands.top and setting operands.s[top] to 'A'. One last observation: The member function top_of had its name changed from the previous implementation because of a naming conflict.

Member functions that are defined within the struct are implicitly inline. As a rule, only short, heavily used member functions should be defined within the struct, as is the case for the example just given. To define a member function outside the struct, the scope resolution operator is used. Let us illustrate this by changing the definition of push to its corresponding function prototype within the struct stack. We write it out fully using the scope resolution operator. In this case the function is not implicitly inline.

```
struct stack {
    //data representation

    char s[max_len];
    int  top;
    enum {EMPTY = -1, FULL = max_len - 1};

    //operations represented as member functions

    void reset() { top = EMPTY; } //implicitly inline
    void push(char c);          //function prototype
    . . .
};

    void stack::push(char c)  //definition, not inline
    {
        top++;
        s[top] = c;
    }
```

The scope resolution operator allows member functions from the different struct types to have the same names. In this case, which member function is invoked will depend on the type of object it acts upon. Member functions within the same struct can be overloaded. Consider adding to the data type stack a pop operation that has an integer parameter that is the number of times the stack should be popped. It could be added as the following function prototype within the struct:

```
char pop(int n);                    //within stack
char stack::pop(int n)
{
   while(n-- > 1)
      top--;
   return (s[top--]);
}
```

The definition that is invoked depends on the actual arguments to pop.

```
data.pop();                    //invokes standard pop
data.pop(5);                   //invokes iterated pop
```

5.5. Visibility private and public

The concept of struct is augmented in C++ to allow structures to have public and private members. Inside a struct, the use of the keyword private followed by a colon restricts the scope of the members that follow this construct. The private members can be used by only a few categories of functions, whose privileges include access to these members. These functions include the member functions of the struct. Other categories of functions having access will be discussed later.

We modify our example of stack to hide its data representation.

```
struct stack {
private:
   char s[max_len];
   int  top;
   enum {EMPTY = -1, FULL = max_len - 1};
public:
   void    reset() { top = EMPTY; }
   void    push(char c) { top++; s[top] = c; }
   char    pop() { return (s[top--]); }
   char    top_of() { return (s[top]); }
   boolean empty() { return (top == EMPTY); }
   boolean full() { return (top == FULL); }
};
```

We now rewrite `main` from Section 5.3 to test the same operations.

```
main()
{
   stack        s;
   static char str[40] = {"My name is Don Knuth!"};
   int          i = 0;

   cout << str << "\n";
   s.reset();                    //s.top = EMPTY; would be illegal
   while (str[i])
      if (!s.full())
         s.push(str[i++]);
   while (!s.empty())            //print the reverse
      cout << s.pop();
   cout << "\n";
}
```

The output from this version of the test program is

```
My name is Don Knuth!
!htunK noD si eman yM
```

As the comment in `main` states, access to the hidden variable `top` is controlled. It can be changed by the member function `reset` but cannot be accessed directly. Also notice how the variable `s` is passed to each member function using the structure member operator form.

The `struct stack` has a private part that contains its data description and a public part that contains member functions to implement stack operations. It is useful to think of the private part as restricted to the implementor's use, and the public part to be an interface specification that clients may use. At a later time, the implementor could change the private part without affecting the correctness of a client's use of the stack type.

Hiding data is an important component of OOP. It allows for more easily debugged and maintained code, because errors and modifications are localized. Client programs need only be aware of the type's interface specification.

5.6. Classes

Classes in C++ are introduced by the keyword `class`. They are a form of `struct` whose default privacy specification is `private`. Thus `struct` and `class` can be used interchangeably with the appropriate privacy specification.

Many scientific computations require complex numbers. Let us write an ADT for complex numbers.

```
struct complex {
private:
    double real, imag;
public:
    void   assign(double r, double i);
    void   print() { cout << real << " + " << imag << "i"; }
};

void complex::assign(double r, double i = 0.0)
{
    real = r;
    imag = i;
}
```

Here is its equivalent `class` representation.

```
class complex {
    double real, imag;
public:
    void   assign(double r, double i);
    void   print() { cout << real << " + " << imag << "i "; }
};

void complex::assign(double r, double i = 0.0)
{
    real = r;
    imag = i;
}
```

Notice the only difference is in the use of the keywords `public` and `private`. Also possible would have been

```
class complex {
private:           //one style is to make this explicit
    double real, imag;
public:
    void   assign(double r, double i);
    void   print() { cout << real << " + " << imag << "i "; }
};
```

It will be our style to prefer `class` to `struct` unless all members are to be treated as `public`.

5.7. static **Member**

Data members can be declared with the storage class modifier `static`. They cannot be declared `auto`, `register`, or `extern`. A data member that is declared `static` is shared by all variables of that class and is stored uniquely in one place. Because of this it can be accessed in the form

class name :: *identifier*

as well as normal member access. This is a further use of the scope resolution operator (see Section 4.5). An example is

```
enum boolean {false, true};

class str {
    char            s[100];
public:
    static boolean  read_only;
    void            print();
    void            assign(char*);
    . . .
};

boolean str::read_only = false;   //file scope initialization
```

In our example this could be used to decide whether an object of type str could be changed in value. So,

```
str s1, s2, s3, s4;
if (!str::read_only)
    s1.assign("Buzz Dolsberry");
```

is a means of conveniently maintaining a value common to the entire class. Classes with static members have some restrictions that will be explained in the next chapter.

5.8. Nested Classes

Classes can be nested. The inner class is not inside the scope of the outer class, but rather has the same scope as the outer class. Since this can lead to confusion, nesting class declarations is normally poor style.

The following incorrectly nested classes illustrate these points:

```
char c;                //external scope

class X {              //outer class declaration
    char c;
    class Y {          //inner class declaration
        char d;
        void foo(char e) { c = e; }
    };
    char goo(X* q) { return (q -> d); }   //illegal
};
```

In class Y the member function foo, when using c, means the external scope c. It is as if class Y were declared at the same level and inside the same block or file scope as class X. In class X the member function goo, when using d, is attempting to access a private member of class Y. Beware! These are Release 2.0 rules and are expected to change.

5.9. An Example: Flushing

We wish to estimate the probability of being dealt a flush. A flush occurs when at least five cards are of the same suit. We will simulate shuffling cards by using a random number generator to shuffle the deck. This is a form of *Monte Carlo* calculation. The program will be written using classes to represent the needed data types and functionality.

```
//A poker calculation on flushing

#include  <stream.h>

int    random(void);                   //random number generator
void   srandom(unsigned int seed);     //if unavailable use
unsigned    seed;                      //rand and srand

enum suit {clubs, diamonds, hearts, spades};

class pips {
    int   p;
public:
    void assign(int n) { p = n % 13 + 1; }
    int  getpip() { return (p); }
    void print();
};

class card {
    int   cd;                          //a cd is from 0 to 51
public:
    suit s;
    pips p;
    void assign(int n) { cd = n; s = n / 13; p.assign(n); }
    void pr_card();
};

class deck {
    card d[52];
public:
    void init_deck();
    void shuffle();
    void deal(int, int, card*);
    void pr_deck();
};
```

We used an enumerated type suit to represent card suits. The enumerated constants are mapped into the integers 0, 1, 2, and 3. So clubs is the integer value 0 and spades is the integer value 3. Each level of declaration hides the complexity of the previous level. Notice also that we can plan to code the functions later on. For example, we will not use the print routines in this example; they can be added as needed.

A most interesting function is the implicitly inline function

```
void assign(int n) { cd = n; s = n / 13; p.assign(n); }
```

which uses the function `void pips::assign(int n);`. We could have used the notation

```
p.pips::assign(n)
```

to show clearly that this function is from the `class pips`, but this is unnecessary. The function maps an integer whose value is between 0 and 51 into a unique pair of `suit` and `pips` values. The value 0 becomes the ace of clubs and the value 51 becomes the king of spades.

The other member functions are not inline and are defined at a later point with the use of the scope resolution operator.

```
void   deck::init_deck()
{
    for (int i = 0; i < 52; ++i)
        d[i].assign(i);
}

void   deck::shuffle()
{
    for (int i = 0; i < 52; ++i) {
        int k = random() % 52;
        card t = d[i]; d[i] = d[k]; d[k] = t; //swap two cards
    }
}

void deck::deal(int n, int pos, card* hand)
{
    for (int i = pos; i < pos + n; ++i)
        hand[i - pos] = d[i];
}
```

The `init_deck` function calls `card::assign` to map the integers into card values. The `shuffle` function uses the library-supplied pseudorandom number generator `random` to exchange two cards for every deck position. Tests show that this gives a reasonable approximation to good shuffling. The `deal` function takes cards in sequence from the deck and arranges them into hands.

It now remains to use these functions to estimate a probability that a flush occurs when poker hands are dealt. The operator can choose to deal out between five and nine cards per hand.

```cpp
main()
{
    card one_hand[9];                        //max hand is 9 cards
    deck dk;
    int   i, j, k, fcnt = 0, sval[4];
    int   ndeal, nc, nhand;

    do {
        cout << "\nEnter no. of cards in each hand (5-9): ";
        cin  >> nc;
    } while (nc < 5 || nc > 9);
    nhand = 52 / nc;

    cout << "\nEnter no. of hands to deal and a random seed: ";
    cin  >> ndeal >> seed;

    srandom(seed);
    dk.init_deck();
    for (k = 0; k < ndeal; k += nhand) {
        if ((nhand + k) > ndeal)
            nhand = ndeal - k;
        dk.shuffle();
        for (i = 0; i < nc * nhand; i += nc) {
            for (j = 0; j < 4; ++j)           //init suit counts to 0
                sval[j] = 0;
            dk.deal(nc, i, one_hand);        //deal next hand
            for (j = 0; j < nc; ++j)
                sval[one_hand[j].s] ++ ;     //increment suit count
            for (j = 0; j < 4; ++j)
                if (sval[j] >= 5)            //5 or more is flush
                    fcnt++;
        }
    }
    cout << "\n\nIn " << ndeal << " ";
    cout << nc << "-card hands there were ";
    cout << fcnt << " flushes\n   ";
}
```

■ DISSECTION OF THE *flush* PROGRAM

```
card one_hand[9];                  //max hand is 9 cards
deck dk;
int  i, j, k, fcnt = 0, sval[4];
int  ndeal, nc, nhand;
```

● These are variables allocated upon block entry when `main` is executed. The variable `one_hand` is an array of nine elements, the maximum hand size allowed. It will be used to store dealt-out hands from the deck. The variable `dk` represents our deck and is automatically allocated. All its data members are created, though some are hidden. The number of cards dealt to each hand is stored as the variable `nc`, and the number of hands to be dealt is kept in the variable `ndeal`. The variable `fcnt` will count the number of flushes. The array `sval` is used to store the number of cards found in the hand of a particular suit value.

```
do {
    cout << "\nEnter no. of cards in each hand (5-9): ";
    cin  >> nc;
} while (nc < 5 || nc > 9);
nhand = 52 / nc;

cout << "\nEnter no. of hands to deal and a random seed: ";
cin  >> ndeal >> seed;

srandom(seed);
```

● We prompt for the number of cards to deal to each hand. The operator must respond with a number between 5 and 9 in order to proceed. The number of hands that can be dealt with the deck is computed and put into the variable `nhand`. We prompt for the number of deals and the initial seed. Different values for `seed` give different random number sequences. Using the same choice leads to the same result.

```
dk.init_deck();
for (k = 0; k < ndeal; k += nhand) {
    if ((nhand + k) > ndeal)
        nhand = ndeal - k;
    dk.shuffle();
```

● The deck variable dk is initialized, and each time through the main loop the deck is reshuffled. The variable dk is implicitly an argument to the called member functions init_deck and shuffle. The test to check whether the value of ndeal has been exceeded ensures that the total number of hands dealt will not exceed the request if the total number of hands is not an even multiple of the number of hands per shuffle.

```
for (i = 0; i < nc * nhand; i += nc) {
    for (j = 0; j < 4; ++j)                //init suit counts to 0
        sval[j] = 0;
    dk.deal(nc, i, one_hand);              //deal next hand
    for (j = 0; j > nc; ++j)
        sval[one_hand[j].s] ++ ;           //increment suit count
    for (j = 0; j < 4; ++j)
        if (sval[j] >= 5)                  //5 or more is flush
            fcnt++;
}
```

● The array sval stores the number of cards of each suit and is initialized to zero for each hand. The function deck::deal deals a card hand into the array one_hand. The expression one_hand[j].s is the suit value of a particular card, for example, 0 if the card were a club. This then is the index of the array sval that counts suits. The variable fcnt winds up with the number of flushes dealt over all these trials. Since the number of trials equals ndeal, the expectation of a flush is fcnt/ndeal.

5.10. Summary

1. The original name given by Stroustrup to his language was "C with classes." A `class` is an extension of the idea of `struct` in traditional C. It is a way of implementing a data type and associated functions and operators. It also is the mechanism in C++ for implementing ADTs, such as complex numbers and stacks.

2. The structure type allows the programmer to aggregate components into a single, named variable. A structure has components, called *members,* that are individually named. Critical to processing structures is the accessing of their members. This is done with either the member operator " . " or the structure pointer operator ->. These operators, along with () and [], have the highest precedence.

3. The concept of `struct` is augmented in C++ to allow functions to be members. The function declaration is included in the structure declaration and is invoked by using access methods for structure members. The idea is that the functionality required by the `struct` data type should be directly included in the `struct` declaration.

4. Member functions that are defined within the `struct` are implicitly inline. As a rule only short, heavily used member functions should be defined within the `struct`. To define a member function outside the `struct`, the scope resolution operator is used.

5. The scope resolution operator allows member functions from the different `struct` types to have the same names. In this case, which member function is invoked will depend on the type of object it acts upon. Member functions within the same `struct` can be overloaded.

6. The concept of `struct` is augmented in C++ to allow functions to have `public` and `private` members. This provides *data hiding*. Inside a `struct`, the use of the keyword `private` followed by a colon restricts the scope of the members that follow this construct. The `private` members can be used by only a few categories of functions, whose privileges include access to these members. These functions include the member functions of the `struct`.

7. Classes in C++ are introduced by the keyword `class`. They are a form of `struct` whose default privacy specification is `private`. Thus `struct` and `class` can be used interchangeably with the appropriate privacy specification.

8. Data members can be declared with the storage class modifier `static`. A data member that is declared `static` is shared by all variables of that class and is stored uniquely in one place. Because of this it can be accessed in the form

   class name :: *identifier*

9. Classes can be nested. The inner class is not inside the scope of the outer class, but rather has the same scope as the outer class. This is not a recommended practice.

5.11. Exercises

1. Design a traditional C structure to store a dairy product's name, portion weight, calories, protein, fat, and carbohydrates. Twenty-five grams of American cheese has 375 calories, 5 grams of protein, 8 grams of fat, and 0 grams of carbohydrates. Show how to assign these values to the member variables of your structure. Write a function that, given a variable of type `struct dairy` and a given weight in grams (portion size), returns the number of calories for that weight.

2. Use the `struct card` defined in Section 5.1 and write a hand-sorting routine. In card games most players keep their cards sorted by pip value. The routine will place aces first, kings next, and so forth, down to twos. A hand will be five cards.

3. The following declarations do not compile correctly. Explain what is wrong.

```
struct brother {
    char            name[20];
    int             age;
    struct sister   sib;
} a;

struct sister {
    char            name[20];
    int             age;
    struct brother  sib;
} a;
```

4. In this exercise use the `struct stack` defined in Section 5.3. Write the function

    ```
    void reverse(char s1[], char s2[]);
    ```

    The strings `s1` and `s2` must be the same size. String `s2` should become a reversed copy of string `s1`. Internal to `reverse` use a `stack` to perform the reversal.

5. Rewrite the functions `push` and `pop` in Section 5.3 to test that `push` is not acting on a full stack and `pop` is not acting on an empty stack. If either condition is detected, print an error message using `cerr` and use `exit(1)` to abort the program.

6. Write `reverse` (see exercise 4) as a member function for type `stack` in Section 5.4. Test it by printing normally and reverse the string

    ```
    Gottfried Leibniz wrote Toward a Universal Characteristic
    ```

7. For the `stack` type in Section 5.4 write as member functions

    ```
    //push n chars from s1[1] onto the stack
    void pushm(int n, char s1[]);

    //pop n chars from stack into char string
    void popm(int n, char s1[]);
    ```

    Hint: Be sure to output a terminator character into the string.

8. What is the difference in meaning between the structure

    ```
    struct a {
        int i, j, k;
    };
    ```

    and the class

    ```
    class a {
        int i, j, k;
    };
    ```

    Explain why the class declaration is not useful. How can you use the keyword `public` to change the class declaration into a declaration equivalent to `struct a`?

9. We wish to define the `class deque` to implement a double-ended queue. A double-ended queue allows push and pop at both ends.

```
class deque {
    char s[max_len];
    int  bottom, top;
public:
    void reset() { top = bottom = max_len / 2; top--; }
      . . .
};
```

Declare and implement push_t, pop_t, push_b, pop_b, out_stack, top_of, bottom_of, empty, and full. The function push_t stands for *push on top*. The function push_b stands for *push on bottom*. The out_stack function should output the stack from its bottom to its top. The pop_t and pop_b functions correspond to *pop from top* and *pop from bottom*. An empty stack is denoted by having the top fall below the bottom. Test each function.

10. Extend the data type deque by adding a member function relocate. If the deque is full, then relocate is called and the contents of the deque are moved to balance empty storage around the center max_len / 2 of array s. Its function declaration header is

```
//returns true if it succeeds, false if it fails
boolean deque::relocate()
```

11. Write a swap function that swaps the contents of two strings. If you pushed a string of characters onto a stack and popped them into a second string, they would come out reversed. In a swap of two strings we want the original ordering. Use a deque to swap two strings. The strings will be stored in two character arrays of the same length, but the strings themselves may be of differing lengths. The function prototype is

```
void swap(char s1[], char s2[]);
```

12. Write the following member functions:

```
void pips::print();
void card::pr_card();
void deck::pr_deck();
```

and add them to the *flush* program found in Section 5.9. Let pr_deck use pr_card and pr_card use print. Print the deck after it is initialized.

13. Write a function pr_hand that prints out card hands. Add it to the *flush* program and use it to print out each flush.

14. In Section 5.9 main detects flushes. Write a function

```
boolean isflush(card hand[], int nc);
```

that returns true if a hand is a flush.

15. Write a function

```
boolean isstraight(card hand[], nc);
```

that returns true if a hand is a straight. A straight is five cards that have sequential pips value. The lowest straight is ace, two, three, four, five and the highest straight is ten, jack, queen, king, ace. Run experiments to estimate the probability that dealt-out cards will be a straight and compare the results of 5-card hands with results of 7-card hands.

   Hint: You may want to set up an array of 15 integers to correspond to counters for each pips value. Be sure that a pip value of 1 (corresponding to aces) is also counted as the high card corresponding to a pip value of 14.

16. Use the previous exercises to determine the probability that a poker hand will be a straight flush. This is a hand that is both a straight and flush. It is the hardest poker hand to get and has the highest

value. Note that in a hand of more than five cards, it is not sufficient to merely check for the presence of both a straight and a flush to determine that the hand is a straight flush.

17. Change the suit declaration from an enumerated type to a class as follows:

```
enum {clubs, diamonds, hearts, spades};

class suit {
    enum {clubs, diamonds, hearts, spades} s;
public:
    void assign(int n) { s = n / 13; }
    int  getsuit() { return (s); }
    void print();
};
```

We use an anonymous enum to define the four integer constants used for suit values. We add the member function getsuit to access the hidden integer value of a suit variable. Now recode all references to suit throughout the program.

CHAPTER 6

Constructors and Destructors

A constructor is a member function whose name is the same as the class name. It *constructs* values of the class type. This process involves initializing of data members and, frequently, allocating free store using new. A destructor is a member function whose name is the class name preceded by the character ~. Its usual purpose is to *destroy* values of the class type, typically by using delete.

Constructors are the more complicated of these two specially named member functions. They may be overloaded and can take arguments, neither of which is possible for destructors. Constructors are invoked when their associated type is used in a declaration. They are also invoked

155

when call-by-value is used to pass a value to a function. Constructors and destructors do not have return types nor can they use `return` statements. Destructors are implicitly invoked when an object of its class must be destroyed, typically upon block exit or function exit.

6.1. Classes with Constructors

The simplest use of a constructor is for initialization. We will develop some examples in this and later sections that will use constructors to initialize the values of the data members of the class.

Our first example is an implementation of a data type `mod_int` to store numbers that are computed with a modulus.

```
// Modulo numbers and constructor initialization

#include <stream.h>

const int modulus = 60;
class mod_int {
    int   v;
public:
    mod_int(int i) { v = i % modulus; }
    void assign(int i) { v = i % modulus; }
    void print() { cout << v << "\t"; }
};
```

The integer v will be restricted in value to 0, 1, 2, . . . modulus − 1. It is the programmer's responsibility to enforce this restriction by having all member functions guarantee this behavior. The member function `mod_int` is a constructor. It does not have a return type. Some examples of declarations using this type are:

```
mod_int   a(0);    // a.v = 0;
mod_int   b(61);   // b.v = 1;
```

but not

```
mod_int   a;        // no parameter list
```

Using this type, we can write code to convert seconds into minutes and seconds as follows.

```
main()
{
    int       seconds = 400;
    mod_int z(seconds);

    cout << seconds << " seconds equals "
         << seconds / 60 << " minutes ";
    z.print();
    cout << " seconds\n";
}
```

It is often convenient to overload the constructor with several function declarations. In our example, it could be desirable to have the default value of v be 0. By adding the constructor

```
mod_int() { v = 0; }
```

as a member function of mod_int, it is possible to have the following declarations:

```
mod_int s1, s2;   // both initialize the private member v to 0
mod_int d[5];     // arrays are properly initialized
```

In both of these declarations the empty parameter list constructor is invoked. Classes with constructors that have a constructor with a void argument list can be the base type of an array declaration. A class with constructors that always require parameters cannot be the base type of an array declaration.

A constructor can also be used to allocate space from free store. We will modify the stack type from Chapter 5 to have its maximum length be initialized by a constructor.

```
//stack implementation with constructor
class stack {
    enum  {EMPTY = -1};
    char* s;              //changed from s[max_len]
    int   max_len;
    int   top;
public:
    //the public interface for the ADT stack
    stack(int size) { s = new char[size];
                      max_len = size; top = EMPTY; }
    void    reset() { top = EMPTY; }
    void    push(char c) { top++; s[top] = c; }
    char    pop() { return (s[top--]); }
    char    top_of() { return (s[top]); }
    boolean empty() { return (top == EMPTY); }
    boolean full() { return (top == max_len - 1); }
};
```

An example of a `stack` declaration invoking this constructor is

```
stack data(1000);     // allocate 1000 element char stack
```

Two alternate constructors would be an empty parameter constructor that would allocate a specific length stack, and a two-parameter constructor whose second parameter is a string used to initialize the stack. They could be written as follows:

```
stack::stack()
{
    s = new char[100];
    max_len = 100;
    top = EMPTY;
}

stack::stack(int size, char str[])
{
    s = new char[size];
    max_len = size;
    for ( int i = 0; i < max_len && str[i] != 0; ++i)
        s[i] = str[i];
    top = --i;
}
```

The corresponding function prototypes would be included as members of the class `stack`.

6.2. Classes with Destructors

Destructors are member functions whose name is the same as the class name preceded by a tilde. They cannot be explicitly called, and usually are associated with classes where data members are dynamically allocated from free store.

Let us augment our stack example with a destructor.

```
//stack implementation with constructors and destructor
class stack {
    enum  {EMPTY = -1};
    char* s;
    int    max_len;
    int    top;
public:
    stack(int size) { s = new char[size];
                      max_len = size; top = EMPTY; }
    stack();
    stack(int size, char str[]);
    ~stack() { delete s; }    //destructor
    . . .
};
```

The external interface of this class remains the same. In other words, all the public member functions perform in exactly the same manner as before. The difference is that the destructor will be implicitly invoked upon block and function exit to clean up storage that is no longer accessible. This is good programming practice and allows programs to execute with less available memory.

6.3. An Example: Dynamically Allocated Strings

A string type is lacking in traditional C. Strings in C are represented as pointer to char and manipulated accordingly. In this representation the end-of-string is denoted by \0. This convention has an important drawback in that many basic string manipulations are proportional to string length. When the string length is known, the efficiency of operations on strings can be significantly improved.

We will develop a useful string ADT in this section that stores its length privately. We want our type to be dynamically allocated, and able to represent arbitrary length strings. A variety of constructors will be coded to initialize and allocate strings, and a set of operations on strings

will be coded as member functions. The implementation will use the
string.h library functions to manipulate the underlying pointer representation of strings.

```
//An implementation of dynamically allocated strings.
#include <string.h>
#include <stream.h>

class string {
    char* s;
    int   len;
public:
    string() { s = new char[81]; len = 80; }
    string(int n) { s = new char[n + 1]; len = n; }
    string(char* p) { len = strlen(p);
                      s = new char[len + 1]; strcpy(s, p); }
    string(string& str);
    ~string() { delete s; }
    void assign(char* str) { strcpy(s, str);
                             len = strlen(str); }
    void print() { cout << s << "\n"; }
    void concat(string& a, string& b);
};

string::string(string& str)
{
    len = str.len;
    s = new char[len + 1];
    strcpy(s, str.s);
}

void string::concat(string& a, string& b)
{
    len = a.len + b.len;
    delete s;
    s = new char[len + 1];
    strcpy(s, a.s);
    strcat(s, b.s);
}
```

This type allows you to declare strings, assign a character array to a
string, print a string, and concatenate two strings. The hidden representation is pointer to char and has a variable len in which to store the
current string length. The constructors all allocate dynamically from free
store.

■ DISSECTION OF THE *string* CLASS

```
string() { s = new char[81]; len = 80; }
string(int n) { s = new char[n + 1]; len = n; }
string(char* p) { len = strlen(p);
                    s = new char[len + 1]; strcpy(s, p); }
string(string& str);
```

● There are four overloaded constructors. The first is the empty parameter default, which also allows us to declare an array of strings. The second has an int parameter that is used to initialize the string length variable len and to retrieve that much store using new. The third constructor has a pointer to char argument that can be used to transform the traditional C representation of strings to our class type. It uses two library functions: strlen and strcpy. We allocate one additional character to store the end-of-string character \0, although this character is not counted by strlen. The fourth constructor will be explained below.

```
~string() { delete s; }
```

● The destructor automatically returns memory allocated to strings back to free store for reuse. The operator delete knows the amount of memory associated with the pointer s as base address.

```
void assign(char* str) { strcpy(s, str);
                          len = strlen(str); }
void print() { cout << s << "\n"; }
```

● These two inline member functions provide an assignment and print operation, respectively. The assignment takes the traditional C representation pointer to char and uses strcpy to copy this to the private member variable s.

```
string::string(string& str)
{
   len = str.len;
   s = new char[len + 1];
   strcpy(s, str.s);
}
```

● This form of constructor is used to perform copying of one string value into another when:

1. A string is initialized by another string

2. A string is passed as an argument in a function

3. A string is returned as the value of a function

In older C++ systems, if this constructor is not present, then these operations are bitwise copy. In newer systems, the default is member-by-member assignment of value.

```
void string::concat(string& a, string& b)
{
    len = a.len + b.len;
    delete s;
    s = new char[len + 1];
    strcpy(s, a.s);
    strcat(s, b.s);
}
```

● This is a form of string concatenation. The two string arguments are not modified. The implicit argument, whose hidden member variables are s and len, is modified to represent the string a followed by the string b. Note that in this member function the use of len, a.len, and b.len is possible. Member functions have access not only to the private members of the implicit argument, but also to the private representation of any of the arguments.

The following code tests this type by concatenating several strings:

```
main()
{
    char*    str = "The wheel that squeaks the loudest\n";
    string   a(str), b, author("Josh Billings\n"), both, quote;

    b.assign("Is the one that gets the grease\n");
    both.concat(a, b);
    quote.concat(both, author);
    quote.print();
}
```

The printout from this program is:

```
The wheel that squeaks the loudest
Is the one that gets the grease
Josh Billings
```

We deliberately used a variety of declarations to show how different constructors would be called. The string variables b, both, and quote all use the empty argument list constructor. The declaration for author uses the constructor whose argument type is char*, which is the type of a literal C string. The concatenation takes place in two steps. First, strings a and b are concatenated into both. Next, strings both and author are concatenated into quote. It is important to understand that both is an argument to concat and is used internally wherever the unqualified member names are written.

6.4. A Class vect

The one-dimensional array in C is a very useful, efficient aggregate type. However, the traditional C array is error prone. A common mistake is to access elements that are *out of bounds*. C++ allows us to control this problem by defining an analogous array type in which bounds can be tested.

```
//Implementation of a safe array type vect
#include <stream.h>

class vect {
    int* p;
    int  size;
public:
    int  ub;                     //upper bound = size - 1
    vect() { size = 10; p = new int[size]; ub = size - 1; }
    vect(int n);
    ~vect() { delete p; }
    int& element(int i);
};

vect::vect(int n)
{
    if (n <= 0) {
        cerr << "illegal vect size " << n << "\n";
        exit(1);
    }
    size = n;
    p = new int[size];
    ub = size - 1;
}

int& vect::element(int i)
{
    if (i < 0 || i > ub) {
        cerr << "illegal vect index " << i << "\n";
        exit(1);
    }
    return (p[i]);
}
```

The constructor `vect::vect(int n)` allows the user to build dynamically allocated arrays. Such arrays are much more flexible than those in traditional C, where array sizes must be constant expressions. The constructor also initializes the variable ub, whose value is the array upper bound. Access to individual elements is through the safe indexing member function int& vect::element(int i). An index that is outside the expected array range 0 through ub will cause an error message and error exit. This safe indexing member function returns a reference to int, that is the address of p[i] and that can be used as the left operand of an assignment or *lvalue*. The technique is much used in C++ and will be an efficient mechanism for operating on complicated types.

As an example, the declarations

```
vect a(10), b(5);
```

construct an array of 10 integers and an array of 5 integers, respectively. Individual elements can be accessed by the member function element, which checks whether the index is out of range. The statements

```
a.element(1) = 5;
b.element(1) = a.element(1) + 7;
cout << a.element(1) - 2;
```

are all legal. In effect we have a safe dynamic array type.

Classes with constructors having an empty argument list can have a derived array type. For example

```
vect a[5];
```

is a declaration that uses the empty argument constructor to create an array a of five objects, each of which is a size 10 vect. The ith element's address in the jth array would be given by a[j].element(i).

6.5. Members That Are Class Types

In this section we will use the type vect as part of a new class. We wish to store multiple values for each index. For example, we may want to store the age, weight, and height of a group of individuals. We could group three arrays together inside a new class.

```
#include "vect.h"

class multi_v {
public:
    vect a, b, c;
    multi_v(int i):a(i), b(i), c(i) { }
};
```

The class has three `vect` members and a constructor, which has an empty body but a list of constructor calls separated by commas. These constructors are executed with the integer argument i creating the three class objects a, b, and c. In early versions of the C++ language the order of constructor invocation was unspecified. In newer versions the order is as written in the comma-separated list, followed by any default initializations.

Let us test this class by writing code to store and print a set of values for age in years, weight in pounds, and height in inches.

```
main()
{
    multi_v a_w_h(5);   //age weight and height

    for (int i = 0; i <= a_w_h.a.ub; ++i) {
        a_w_h.a.element(i) = 21 + i;
        a_w_h.b.element(i) = 135 + i;
        a_w_h.c.element(i) = 62 + i;
    }
    for (i = 0; i <= a_w_h.a.ub; ++i) {
        cout << a_w_h.a.element(i) << " years ";
        cout << a_w_h.b.element(i) << " pounds ";
        cout << a_w_h.c.element(i) << " inches\n";
    }
}
```

The declaration of a_w_h creates three `vect` members each of five elements. When the program is executed, the individual destructors for each `vect` member will be called upon block exit from `main`. The ordering of destructor calls in newer C++ systems is to be the reverse of the call on constructors. When executed, the above program will print:

```
21 years 135 pounds 62 inches
22 years 136 pounds 63 inches
23 years 137 pounds 64 inches
24 years 138 pounds 65 inches
25 years 139 pounds 66 inches
```

6.6. An Example: A Singly Linked List

In this section we develop a singly linked list data type. This is the prototype of many useful dynamic data structures called *self-referential* structures. These data types have pointer members that refer to objects of their own type. A linked list is like a clothes line on which the data elements hang sequentially. The head of the line is the only immediate access point, and items can readily be added to or deleted from it. The following class declaration implements such a type.

```
//A singly linked list

#include <stream.h>

struct listelem {
    char        data;
    listelem*   next;
};

class list {
    listelem*   h;              //head of list
public:
    list() { h = 0; }           //0 is the NULL pointer value
    ~list() { release(); }
    void        add(char c);    //adds to front of list
    void        del() { listelem* temp = h;
                        h = h -> next;
                        delete temp; }
    listelem* first() { return (h); }
    void        pr_list();
    void        release();
};
```

The link member next is self-referential. The variable data in this example is a simple variable, but it could be replaced by a complicated type capable of storing a range of information. The constructor initializes the head of list pointer h to the value 0, which is called the *null pointer constant*. It can be assigned to any pointer type. In linked lists it typically denotes the empty list or end-of-list value. The member function add is used to build the list structure.

```
void list::add(char c)
{
    listelem* temp = new listelem;      //create new element

    temp -> next = h;                   //link to list
    temp -> data = c;
    h = temp;                           //update head of list
}
```

A list element is allocated from free store and its data member is initialized from the single argument c. Its link member next points at the old head of list. The head pointer h is then updated to point at this element as the new first element of the list.

The inline member function del has the inverse role. It returns the first element of the list to free store. It does this by using the delete operator on the head of list pointer h. The new head of list is the value of the next member.

Much of list processing is repetitively chaining down the list until the null pointer value is found. The following two functions use this technique.

```
void list::pr_list()
{
    listelem*  temp = h;

    while (temp != 0) {              //detect end of list
        cout << form("%c -> ", temp -> data);
        temp = temp -> next;
    }
    cout << "\n###\n";
}

void list::release()   //elements are returned to free store
{
    while (h != 0)
        del();
}
```

■ DISSECTION OF THE *pr_list* AND *release* FUNCTIONS

```
void list::pr_list()
{
    listelem*  temp = h;
```

- An auxiliary pointer temp will be used to chain down the list. It is initialized to the address of the list head h. The

pointer h cannot be used because its value would be lost,
in effect destroying access to the list.

```
while (temp != 0) {                         //detect end of list
   cout << form("%c -> ", temp -> data);
   temp = temp -> next;
}
```

- The value 0 represents the end-of-list value. It is guaranteed to be such because the constructor list::list initialized it and the list::add function maintains it as the end-
  of-list pointer value. Notice that the internals of this loop
  could be changed to process the entire list in some other
  manner.

```
void list::release()    //each element is returned to free store
```

- The release function is used to return all list elements to
  free store. It marches down the list doing so.

```
while (h != 0)
   del();
```

- Each element of the list must be returned to free store in
  sequence. This is done for a single element by the member
  function del, which manipulates the hidden pointer h. Since
  we are destroying the list, it is unnecessary to preserve the
  original value of pointer h. This function's chief use is as
  the body of the destructor list::~list. We could not use
  a destructor written

```
list::~list()
{
   delete h;
}
```

because it only deletes the first element in the list.

We demonstrate the use of this type in the following code:

```
main()
{
   list*  p;
   {
      list        w;

      w. add('A');
      w. add('B');
      w. pr_list();
      w. del();
      w. pr_list();
      p = &w;
      p -> pr_list();
   }
   p -> pr_list();
}
```

Notice that there is an inner block in main. That block is included to test that the destructor is invoked upon block exit, returning storage associated with w to free store. The output of this program is

```
B -> A ->
###
A ->
###
A ->
###

###
```

The first pr_list call prints the two-element list storing B and A. After a del operation is performed, the list contains one element storing A. The outer block pointer to list p is assigned the address of the list variable w. When the list is accessed through p in the inner block, it prints A. After block exit the same print command prints the empty list. This output shows that the destructor works at block exit on the variable w.

6.7. Two-Dimensional Arrays

Traditional C does not have authentic higher dimensional arrays. Instead, the programmer must be careful to map such an abstract data structure into a pointer to pointer to . . . base type. In C++ the programmer can implement flexible safe dynamic higher dimensional arrays. We will demonstrate this by implementing a two-dimensional array type `matrix`. The observant reader will notice the strong parallels with the class `vect`.

```
//A two-dimensional safe array type matrix
#include <stream.h>

class matrix {
    int**   p;
    int     s1, s2;
public:
    int     ub1, ub2;
    matrix(int d1, int d2);
    ~matrix();
    int& element(int i, int j);
};
```

The type `matrix` has a size for each dimension and a corresponding public upper bound. The hidden representation uses the pointer to pointer to `int` type. This will store the base address of a vector of pointers to `int` that in turn store a base address for each row vector of the `matrix` type.

```
matrix::matrix(int d1, int d2)
{
    if (d1 < 0 || d2 < 0) {
        cerr << "illegal matrix size "
             << d1 << " by " << d2 << "\n";
        exit(1);
    }
    s1 = d1;
    s2 = d2;
    p = new int*[s1];
    for (int i = 0; i < s1; ++i)
        p[i] = new int[s2];
    ub1 = s1 - 1;
    ub2 = s2 - 1;
}
```

```
matrix::~matrix()
{
    for (int i = 0;  i <= ub1;  ++i)
        delete p[i];
    delete p;
}
```

What is novel here are the ways in which the constructor and destructor work. The constructor allocates a vector of pointer to `int`. The number of elements in this vector is the value of `s1`. Next the constructor iteratively allocates a vector of `int` pointed at by each element `p[i]`. Therefore there is space for `s1 * s2` integers allocated from free store, and additionally the space for `s1` pointers is allocated from free store. The destructor deallocates store in the reverse order. All of this generalizes to higher dimensions.

Obtaining the reference to (lvalue of) an element in this two-dimensional array requires two index arguments.

```
int& matrix::element(int i, int j)
{
    if (i < 0 || i > ub1 || j < 0 || j > ub2) {
        cerr << "illegal matrix index "
             << ub1 << ", " << ub2 << "\n";
        exit(1);
    }
    return (p[i][j]);
}
```

Both arguments are tested to see that they are in range. This is a generalization of the one index case.

6.8. The this Pointer

The keyword `this` denotes an implicitly declared self-referential pointer. It can be used in a non-static member function. A simple illustration of its use is as follows:

```
// Use of the this pointer

#include <stream.h>

class X {
    char     c;    // X* const this is implicit
public:
    void     init(char b) { c = b; }
    char     valc() { return (this -> c); }
    unsigned where_am_I () { return((unsigned)this); }
};

main()
{
    X   a, b, c;
    a.init('A');
    b.init('B');
    c.init('C');
    cout << a.valc() << " is at " << a.where_am_I() << "\n";
    cout << b.valc() << " is at " << b.where_am_I() << "\n";
    cout << c.valc() << " is at " << c.where_am_I() << "\n";
}
```

The member function valc() uses the implicitly provided pointer this to access the member variable c. Of course, it is unnecessary because the member variable is directly available. The member function where_am_I() returns the address of the given object.

Early C++ systems allowed memory management for objects to be controlled by assignment to the this pointer. Such code is obsolete because the this pointer is nonmodifiable.

6.9. Summary

1. A constructor is a member function whose name is the same as the class name. It *constructs* objects of the class type. This process may involve initializing data members and allocating free store using new.

2. A destructor is a member function whose name is the class name preceded by the character ~. Its usual purpose is to *destroy* values of the class type, typically by using delete.

3. A class with constructors that has a constructor with a void argument list can be the base type of an array declaration. A class with constructors that always require parameters cannot be the base type of an array declaration.

4. An example of a class with both a constructor and destructor is

```
class stack {
   char* s;
   int    max_len;
   int    top;
public:
   stack(int size) { s = new char[size];
                        max_len = size; top = 0; }
   ~stack() { delete s; }
   . . .
};
```

5. A constructor of the form

   type: : *type* (*type*& x)

   is used to perform copying of one *type* value into another when:

   A *type* variable is initialized by a *type* value.
   A *type* value is passed as an argument in a function.
   A *type* value is returned from a function.

   In older C++ systems, if this constructor is not present, then these operations are bitwise copy. In newer systems, the default is member-by-member assignment of value.

6. Classes with constructors having an empty argument list can have a derived array type. For example, in Section 6.4

```
vect a[5];
```

is a declaration that uses the empty argument constructor to create an array a of five objects, each of which is a size 10 vect.

7. A class having members whose type requires a constructor may have these specified after the argument list for its own constructor. The constructor has a comma-separated list, following a colon, of constructor calls. The constructor is invoked by using the member name followed by a parenthesized argument list. In early versions of the C++ language, the order of constructor invocation was unspecified. In newer versions the order is as written in the comma-separated list, followed by any default initializations.

8. A singly linked list is the prototype of many useful dynamic data structures called *self-referential* structures. A linked list is like a clothes line on which the data elements hang sequentially. The head of the line is the only immediate access point, and items can readily be added to or deleted from this point.

9. The value 0 is called the *null pointer constant*. It can be assigned to any pointer type. In linked lists it typically denotes the empty list or end-of-list value.

10. The keyword this denotes an implicitly declared self-referential pointer. The this pointer can only be used inside a class member function to refer to non-statically declared members.

6.10. Exercises

1. Discuss why constructors are almost always public member functions. What goes wrong if they are private?

2. Write a member function for the class mod_int

```
void add_to(int i);    //add i to v modulo 60.
```

It should add the number of seconds in `i` to the current value of `v`, while retaining the modulo 60 feature of `v`.

3. Run the following program and explain its behavior. Placing debugging information inside constructors and destructors is a very useful step in developing efficient and correct classes.

```
//Constructors and destructors invoked

#include <stream.h>

class A {
    int xx;
public:
    A(int n) { xx = n;
               cout << form("A(int %d) called\n", n); }
    A(double y) { xx = y + 0.5;
                  cout << form("A(fl %f) called\n", y); }
    ~A() { cout << form("~A() called A::xx = %d\n", xx); }
};

main()
{
    cout << "enter main\n";
    int x = 14;
    double y = 17.3;
    A z(11), zz(11.5), zzz(0);

    zzz = A(x);
    zzz = A(y);
    cout << "exit main\n";
}
```

4. Add an empty parameter list constructor for `class A`.

```
A() { xx = 0; cout << "A() called\n"; }
```

Now modify the previous program by declaring a vector of type `A`

```
A d[5];      //declares a vector of 5 elements of type A
```

Assign the values 0, 1, 2, 3, and 4 to the data member `xx` of each `d[i]`. Run the program and explain its behavior.

5. Use the `stack` type in Section 6.1 in this exercise and include the empty argument constructor to allocate a stack of 100 elements. Write a program that swaps the contents of two stacks, using a vector

of stacks to accomplish the job. The two stacks will be the first two stacks in the vector. One method would be to use four stacks: `st[0]`, `st[1]`, `st[2]` and `st[3]`. Push the contents of `st[1]` into `st[2]`. Push the contents of `st[0]` into `st[3]`. Push the contents of `st[3]` into `st[1]`. Push the contents of `st[2]` into `st[0]`. Verify that the stacks have their contents in the same order by implementing a print function that outputs all elements in the stack. Can this be done with three stacks only?

6. Add a constructor to the type `stack` with the following prototype:

```
stack::stack(char* c);     //initialize from string array
```

7. Use the `string` type in Section 6.3 in this exercise and code the following member functions:

```
//strcmp is negative if s < s1,
//        is 0 if s == s1,
//        and is positive if s > s1
//        where s is the implicit string argument
int string::strcmp(string& s1);

//strrev  reverses the implicit string argument
void string::strrev();

//print  is overloaded to print the first n characters
void string::print(int n);
```

8. Write a function that swaps two strings. Use it and `string::strcmp` from the previous exercise to write a program that will sort an array of strings.

9. Use the `vect` type in Section 6.4 in this exercise and code the following member functions:

```
//adds up all the element values and returns their sum
int vect::sumelem();

//prints all the elements
void vect::print();

//adds two vectors into a third   v(implicit) = v1 + v2
void vect::add(vect& v1, vect& v2);

//adds two vectors and returns  v(implicit) + v1
vect vect::add(vect& v1);
```

10. Write a further constructor for vect that accepts an int array and its size and constructs a vect with these initial values.

```
vect::vect(int* d, int sz);
```

11. Try to benchmark the speed differences between safe arrays as represented by class vect and ordinary integer arrays. Repeatedly run an ordinary element summation routine on int a[10000] and one using the vect a(10000). Time your trials.

12. Define the class multi_v as follows:

```
class multi_v {
    vect a, b, c;
    int  size;
public:
    int  ub;
    multi_v(int i):a(i), b(i), c(i) { size = i;
                                      ub = size -1; }
    void assign(int ind, int i, int j, int k);
    void retrieve(int ind, int& i, int& j, int& k);
    void print(int ind);
};
```

Write and test code for each member function: assign, retrieve, and print. The function assign should assign i, j, and k to a[ind], b[ind], and c[ind], respectively. The function retrieve does the inverse of assign. The function print should print the three values a[ind], b[ind], and c[ind].

13. Use the list type in Section 6.6 in this exercise and code the following member functions:

```
//list a constructor whose initializer is a char array
list::list(char* c);

//length returns the length of the list
int list::length();

//return the number of elements whose data value is c
int list::count_c(char c);
```

14. Write a member function append that will add a list to the rear of the implicit list argument, then clear the appended string by zeroing the head.

```
void list::append(list& e);
```

15. Write a member function copy that will copy a list.

```
//the implicit argument ends up a copy of e
void list::copy(list& e);
```

Be sure you destroy the implicit list before you do the copy.

16. Use the list type and add the equivalent five member functions that give you stack functions.

```
reset    push    pop   top_of   empty
```

17. The following function is a traditional C two-dimensional matrix multiply.

```
void mmpy(int a[M][N], int b[N][R], int c[M][R])
{
    int   i, j, k, t;

    for (i = 0; i < M; ++i)
        for (j = 0; j < R; ++j) {
            t = 0;
            for (k = 0; k < N; ++k)
                t += a[i][k] * b[k][j];
            c[i][j] = t;
        }
}
```

Write the corresponding function for class matrix

```
void matrix::mmpy(matrix& a, matrix& b);
```

where the result of the multiply is the implicit matrix argument.

18. Construct a three-dimensional safe array type called v_3_d.

```
//Implementation of a three-dimensional safe array
class v_3_d {
    int*** p;
    int     s1, s2, s3;
public:
    int     ub1, ub2, ub3;
    v_3_d(int l1, int l2, int l3);
    ~v_3_d();
    int& element(int i, int j, int k);
    void print();
};
```

Initialize and print a three-dimensional array.

19. We wish to define a C++ class that will resemble sets in Pascal.
The underlying representation will be a 32-bit machine word.

```
//Implementation of an ADT for type set.
const unsigned masks[32] = {
    0x80000000, 0x40000000, 0x20000000, 0x10000000,
    . . .

    0x80, 0x40, 0x20, 0x10, 0x8, 0x4, 0x2, 0x1};

class set{
    private:
        unsigned t;
    public:
        set (unsigned i){ t = i;}
        set () { t = 0x0;}
        void u_add(int i){ t |= masks[i];}
        void u_sub(int i){ t &= ~masks[i];}
        boolean in(int i){ return((t  & masks[i]) == masks[i]);}
        void pr_mems();
        set unite(set& v){set temp; temp.t  = v.t  | t; return(temp);}
};
```

Write the code for pr_mems() to print out all the elements of the set.
Write the code for the member function intersection() to return
the resulting set intersection.

CHAPTER 7

Operator Overloading and Conversions

This chapter describes operator overloading and conversions of data types. Overloading operators gives them new meanings for ADTs. The ADT can then be used in much the same way as a built-in type. For example, the expression a + b will have a different meaning depending on the types of the variables a and b. The expression could mean string concatenation, complex number addition, or integer addition depending, respectively, on whether the variables were the ADT string, the ADT complex, or the built-in type int. Mixed type expressions are also possible by defining conversion functions. This chapter also discusses friend functions and how they are crucial to operator overloading.

7.1. The Traditional Conversions

An arithmetic expression such as x + y has both a value and a type. For example, if x and y are both variables of the same type, say int, then x + y is also an int. However, if x and y are of different types, then x + y is a *mixed expression*. Suppose x is a short and y is an int. Then the value of x is converted to an int, and the expression x + y has type int. Note carefully that the value of x as stored in memory is unchanged. It is only a temporary copy of x that is converted during the computation of the value of the expression. Now suppose that both x and y are of type short. Even though x + y is not a mixed expression, automatic conversions again take place; both x and y are promoted to int and the expression is of type int. The general rules are straightforward.

Automatic conversion in an arithmetic expression *x op y*

First:
   Any char, short, or enum is promoted to int.
   Integral values unrepresentable as int are promoted to unsigned.

Second:
   If after the first step the expression is of mixed type, then according to the hierarchy of types

```
int < unsigned < long < unsigned long
     < float < double < long double
```

   the operand of lower type is promoted to that of the higher type and the value of the expression has that type.

To illustrate implicit conversion, we first make the following declarations:

```
char c;        double d;      float f;       int i;
long lg;       short s;       unsigned u;
```

Now we can list a variety of mixed expressions along with their corresponding types:

Expression	Type	Expression	Type
c - s / i	int	u * 3 - i	unsigned
u * 3.0 - i	double	f * 3 - i	float
c + 1	int	3 * s * lg	long
c + 1.0	double	d + s	double

In addition to automatic conversions in mixed expressions, an automatic conversion also can occur across an assignment. For example

```
d = i
```

causes the value of i, which is an int, to be converted to a double and then assigned to d; double is the type of the expression as a whole. A promotion or widening such as d = i will usually be well behaved, but a narrowing or demotion such as i = d can lose information. Here, the fractional part of d will be discarded. Precisely what happens in each case is machine-dependent.

In addition to implicit conversions, which can occur across assignments and in mixed expressions, there are explicit conversions called *casts*. If i is an int, then

```
(double) i
```

will cast the value of i so that the expression has type double. The variable i itself remains unchanged. Casts can be applied to expressions. Some examples are

```
(char) ('A' + 1.0)
x = (float) ((int) y + 1)
(double) (x = 77)
```

The cast operator (*type*) is a unary operator having the same precedence and right-to-left associativity as other unary operators. Thus the expression

```
(float) i + 3      is equivalent to      ((float) i) + 3
```

because the cast operator (*type*) has higher precedence than +.

These conversions are all found in C. In C++, we also have implicit pointer conversions. As we mentioned in Chapter 4 any pointer type can be converted to a generic pointer of type void*. Other pointer conversions include: the name of an array is a pointer to its base element;

the null pointer value can be converted to any type; the type function returning x is converted to pointer to function. C++ is generally stricter than traditional C and does not allow mixing of pointer types unless they are correctly cast.

7.2. ADT Conversions

Explicit type conversion of an expression is necessary when either the implicit conversions are not desired or the expression will not otherwise be legal. Traditional C casts are augmented in C++ by a functional notation as a syntactic alternative. C++ has as one aim: the integration of user-defined ADTs and built-in types. To achieve this, there is a mechanism for having a member function provide an explicit conversion.

A functional notation of the form

type-name   (*expression*)

is equivalent to a cast. The type must be expressible as an identifier. Thus, the two expressions

```
x = float(i);     //C++ functional notation
x = (float) i;
```

are equivalent. The expression

```
p = (int*) q;     //legal cast
```

cannot be directly expressed functionally as

```
p = int*(q);      //illegal
```

However, a `typedef` can be used to achieve this result:

```
typedef  int*  int_ptr;
p = int_ptr(q);
```

Functional notation is the preferred style.

A constructor of one argument is de facto a type conversion from the argument's type to the constructor's class type. In Section 6.3 the string type had a constructor

```
string(char* p) { len = strlen(p);
                  s = new char[len + 1]; strcpy(s, p); }
```

This is automatically a type transfer from char* to string. It is available both explicitly and implicitly. Explicitly it is used as a conversion operation in either cast or functional form. Thus

```
string s;
char*  logo = "Geometrics Inc";

s = string(logo);     //performs conversion then assignment
```

and

```
s = logo;             //implicit invocation of conversion
```

both work.

These are conversions from an already defined type to a user-defined type. However, it is not possible for the user to add a constructor to a built-in type such as int or double. In the string example, one may also want a conversion from string to char*. This can be done by defining a special conversion function inside the string class, as follows:

```
operator char*() { return (s); }   //char* s is a member
```

The general form of such a member function is

```
operator type() { . . . }
```

These conversions occur implicitly in assignment expressions, in arguments to functions, and in values returned from functions.

7.3. Overloading and Function Selection

Overloaded functions are an important addition in C++. The overloaded meaning is selected by matching the argument list of the function call to the argument list of the function declaration. When an overloaded function is invoked, the compiler must have a selection algorithm with which to pick the appropriate function. The algorithm that accomplishes this depends on what type conversions are available. A best match must be unique. It must be best on at least one argument and as good on all other arguments as any other match.

The matching algorithm for each argument is as follows:

Overloaded Function Selection Algorithm

1. Use an exact match if found.
2. Try standard type conversions.
3. Try user-defined conversions.
4. Use a match to ellipsis if found.

Let us write an overloaded function `greater` and follow our algorithm for various invocations. In this example the user type `complex` is available.

```
//overloading functions

#include <stream.h>
double sqrt(double);

class complex {
   double real, imag;
public:
   complex(double r) { real = r; imag = 0; }
   void assign(double r, double i) { real = r; imag = i; }
   void print() { cout << real << " + " << imag << "i "; }
   operator double() {return(sqrt(real * real + imag * imag));}
};

inline int     greater(int i, int j)
               { return ( i > j ? i : j); }
inline double  greater(double x, double y)
               { return ( x > y ? x : y); }
inline complex greater(complex w, complex z)
               { return ( w > z ? w : z); }
```

```
main()
{
    int      i = 10, j = 5;
    double   x = 7.0, y = 14.5;
    complex w(0), z(0), zmax(0);

    w.assign(x, y);
    z.assign(i, j);
    cout << form("compare %d  and  %d  greater is %d\n",
                    i, j, greater(i,j));
    cout << form("compare %g  and  %d  greater is %g\n",
                    y, j, greater(y, (double)j));
    cout << "compare " << y << "  and  ";
    z.print();
    cout << "  greater is " << greater(y, double(z)) << "\n";
    zmax = greater(w, z);
    cout << "compare ";
    w.print();
    cout << "  and  ";
    z.print();
    cout << "  greater is   ";
    zmax.print();
    cout << "\n\n";
}
```

The output from this program is:

```
compare 10   and   5  greater is 10
compare 14.5   and   5  greater is 14.5
compare 14.5   and   10 + 5i   greater is 14.5
compare 7 + 14.5i   and   10 + 5i   greater is   7 + 14.5i
```

A variety of conversion rules, both implicit and explicit, are being applied. We explain these in the following dissection.

■ DISSECTION OF THE *overloading* PROGRAM

```
complex(double r) { real = r; imag = 0; }
```

- This constructor provides a conversion from `double` to `complex`.

```
operator double() {return(sqrt(real * real + imag * imag));}
```

- This member function provides a conversion from `complex` to `double`.

```
inline int      greater(int i, int j)
                { return ( i > j ? i : j); }
inline double   greater(double x, double y)
                { return ( x > y ? x : y); }
inline complex  greater(complex w, complex z)
                { return ( w > z ? w : z); }
```

- Three distinct functions are overloaded. The most interesting has `complex` type for its argument list variables and its return type. The conversion member function `operator double` is required to evaluate `w > z`. The `complex` variables `w` and `z` are converted to `double`. Later in this chapter we will discuss overloading operators, a construct that will allow us to provide new meanings to existing C++ operators. No conversion is necessary for the return type.

```
w.assign(x, y);
z.assign(i, j);
```

- The first invocation of the member function `assign` has both arguments as `double`, requiring no conversion. The second invocation has both arguments as `int`, requiring conversion. Integer arguments are assignment compatible with `double`.

```
cout << form("compare %d  and  %d  greater is %d\n",
             i, j, greater(i,j));
cout << form("compare %g  and  %d  greater is %g\n",
             y, j, greater(y, (double)j));
```

- The first statement selects the first definition of `greater` because of the exact match rule. The second statement selects the second definition of `greater` because of the use of a cast to convert `int` to `double`. The value of variable `j` is widened to `double`.

```
cout << "  greater is " << greater(y, double(z)) << "\n";
```

- The second definition of `greater` is selected because of the exact match rule. The explicit conversion `double(z)` is necessary to avoid ambiguity. The function call

```
greater(y, z);
```

would have two available conversions to achieve a match. The user-defined conversion of `double` to `complex` for the argument `y` matches the third definition. The user-defined conversion from `complex` to `double` for the argument `z` matches the second definition. This violates the uniqueness provision for matching when user-specified conversions are involved.

```
zmax = greater(w, z);
```

- An exact match for definition three.

7.4. Friend Functions

The keyword `friend` is a function specifier. It gives a nonmember function access to the hidden members of the class. Its use is a method of escaping the strict strong typing and data hiding restrictions of C++. However, we must have a good reason for escaping these restrictions, as they are both important to reliable programming. This feature of the C++ language is controversial.

One reason for using `friend` functions is that some functions need privileged access to more than one class. A second reason is that `friend` functions pass all their arguments through the argument list, and each argument value is subject to assignment-compatible conversions. Conversions would apply to a class variable passed explicitly and would be especially useful in cases of operator overloading, as seen in the next section.

A `friend` function must appear inside the class declaration to which it is a friend. The function is prefaced by the keyword `friend` and can appear in either the public or private part of the class without affecting its meaning. Member functions of one class can be `friend` functions of another class. In this case they are written in the friend's class using the scope resolution operator to qualify its function name. If all member functions of one class are `friend` functions of a second class, this can be specified by writing `friend class` *class name*.

The following declarations illustrate the syntax:

```
class tweedledee {
    . . .
    friend void alice();                //friend function
    int         cheshire();             //member function
    . . .
};

class tweedledum {
    . . .
    friend int tweedledee::cheshire();
    . . .
};

class tweedledumber {
    . . .
    friend class tweedledee;       //all member functions
                                   //of tweedledee have access
    . . .
};
```

Consider the `class matrix` and the `class vect` in Chapter 6. A function multiplying a vector by a matrix as represented by these two classes could be written efficiently if it had access to the private members of both classes. It would be a `friend` function of both classes. In our discussion in Chapter 6, safe access was provided to the elements of `vect` and `matrix` with their respective member function `element`. One could write a function using this access that would multiply without requiring `friend` status. However, the price in functional call overhead and array bounds checking would make such a matrix multiply unnecessarily inefficient.

```
class matrix;                    //forward reference

class vect {
   int*        p;
   int         size;
   friend vect mpy(vect& v, matrix& m);
public:
   . . .
};

class matrix {
   int**       p;
   int         s1, s2;
   friend vect mpy(vect& v, matrix& m);
public:
   . . .
};

vect mpy(vect& v, matrix& m)
{
   if (v.size != m.s1) {      //incorrect sizes
      cerr << "multiply failed - sizes incorrect "
           << v.size << " and " << m.s1 << "\n";
      exit(1);
   }
   //use privileged access to p in both classes
   vect ans(m.s2);
   for (int i = 0; i <= m.ub2; ++i) {
      ans.p[i] = 0;
      for (int j = 0; j <= m.ub1; ++j)
         ans.p[i] += v.p[j] * m.p[j][i];
   }
   return (ans);
}
```

A minor point is the necessity of an empty declaration of the class matrix. This is necessary because the function mpy must appear in both classes and it uses each class as an argument type.

Friends are controversial because they break through the encapsulating wall surrounding private members of classes. The OOP paradigm is that objects (in C++ these are class variables) should be accessed through their public members. Only member functions should have access to the hidden implementation of the ADT. This is a neat, orderly design principle. The friend function, however, straddles this boundary. It is neither fish nor fowl. It has access to private members but is not itself a member function. It can be used to provide quick fixes to code that needs access to the implementation details of a class. But the mechanism is easily abused. However, as in the previous example, some coding situations require its use.

7.5. Overloading Operators

The keyword `operator` is used to define a type conversion member function. It is also used to overload the built-in C operators. Just as a function name, such as `print`, can be given a variety of meanings that depend on its arguments, so can an operator, such as `+`, be given additional meanings. Overloading operators allows infix expressions of both ADTs and built-in types to be written. It is an important notational convenience and in many instances leads to shorter and more readable programs.

The previous section's `mpy` function could have been written as:

```
vect operator* (vect& v, matrix& m)
   .  .  .
```

If this had been done, and if `r` and `s` were `vect` and `t` was a `matrix`, then the natural looking expression

```
r = s * t;
```

would invoke the multiply function. This replaces the functional notation

```
r = mpy(s, t);
```

Although meanings can be added to operators, their associativity and precedence remain the same. For example, the multiplication operator will remain of higher precedence than the add operator. The operator precedence table for C++ is included in Appendix B. Almost all operators can be overloaded. The exceptions are the member operator `.`, the member object selector operator `.*` (see Chapter 10), the ternary conditional expression operator `? :`, the `sizeof` operator, and the scope resolution operator `: :`.

Available operators include all the arithmetic, logical, comparison, equality, assignment, and bit operators. The subscript operator `[]` and the function call `()` can also be overloaded. It is also possible to overload `new` and `delete`.

7.6. Unary Operator Overloading

We will continue our discussion of operator overloading by demonstrating how to overload unary operators, such as !, ++, ~, and []. For this purpose we develop the `class clock`, which can be used to store time as days, hours, minutes, and seconds. We will develop familiar operations on this `clock`.

```
class clock {
    unsigned int  tot_secs, secs, mins, hours, days;
public:
    clock(unsigned int i);      //constructor and conversion
    void print();               //formatted printout
    void tick();                //add one second
    clock operator ++() { this -> tick(); return(*this); }
};
```

This class overloads the autoincrement operator. The overloaded operator is a member function and can be invoked on its implicit single argument. The member function `tick` adds one second to the implicit argument of the overloaded ++ operator.

```
inline clock::clock(unsigned int i)
{
    tot_secs = i;
    secs = tot_secs % 60;
    mins = (tot_secs / 60) % 60;
    hours = (tot_secs / 3600) % 24;
    days = tot_secs / 86400;
}

void clock::tick()
{
    clock  temp = clock(++tot_secs);

    secs = temp.secs;
    mins = temp.mins;
    hours = temp.hours;
    days = temp.days;
}
```

The constructor performs the usual conversions from `tot_secs` to days, hours, minutes, and seconds. For example, there are 86,400 seconds in a day, and therefore integer division by this constant gives the whole number of days. The member function `tick` constructs `clock temp`, which adds one second to the total time. The constructor acts as a conversion function that properly updates the time.

The overloaded member function ++ also updates the implicit `clock` variable, but returns the updated value as well. It could have been coded in the same way as `tick`, except that the statement

```
return(temp);
```

would be added.

Adding the following code, we can test our functions:

```
void clock::print()
{
    cout << days << " d :" << hours << " h :"
         << mins << " m :" << secs << " s\n";
}

main()
{
    clock t1(59), t2(172799);   //min - 1 sec and 2 days - 1 sec
    cout << "initial times are\n";
    t1.print();
    t2.print();
    ++t1;   ++t2;              //t1++; t2++ are also possible
    cout << "after one second times are\n";
    t1.print();
    t2.print();
}
```

The output is

```
initial times are
0 d :0 h :0 m :59 s
1 d :23 h :59 m :59 s
after one second times are
0 d :0 h :1 m :0 s
2 d :0 h :0 m :0 s
```

It would have been possible to overload ++ using a `friend` function as follows:

```
friend clock clock::operator ++(clock& cl)
                { cl.tick(); return(cl); }
```

Note, since the clock variable must advance by one second, we call it by reference. The decision to choose between a `friend` representation and a member function representation typically depends on whether or not implicit conversion operations are available and desirable. Explicit argument passing, as in `friend` functions, allows the argument to be automatically coerced if necessary and possible.

7.7. Binary Operator Overloading

We continue with our `clock` example and show how to overload binary operators. Basically the same principles hold. When a binary operator is overloaded using a member function, it has as its first argument the implicitly passed class variable and as its second argument the lone argument list parameter. Friend functions or ordinary functions have both arguments specified in the parameter list. Of course ordinary functions cannot access private members.

Let us create an adding operation for type `clock` that will add two values together.

```
class clock {
    . . .
    friend clock operator +(clock c1, clock c2);
};

clock operator +(clock c1, clock c2)
{
    unsigned total_sec = c1.tot_secs + c2.tot_secs;
    clock temp = total_sec;
    return (temp);
}
```

Both arguments are specified explicitly. They are both candidates for assignment conversions. The line of code

```
clock temp = total_sec;
```

uses the constructor to convert `total_sec` into a `clock` value. This could have also been written

```
clock temp(total_sec);
```

In contrast, let us overload binary minus with a member function.

```
class clock {
   . . .
   clock operator -(clock c);
};

clock clock::operator -(clock c)
{
   unsigned total_sec = tot_secs - c.tot_secs;
   clock temp = total_sec;
   return (temp);
}
```

Remember that there is an implicit first argument. This takes some getting used to.

We will define a multiplication operation as a binary operation with one argument an unsigned int and the second argument a clock variable. The operation will require the use of a friend function. A member function must have the first argument from its class.

```
clock operator *(unsigned int m, clock c)
{
   unsigned total_sec = m * c.tot_secs;
   clock temp = total_sec;
   return (temp);
}
```

This requirement forces the multiplication to have a fixed ordering that is type-dependent. To avoid this, it is common practice to write a second overloaded function:

```
clock operator *(clock c, unsigned int m)
   . . .
```

7.8. Overloading Assignment and Subscripting Operators

In C++ there are reference declarations. In effect, such type modifiers produce lvalues. On the right side of an assignment expression, an lvalue is automatically dereferenced. On the left side of an assignment expression, it specifies where an appropriate value is to be stored. Both subscripting and assignment make use of these properties of lvalues. For

ADTs, we must define such expressions unless satisfactory defaults are available. We will reimplement the `class vect` from Section 6.4, extending its functionality by applying operator overloading.

The reimplemented class will have several improvements to make it both safer and more useful. A constructor that converts an ordinary integer array to a safe array will be added. This will allow us to develop code using safe arrays and later run the same code efficiently on ordinary arrays. The public data member `ub` has been changed to a member function. This prevents a user from inadvertently introducing a program error by modifying the member. Finally, the subscript operator `[]` is overloaded and replaces the member function `element`.

```
//A safe array type vect with [] overloaded
#include <stream.h>

class vect {
    int* p;                          //base pointer
    int size;                        //number of elements
public:
    //constructors and destructor
    vect();                          //create a size 10 array
    vect(int n);                     //create a size n array
    vect(vect& v);                   //initialization by vect
    vect(int a[], int n);            //initialization by array
    ~vect() { delete p; }
    //other member functions
    int  ub() { return (size - 1); } //upper bound
    int& operator [](int i);         //range checked element
};

vect::vect()
{
    size = 10;
    p = new int[size];
}

vect::vect(int n)
{
    if (n <= 0) {
        cerr << "illegal vect size: " << n << "\n";
        exit(1);
    }
    size = n;
    p = new int[size];
}
```

```
vect::vect(int a[], int n)
{
    if (n <= 0) {
        cerr << "illegal vect size: " << n << "\n";
        exit(1);
    }
    size = n;
    p = new int[size];
    for (int i = 0; i < size; ++i)
        p[i] = a[i];
}

vect::vect(vect& v)
{
    size = v.size;
    p = new int[size];
    for (int i = 0; i < size; ++i)
        p[i] = v.p[i];
}

int& vect::operator [](int i)
{
    if (i < 0 || i > ub()) {
        cerr << "illegal vect index: " << i << "\n";
        exit(1);
    }
    return (p[i]);
}
```

An overloaded subscript operator can have any return type and any argument list type. However, it is good style to maintain the consistency between a user-defined meaning and standard usage. Thus a most common function prototype is:

class name& operator [] (*integral type*);

A reference value is returned in such functions that can be used on either side of an assignment expression.

It is also convenient to be able to assign one array to another. The user can specify the behavior of assignment by overloading it. It is good style to maintain consistency with standard usage. The following member function overloads assignment for class vect:

```
vect& vect::operator =(vect& v)
{
    int s = (size < v.size) ? size : v.size;

    if (v.size != size)
        cerr << "copying different size arrays "
             << size << " and " << v.size << "\n";
    for (int i = 0; i < s; ++i)
        p[i] = v.p[i];
    return (*this);
}
```

■ DISSECTION OF THE *vect::operator =(vect& v)* FUNCTION

```
vect& vect::operator =(vect& v)
```

- The operator = function returns reference to vect and has one explicit argument of type reference to vect. The first argument of the assignment operator is the implicit argument. The function could have been written to return void, but then it would not have allowed multiple assignment.

```
int s = (size < v.size) ? size : v.size;
```

- The smaller size will be used in the element-by-element assignment. This function will allow a smaller array to have its contents copied into the beginning of a larger array. When assigning from the larger array, it will use only as many elements as are in the smaller array.

```
if (v.size != size)
    cerr << "copying different size arrays "
         << size << " and " << v.size << "\n";
```

- A warning to the user in case this use was inadvertent.

```
for (int i = 0; i < s; ++i)
   p[i] = v.p[i];
return (*this);
```

- The explicit argument v.p[] will be the right-hand side of the assignment; the implicit argument, as represented by p[], will be the left-hand side of the assignment. The self-referential pointer is dereferenced and passed back as the value of the expression. This allows multiple assignment with right-to-left associativity to be defined.

■

Expressions of type vect can be evaluated by overloading in appropriate ways the various arithmetic operators. As an example, let us overload binary plus to mean element-by-element addition of two vect variables.

```
vect vect::operator +(vect& v)
{
   int s = (size < v.size) ? size : v.size;
   vect  sum(s);

   if (v.size != size)
      cerr << "adding different size arrays"
           << size << " and " << v.size << "\n";
   for (int i = 0; i < s; ++i)
      sum.p[i] = p[i] + v.p[i];
   return (sum);
}
```

Now with the class vect, as extended, all of the following expressions are meaningful:

```
a = b;                      //a, b are type vect
a = b = c;                  //a, b, c are type vect
a = vect(data, DSIZE);      //convert array data[DSIZE]
a = b + a;                  //assignment and addition
a = b + (c = a) + d;        //complicated expression
```

The class vect is a full-fledged ADT. It behaves and appears in client code much as any built-in type behaves and appears.

7.9. Summary

1. Overloading operators gives them new meanings for ADTs. The ADT can then be used in much the same way as a built-in type. For example, the expression a + b will have a different meaning depending on the types of the variables a and b. The expression could mean string concatenation, complex number addition, or integer addition depending, respectively, on whether the variables were the ADT string, the ADT complex, or the built-in type int.

2. A functional notation of the form

   type-name   (*expression*)

   is equivalent to a cast. The type must be expressible as an identifier. Thus, the two expressions

   ```
   x = float(i);    //C++ functional notation
   x = (float) i;
   ```

   are equivalent.

3. A constructor of one argument is de facto a type conversion from the argument's type to the constructor's class type. A conversion from a user-specified type to a built-in type can be made by defining a special conversion function. The general form of such a member function is

   ```
   operator type()   { . . . }
   ```

   These conversions occur implicitly in assignment expressions, in arguments to functions, and in values returned from functions.

4. Overloaded functions are an important addition in C++. A best match must be unique. It must be best in at least one argument and as good on all other arguments as any other match. The matching algorithm simplified is as follows:

   1. Use an exact match if found.
   2. Try standard type conversions.
   3. Try user-defined conversions.
   4. Use a match to ellipsis if found.

5. The keyword `friend` is a function specifier. It allows a nonmember function access to the hidden members of the class of which it is a friend. Its use is a method of escaping the strict strong typing and data hiding restrictions of C++.

6. The keyword `operator` is also used to overload the built-in C operators. Just as a function name, such as `print`, can be given a variety of meanings that depend on its arguments, so can an operator, such as `+`, be given additional meanings. Overloading operators allows infix expressions of both user types and built-in types to be written. The precedence and associativity remain fixed.

7. Operator overloading typically uses either member functions or friend functions because they both have privileged access. When a unary operator is overloaded using a member function, it has an empty argument list because the single operator argument is the implicit argument. When a binary operator is overloaded using a member function, it has as its first argument the implicitly passed class variable and as its second argument the lone argument list parameter. Friend functions or ordinary functions have both arguments specified in the parameter list.

8. An overloaded subscript operator can have any return type and any argument list type. However, it is good style to maintain the consistency between a user-defined meaning and standard usage. Thus a most common function prototype is:

> *class name*& operator [] (*integral type*);

A reference value is returned in such functions that can be used on either side of an assignment expression.

7.10. Exercises

1. The following table has a variety of mixed type expressions. You are to fill in both the type the expression is converted to and its value when well defined.

Declarations and initializations		

int   i = 3, *p = &i;
char   c = 'b';
float x = 2.14, *q = &x;		

Expression	Type	Value
i + c		
x + i		
p + i		
p == & i		
* p - * q		
(int)x + i		

2. For the type `complex` provide a constructor that converts an `int` to a `complex`. Explain why this is redundant where a constructor from `double` has been provided. Write an explicit conversion that converts `complex` to `double` with the meaning that its value is its real component.

3. If the following line of code from the `greater` program

   ```
   cout << "  greater is " << greater(y, double(z)) << "\n";
   ```

   is replaced by

   ```
   cout << "  greater is " << greater(y, z) << "\n";
   ```

   what goes wrong?

4. Write a function that adds a `vect` v to a `matrix` m. The prototype to be added to `class matrix` and `class vect` is

   ```
   friend vect add(vect& v, matrix& m);
   ```

   The `vect` v will be added element by element to each row of m.

5. The class `complex` as defined in this chapter is:

```
class complex {
   double real, imag;
public:
   complex(double r) { real = r; imag = 0; }
   void assign(double r, double i) { real = r; imag = i; }
   void print() { cout << real << " + " << imag << "i "; }
   operator double()
           { return(sqrt(real * real + imag * imag)); }
};
```

We wish to augment it by overloading a variety of operators. For example, the member function `print` could be replaced by overloading the `~` operator:

```
void operator ~() { cout << real << " + " << imag << "i "; }
```

Rewrite this as a `friend` function. Also code and test a unary minus operator. It should return a `complex` whose value in each part is negated.

6. For the type `complex` write the following binary operator functions: add, multiply, and subtract. Each should return `complex`. Write two versions, a `friend` version and a member function version.

7. Write two `friend` functions

```
friend complex operator +(complex, double);
friend complex operator +(double, complex);
```

In the absence of a conversion from type `double` to type `complex`, both types are needed in order to allow completely mixed expressions of `complex` and `double`. Explain why writing one with an `int` parameter is unnecessary when these `friend` functions are available.

8. Overload assignment for `complex`. In the presence of the conversion operator for converting `complex` to `double`, what is the effect of assigning a `complex` to `double`?

9. Program a `class vec_complex` that is a safe array type whose element values are `complex`. Overload the operators + and * to mean element-by-element `complex` addition and dot-product of two `complex` vectors, respectively. For added efficiency you can make the `class vec_complex` a friend of `class complex`.

10. The following member function is a form of *iterator*:

    ```
    int& vect::iterate()
    {
        static int i = 0;
        i = i % size;
        return (p[i++]);
    }
    ```

    It is called an iterator because it returns each element value of a vect in sequence. Use it to write a print function that is not a member function and that writes out all element values of a given vect.

11. Exercise 10 has a serious limitation. By providing an iterator that is contained in the class, the element sequencing will not depend on the individual vect variable. Thus, if a and b are both vect variables, the first call of a.iterate() will get the first element of a and a subsequent call of b.iterate() will get the second element of b. So instead we will define a new class vect_iterator as follows:

    ```
    class vect_iterator {
        int   i;
        int   *p;
    public:
        vect_iterator(vect& v) { p = v.p; i = 0; }
        int& iterate();
    };
    ```

    This class is to be a friend of vect. Write the code for iterate(). Then for each declaration of a vect there will be a corresponding declaration of its iterator. For example,

    ```
    vect a(5), b(10);
    vect_iterator it_(a), it_(b);
    ```

    Use this to write a function that finds the maximum element value in a vect.

12. Define a new class matrix_iterator as the iterator that sequences through all elements of a matrix (Section 6.7). Use it to find the maximum element in a matrix.

13. Redo the string ADT of Section 6.3 by using operator overloading. The member function assign should be changed to become operator=.

The member function `concat` should be changed to become `operator+`. Also, overload `operator[]` to return the `i`th character in the string. If there is no such character, the value -1 is to be returned.

14. Redo the list ADT of Section 6.6 by using operator overloading. The member function `add` should be changed to become `operator+`. The member function `del` should be changed to become `operator--`. Also, overload `operator[]` to return the `i`th element in the list.

15. Modify the `class set` in chapter 6, exercise 19, to have overloaded operators $+$, $-$, and $*$.

```
class set {
    . . .
    set operator+ (set& v); //define union
    set operator* (set& v); //define intersection
    set operator- (set& v); //define difference
};
```

Test your complete set ADT with the following:

```
main()
{
    set    s(0×5555), t(0×10303021), w, x;
    s.pr_mems(); t.pr_mems(); w.pr_mems(); x.pr_mems();
    w = s + t;          //set union
    x = s * t;          //set intersection
    t = t - s;          //set difference
    s.pr_mems(); t.pr_mems(); w.pr_mems(); x.pr_mems();
}
```

Notice that we now have added a set type that is similar to the built-in Pascal set type.

CHAPTER 8

Inheritance

This chapter describes inheritance in C++. Inheritance is the mechanism of *deriving* a new class from an old one. That is, the existing class can be added to or altered to create the derived class. Through inheritance, a hierarchy of related ADTs can be created that share code, a feature critical to the ability to reuse code. Inheritance is an important component of OOP (for multiple inheritance see Chapter 10).

Many useful data structures are variants of one another, and it is frequently tedious to produce the same code for each. A derived class inherits the description of the *base* class. It can then be altered by adding members, overloading existing member functions, and modifying access privileges. The usefulness of this concept can be seen by examining how taxonomic classification compactly summarizes large bodies of knowl-

207

edge. For example, knowing the concept mammal and knowing that an elephant and mouse are both mammals allows our descriptions of them to be considerably more succinct than they would be otherwise. The root concept mammal contains the information that mammals are warm-blooded animals and higher vertebrates, and that they nourish their young using milk-producing mammary glands. This information is inherited by both the mouse and the elephant, but it is expressed only once: in the root class. In C++ terms, both elephant and mouse are derived from the base class mammal.

C++ supports `virtual` member functions. These are functions declared in the base class and overloaded in a derived class. An ADT hierarchy that is defined by inheritance creates a related set of user types, all of whose objects may be pointed at by a base class pointer. By accessing the `virtual` function through this pointer, C++ selects the appropriate overloaded function at run-time. The object being pointed at must carry around type information so that this distinction can be made dynamically, a feature typical of OOP code. Each object "knows" how it is to be acted on. We briefly touched on this in Section 3.7 and we will explain it in detail in this chapter.

The OOP design methodology becomes:

1. Decide on an appropriate set of ADTs.

2. Design in their relatedness and use inheritance to share code.

3. Use virtual functions to process related objects dynamically.

8.1. A Derived Class

A class can be derived from an existing class using the form:

```
class class-name :   (public|private) optional base-class-name
{
    member declarations
};
```

As usual, the keyword `class` can be replaced by the keyword `struct`, with the usual implication that members are default `public`. The most complicated aspect of the derived class is the visibility of its inherited members. One of two keywords, `public` and `private`, can optionally be used to specify how the base class members are to be accessible to the derived class. We will explore this in detail in the next section.

An example of deriving a class is:

```
class student {
public:
    int    student_id;
    float gpa;
    char   name[30];
    char   college[20];
    enum   {fresh, soph, junior, senior} year;
    char   major[10];
    void   print();
};

class grad_student:public student {
public:
    enum {ta, ra, fellowship, other} support;
    char dept[10];
    char thesis[80];
    void print();
};
```

In this example, grad_student is the derived class and student is the base class. The use of the keyword public following the colon in the derived class header means that the public members of student are to be public members of grad_student.

A derived class is a modification of the base class that inherits the public members of the base class. Thus, in the example of grad_student, the student members—student_id, gpa, name, college, year, major, and print —are inherited. Frequently, a derived class adds new members to the existing class members. This is the case with grad_student, which has three new data members and a redefined member function print. A derived class can also be restrictive. The derived class can change the visibility of members and it can alter their meanings.

8.2. public, private, **and** protected

The keywords public, private, and protected are available as visibility modifiers for class members. A public member is visible throughout its scope. A private member is visible to other member functions within its own class. A `protected` member is visible to other member functions within its class and any class immediately derived from it. These visibility modifiers can be used within a class declaration in any order and with any frequency. The usual style is:

```
class foo {
private:   //optional
   . . .
protected:
   . . .
public:
   . . .
};
```

This ordering is from least visible to most visible. In older compilers, where `private` and `protected` are not available, the ordering conforms to the omission of the keyword `private`.

The visibility modifiers can be explicitly used in the class declaration header. If not used there, the default-inherited visibility for `class` is `private` and for `struct` is `public`. The recommended style is to always be explicit. The most frequent use is to make the base class publicly visible to the derived class. This was seen in the example of `grad_student` in the previous section. In `public` derivation, the derived class inherits both the `public` and `protected` members of the base class and retains these visibilities. Thus a `public` member of the base class is also a public member of the derived class. The private members of the base class are not accessible to the derived class. In `private` derivation, the derived class has access to both the `public` and `protected` members of the base class, but within the derived class they are considered `private`.

As can be seen, visibility modifiers in the header can be used to restrict access to members. It is possible to alter this for individual members in the derived class. If a member is transmitted to its derived class as `private`, this can be altered to `public` or `protected`, as in the following:

```
class b {
protected:
    int g;
public:
    int f;
    int h;
    . . .
};

class d : private b { //f,g,h default to private
protected:
    b::g;     //g is converted to protected
public:
    b::f;     //f is converted to public
    . . .
};
```

In the same manner, a publicly transmitted member can be explicitly converted to `private` or `protected`. Such a declaration is called an *access declaration*. In general they cannot be used to prevent access to a member accessible in the base class, and they cannot be used to make members visible in the derived class that are inaccessible in the base class. The key design rule is to limit visibility as much as possible, which enhances the modularity of the resulting code. When using classes to implement an ADT, such as a stack, the public code should reflect the operations and functions that client code needs in using the ADT. The implementation details of an ADT, such as the choice of array or list to represent the stack, should be hidden in `private` and `protected` parts of the class.

8.3. A Derived Safe Array Type vect_bnd

In this section we will develop a safe array type that will be declared with both a lower bound and an upper bound. This style of array declaration was used in Algol 60 and PL/1. It will be derived from the `class vect` found in Section 7.8. The following program implements `class vect_bnd`, which allows safe array declaration using both lower and upper bound specification. It includes a simple test of the class in `main`.

```
//Derived safe array type vect_bnd
#include <stream.h>

class vect {
    int* p;                          //base pointer
    int  size;                       //number of elements
public:
    //constructors and destructor
    vect();                          //create a size 10 array
    vect(int n);                     //create a size n array
    vect(vect& v);                   //initialization by vect
    vect(int a[], int n);            //initialization by array
    ~vect(){ delete p; }
    //other member functions
    int  ub() { return (size - 1); }     //upper bound
    int& operator [](int i);      //a range checked element
    vect& operator =(vect& v);
    vect operator +(vect& v);
};

class vect_bnd : public vect {
    int l_bnd, u_bnd;
public:
    vect_bnd();
    vect_bnd(int, int);
    int& operator[](int);
    int  ub() { return (u_bnd); }
    int  lb() { return (l_bnd); }
};
```

The derived class vect_bnd has its own constructors, which will invoke the base class constructor. There is a special syntax to pass arguments from the derived class constructor back to the base class constructor.

function header : base-class-name (argument list)

This syntax is illustrated by the definitions of the derived class constructors.

```
vect_bnd::vect_bnd()  :vect(10)
{
    //invokes the constructor vect(10);
    l_bnd = 0;
    u_bnd = 9;
}

vect_bnd::vect_bnd(int lb, int ub) :vect(ub - lb + 1)
{
    //invokes the constructor vect(ub - lb + 1);
    l_bnd = lb;
    u_bnd = ub;
}

int& vect_bnd::operator[](int i)
{
    if (i < l_bnd || u_bnd < i) {
        cerr << "index out of range: " << i << "\n";
        exit(1);
    }
    return (vect::operator[](i - l_bnd));
}

main()
{
    vect_bnd s(-5, 5);

    for (int i = s.lb(); i <= s.ub(); ++i) {
        s[i] = i;
        cout << i << "  ";
    }
    cout << "\n";
}
```

The declaration vect_bnd s(-5, 5) creates a one-dimensional safe array whose lower bound is −5 and whose upper bound is 5, a total of eleven elements. The output from this program is a series of values that is the index sequence of this array:

```
-5  -4  -3  -2  -1  0  1  2  3  4  5
```

■ DISSECTION OF THE *vect_bnd* CLASS

```
class vect_bnd : public vect {
    int l_bnd, u_bnd;
public:
    vect_bnd();
    vect_bnd(int, int);
    int& operator[](int);
    int  ub() { return (u_bnd); }
    int  lb() { return (l_bnd); }
};
```

- This is a publicly derived class incorporating the base class vect. The class vect has as private members the pointer p and the int variable size, which are not directly accessible to vect_bnd. They are implementation details that are hidden from clients of this class. The publicly accessible members of vect are also publicly accessible members of vect_bnd. The identifier ub is overloaded. The operator[] is also overloaded. Selection will depend on type matching unless explicit use of the scope resolution operator is made.

```
vect_bnd::vect_bnd() :vect(10)
{
    l_bnd = 0;
    u_bnd = 9;
}

vect_bnd::vect_bnd(int lb, int ub) :vect(ub - lb + 1)
{
    l_bnd = lb;
    u_bnd = ub;
}
```

- These are the two different constructors for vect_bnd. The first is an empty argument default constructor that creates a ten-element array. The parenthesized expression following the colon in the constructor header is the argument to the constructor for vect. The argument 10 is first passed back to the appropriate vect constructor and when executed creates a ten-element array. Then the body of this (the derived class) constructor is executed, assigning values to l_bnd and u_bnd. If a base class has a constructor, it is invoked for the derived class. If the constructor needs an argument list, this is provided in the derived class constructor heading as a parenthesized list following a colon. The second constructor is a two-argument constructor whose arguments are the bound's pair values for the safe array variable. Note how they get used in the implicit argument for the base class constructor.

```
int& vect_bnd::operator[](int i)
{
   if (i < l_bnd || u_bnd < i) {
      cerr << "index out of range: " << i << "\n";
      exit(1);
   }
   return (vect::operator[](i - l_bnd));
}
```

● This function will accomplish range checked indexing into the safe array. Once the index is found to be legal, we wish to return the appropriate element's address. This is an address offset from the base pointer p that is inaccessible to this routine. However, the public member vect::operator[](int i) is accessible by use of the scope resolution operator. This base class member does have access to p and can return with the appropriate reference value. If vect:: were omitted in the return statement, the function would be a nonterminating recursion.

■

8.4. Typing Conversions and Visibility

A publicly derived class is a *subtype* of its base class. A variable of the derived class can in many ways be treated as if it were the base class type. A pointer whose type is pointer to base class can point to objects having the derived class type. This can be confusing since subtle implicit conversions are occurring between base and derived type, and it is sometimes difficult to follow what member is being accessed if the base and derived class overloaded the same member name.

We will modify our earlier example of student and grad_student.

```
enum year {fresh, soph, junior, senior};
enum support {ta, ra, fellowship, other};

class student {
protected:
    int    student_id;
    float gpa;
public:
    grad_student(support x, int id, float g):student(id, g) { s = x
    char name[30];
    char college[20];
    year yr;
    char major[10];
    void print();
    void read();
};

class grad_student : public student {
    support  s;
public:
    grad_student(support x, int id, float g):student(id, g) { s =
    char dept[10];
    char thesis[80];
    void print();
    void read();
};
```

The grad_student is a publicly derived type whose base class is student.
In the class student, the members student_id and gpa are protected.
This makes them visible to the derived class but otherwise treated as
private. The class grad_student has one private member s, with all
other members public.

Both classes have constructors and both classes have overloaded
read and print as member functions. The constructors act to initialize the non–publicly accessible data members. The constructor for
grad_student, as is usual, invokes the constructor for student.

A reference to the derived class may be implicitly converted to a
reference to the public base class. For example,

```
grad_student gs(ta, 201, 88.9);
student& rs = &gs;
```

In this case the variable rs is a reference to student. The base class of
grad_student is student. Therefore this reference conversion is appropriate.

The `print` and `read` member functions are overloaded. We will implement the `print` functions and leave as an exercise the coding of the `read` functions.

```
void student::print()
{
    cout << form("%-30s %4d %-20s %-10s %1d %5.4f\n",
                    name, student_id, college, major, yr, gpa);
}

void grad_student::print()
{
    student::print();
    cout << form("%-10s %2d\n%-79s\n", dept, s, thesis);
}
```

For `grad_student::print` to invoke the `student::print` function, the scope-resolved identifier `student::print` must be used. Otherwise, there will be an infinite loop. To see which versions of these functions get called and to demonstrate some of the conversion relationships between base and publicly derived classes, we write a simple test program.

```
//Test pointer conversion rules.
#include "stud.h"   //include relevant declarations

main()
{
    student        s1(100, 87.6), s2(101, 67.0);
    student*       ps;
    grad_student   gs1(ta, 200, 88.8);
    grad_student*  pgs;

    ps = &s1;
    strcpy(ps -> name, "Mae Pohl");
    ps -> print();
    ps = pgs = &gs1;
    strcpy(ps -> name, "Morris Pohl");
    strcpy(pgs -> dept, "pharmacy");
    strcpy(pgs -> thesis, "Pharmacies as retail outlets.");
    ps -> print();
    pgs -> print();     //grad_student::print
}
```

This function declares both class variables and pointers to them. The conversion rule is that a pointer to a publicly derived class may be converted to a pointer to its base class. In our example, the pointer variable ps can point at objects of both classes, but the pointer variable pgs can only point at objects of type grad_student. We wish to study how different pointer assignments affect the invocation of a version of print. The first instance of the statement

```
ps -> print();
```

invokes student::print. It is pointing at the variable s1 of type student. The multiple assignment statement

```
ps = pgs = &gs1;
```

has both pointers pointing at an object of type grad_student. The assignment to ps involves an implicit conversion. The second instance of the statement

```
ps -> print();
```

again invokes student::print. The fact that this pointer is pointing at a grad_student variable gs1 is not relevant. The statement

```
pgs -> print();     //grad_student::print
```

invokes grad_student::print. The variable pgs is of type pointer to grad_student and when invoked with an object of this type selects a member function from this class.

8.5. Virtual Functions

Overloaded member functions are selected to be invoked by a type matching algorithm that includes having the implicit argument matched to an object of that class type. All of this is known at compile-time and allows the compiler to select the appropriate member directly. As will become apparent, it would be nice to dynamically select at run-time the appropriate member function from among base and derived class functions. The keyword `virtual` is a function specifier that provides such a mechanism, but it may be used only to modify member function declarations.

A `virtual` function must be executable code. When invoked, its semantics are the same as other functions. In a derived class, its name can be overloaded and the function prototype of the derived function must have matching type. The selection of which function to invoke from among a group of overloaded `virtual` functions is dynamic. The typical case is where a base class has a virtual function and derived classes have their versions of this function. A pointer to base class can point at either a base class object or a derived class object. The member function selected will depend on the class of the object being pointed at, not on the pointer type. In the absence of a derived type member, the base class virtual function is used by default.

Consider the following example:

```
//virtual function selection
#include <stream.h>

class B {
public:
    int  i;
    virtual void print_i() { cout << i << " inside B\n"; }
};

class D1 : public B {
public:
    void print_i() { cout << i << " inside D1\n"; }
};

class D2 : private B {
public:
    D2() {B::i = 0;}
    int i;
    void print_i() { cout << i << " inside D2 B::i is "
                          << B::i << "\n"; }
};
```

```
main()
{
    B    b;
    B*   pb = &b;
    D1   f;
    D2   h;

    h.i = 1 + (f.i = 1 + (b.i = 1));
    pb -> print_i();
    pb = &f;
    pb -> print_i();
    pb = (B*)&h;
    pb -> print_i();
}
```

The output from this program is

```
1 inside B
2 inside D1
3 inside D2 B::i is 0
```

In each case a different version of print_i is executed. Selection depends dynamically on the object being pointed at. Different class objects are processed by different functions determined at run-time. Facilities that allow the implementation of ADTs, inheritance, and the ability to process objects dynamically are the essentials of OOP.

The last line of output requires some explanation. The derived class D2 has both a private and public variable i. Its private variable was inherited privately from the base class variable i, and it can be accessed by the member function print_i using scope resolution. Because D2 is privately derived, it is not a subtype of B and the cast is required to allow pb to point at h.

Only member functions can be virtual. One last restriction: Constructors cannot be virtual. Destructors can be virtual.

8.6. An Example: A Class Hierarchy

We will further demonstrate object-oriented programming. The stack implementation of Chapter 6 will be modified to store pointers, and a class hierarchy will be used to create various ADTs. In this hierarchy, the base class proc_data is the common ancestor of the derived classes.

Processing of these varied data types will be dynamic because it will involve a virtual function in the base class.

We begin by showing the hierarchy of derived classes.

```
class proc_data {
public:
    virtual void print() { cout << "virtual\n"; }
};

struct X {
    int   age;
    char name[20];
};

class X_data : public proc_data {
    X* d;
public:
    X_data(int i, char* n)
        { d = new X; d -> age = i; strcpy(d -> name, n); }
    ~X_data() { delete d; }
    void print() { cout << form("%20s %d yrs ",
                                    d -> name, d -> age); }
};

struct Y {
    int   salary;
    char name[20];
};

class Y_data : public proc_data {
    Y* d;
public:
    Y_data(int i, char* n)
        { d = new Y; d -> salary = i; strcpy(d -> name, n); }
    ~Y_data() { delete d; }
    void print() { cout << form("%20s $%d ",
                                    d -> name, d -> salary); }
};

struct Z {
    int   phone;
    char state[5];
};
```

```
class Z_data : public Y_data {
   Z* z;
public:
   Z_data(int i, char* n, int ph, char* st):Y_data (i, n)
      { z = new Z; z -> phone = ph; strcpy(z -> state, st); }
   ~Z_data() {delete z; }
   void print()
   {
      Y_data::print();
      cout << form("%9d ph %5s\n", z -> phone, z -> state);
   }
};
```

The root of this class hierarchy is proc_data, which can be used to hold a variety of virtual functions that will be used to process the objects derived from it. This feature leads to a high degree of code sharing and encapsulation. Each class is separately responsible for defining its functionality, and each class can employ routines from an ancestor class.

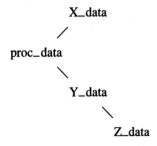

Type hierarchy with base class proc_data

■ DISSECTION OF THE *proc_data* CLASSES

```
class proc_data {
public:
   virtual void print() { cout << "virtual\n"; }
};
```

- This class will house all of the virtual and default functions. Sometimes, as is the case here, the virtual function is only for diagnostic purposes.

```
struct X {
    int   age;
    char  name[20];
};

class X_data : public proc_data {
    X* d;
public:
    X_data(int i, char* n)
        { d = new X; d -> age = i; strcpy(d -> name, n); }
    ~X_data() { delete d; }
    void print() { cout << form("%20s %d yrs ",
                                    d -> name, d -> age); }
};
```

- The derived class X_data manipulates pointers to type struct X. A record-keeping system could be gradually developed that implemented a variety of such types that could be used to contain, access, and operate on different structure types. Our example system will only implement print for these various classes.

```
struct Y {
    . . .
};

class Y_data : public proc_data {
    Y* d;
    . . .
};

struct Z {
    int   phone;
    char  state[5];
};
```

```
class Z_data : public Y_data {
   Z* z;
public:
   Z_data(int i, char* n, int ph, char* st):Y_data(i, n)
      { z = new Z; z -> phone = ph; strcpy(z -> state, st); }
   ~Z_data() { delete z; }
   void print()
   {
      Y_data::print();
      cout << form("%9d ph %5s\n", z -> phone, z -> state);
   }
};
```

- Class z_data derives from Y_data, which derives from
  proc_data. The z_data constructor invokes the Y_data constructor, building an anonymous object of type struct Y.
  The overloaded print invokes its parent's member function
  Y_data::print to process the name and salary information,
  before printing phone and state information. Similar code
  sharing can be distributed throughout this class hierarchy
  for other needed functions.

We modify the stack type to be a stack of pointers of type
proc_data*. Using this pointer type will allow any item of information
to be manipulated dynamically by an overloaded virtual function.

```
typedef proc_data* p_type;
enum boolean {false, true};
enum {EMPTY = -1};

class stack {
   p_type* s;
   int      max_len;
   int      top;
public:
   stack(int size)
      { s = new p_type[size]; max_len = size; top = EMPTY; }
   void    reset() { top = EMPTY; }
   void    push(p_type& c) { top++; s[top] = c; }
   p_type  pop() { return (s[top--] ); }
   p_type  top_of() { return (s[top] ); }
   boolean empty() { return (top == EMPTY); }
   boolean full() { return (top == max_len - 1); }
};
```

This modification of an existing class required mostly changes from type char to p_type. It is another potent demonstration of the ease in which such a type system is extended.

Let us see how all this works in a simple test.

```
main()
{
    proc_data*  temp[10];
    stack st(10);

    temp[0] = new Y_data(24000, "Sue Hawkins");
    temp[1] = new X_data(18, "Ken Hawkins");
    temp[2] = new Z_data(19990, "Igon Hawkins", 5551110, "CA");

    for (int i = 0; i < 3; ++i)
        st.push(temp[i]);
    for (i = 0; i < 3; ++i) {
        st.pop() -> print();
        cout << "\n";
    }
}
```

The output produced is

```
        Igon Hawkins $19990    5551110 ph    CA

        Ken Hawkins 18 yrs
        Sue Hawkins $24000
```

8.7. A Binary Tree Class

Let us define a generic binary tree class, which will be used to store generic pointers. Since such a class is not very useful, we will derive from it a class that can store useful information.

```
//binary search tree

#include <stream.h>

typedef void    (*pfct)(void*);
typedef void*    p_gen;

class bnode {
    friend   class bstree;
    bnode*   left;
    bnode*   right;
    p_gen    data;
    int      count;
    bnode(p_gen d, bnode* l, bnode* r)
         { data = d; left = l; right = r; count = 1; }
    friend int comp(p_gen a, p_gen b);
    friend void prt(bnode* n);
};

class bstree {
    bnode* root;
public:
    bstree() { root = 0; }
    void insert(p_gen d);
    p_gen find(p_gen d) { return (find(root, d)); }
    p_gen find(bnode* r, p_gen d);
    void apply(pfct f) { traverse(root, f); }
    void traverse(bnode* r, pfct f);
};
```

The individual nodes in this binary tree store a generic pointer data and an int count that will count duplicate entries. The pointer data will match a pointer type in the derived class. The tree will be a binary search tree that will store nodes of smaller value to the left, and larger or equal values to the right. We need a method of comparing values that is appropriate to the specific derived type. We use a friend function comp that is a friend of bnode and will be coded appropriately for the derived class.

The insert function places nodes in a tree, and it must find the position in the tree for the new nodes. The function p_gen(bnode* r, p_gen d) searches the subtree rooted at r, for the information represented by d. The overloaded function p_gen find(p_gen d) searches the entire tree. The member function void traverse(bnode* r, pfct f) walks around the subtree rooted at r, applying the argument function f to each node in turn. This is done for the entire tree by void apply(pfct f).

```
void bstree::insert(p_gen d)
{
    bnode* temp = root;
    bnode* old;

    if (root == 0) {
        root = new bnode(d, 0, 0);
        return;
    }
    while (temp != 0) {
        old = temp;
        if (comp(temp -> data, d) == 0) {
            (temp -> count)++;
            return;
        }
        if (comp(temp -> data, d) > 0)
            temp = temp -> left;
        else
            temp = temp -> right;
    }
    if (comp(old -> data, d) > 0)
        old -> left = new bnode(d, 0, 0);
    else
        old -> right = new bnode(d, 0, 0);
}
```

The insert function creates a one-node tree if the tree is initially empty.
If the information as represented by the pointer d matches existing information as determined by comp, then count is incremented. Otherwise
comp navigates through the tree to the appropriate leaf position, where
the new node is constructed and attached. Note that the function comp
can be computationally expensive, and multiple evaluations of it can be
eliminated (see exercise 16).

```
p_gen bstree::find(bnode* r, p_gen d)
{
    if (r == 0)
        return (0);
    else if (comp(r -> data, d) == 0)
        return (r -> data);
    else if (comp(r -> data, d) > 0)
        return (find( r -> left, d));
    else
        return (find( r -> right, d));
}
```

This is a standard recursion. If the information as pointed at by d is not found, 0 is returned.

The following is also a standard recursion. At each node the formal argument f is applied.

```
void bstree::traverse(bnode* r, pfct f)
{
    if (r != 0) {
        traverse (r -> left, f);
        (*f) (r);
        traverse (r -> right, f);
    }
}
```

We derive a class capable of storing a pointer to char as its data member.

```
#include "gtree.h"
#include <string.h>

class s_tree : bstree {
public:
    s_tree() {}
    void   insert(char* d) { bstree::insert(p_gen(d)); }
    char* find(char* d)
            { return ((char*)bstree::find(p_gen(d))); }
    void   print() { bstree::apply((pfct)prt); }
};
```

The base class insertion function bstree::insert takes a generic pointer type as its argument. The derived class insertion function s_tree::insert takes a pointer to char as its argument. Therefore in the derived class s_tree

```
void   insert(char* d) { bstree::insert(p_gen(d)); }
```

uses the explicit conversion p_gen(d).

We need a function to perform comparison: the promised friend function to class bnode.

```
int comp(p_gen i, p_gen j)
{
    return (strcmp((char*)i, (char*)j));
}
```

We also show how to use the traversal mechanism to provide a `print` routine for the entire tree. This requires a function of type `pfct` that is applied at each node.

```
void prt(bnode* n)
{
    cout << (char*)n -> data << "\t" ;
    cout << n -> count << "\t";
}
```

There is a good deal more abstraction in the design of `s_tree` than would be the case for a like structure written in C. The payback for this is the ease with which further classes that utilize the underlying binary tree structure can be derived.

8.8. Summary

1. Inheritance is the mechanism of *deriving* a new class from an old one. That is, the existing class can be added to or altered to create the derived class. Through inheritance a hierarchy of related ADTs can be created that share code.

2. A class can be derived from an existing class using the form:

   class *class-name* : (public|private) *optional* *base-class-name*
   {
       member declarations
   };

   As usual, the keyword `class` can be replaced by the keyword `struct`, with the usual implication that members are default `public`.

3. The keywords `public`, `private`, and `protected` are available as visibility modifiers for class members. A `public` member is visible throughout its scope. A `private` member is visible to other member functions within its own class. A `protected` member is visible to other member functions within its class and any class immediately derived from it. These visibility modifiers can be used within a class declaration in any order and with any frequency.

4. The derived class has its own constructors, which will invoke the base class constructor. There is a special syntax to pass arguments from the derived class constructor back to the base class constructor.

function header : base-class-name (argument list)

5. A publicly derived class is a *subtype* of its base class. A variable of the derived class can in many ways be treated as if it were the base class type. A pointer whose type is pointer to base class can point to objects of the publicly derived class type.

6. A reference to the derived class may be implicitly converted to a reference to the public base class. It is possible to declare a reference to a base class and initialize it to a reference to an object of the publicly derived class.

7. The keyword `virtual` is a function specifier that provides a mechanism to dynamically select at run-time the appropriate member function from among base and derived class functions. It may be used only to modify member function declarations.

8. Facilities that allow the implementation of ADTs, inheritance, and the ability to process objects dynamically are the essentials of OOP.

8.9. Exercises

1. Change the declaration of `grad_student` found in Section 8.1 to

```
class grad_student : student {
public:
    enum {ta, ra, fellowship, other} support;
    char dept[10];
    char thesis[80];
    void print();
};
```

Explain what goes wrong in the following code:

```
main()
{
    grad_student s;

    strcpy(s.name, "Charles Babbage");
    . . .
}
```

Does this work if the default `private` derivation is changed to an explicit `protected` derivation?

2. The safe array member `vect_bnd::operator[]` in Section 8.3 is guaranteed to be passed a properly indexed element in the `return` statement

```
return (vect::operator[](i - l_bnd));
```

This means that the array index is unnecessarily checked twice. Add an unchecked access function as a member function of `class vect`

```
int& elem(int i);    //unchecked indexing
```

Use this to modify the `return` statement so as not to recheck the index.

3. Write a member function `print()` that prints out a variable of type `vect_bnd`.

4. Write two new constructors for `vect_bnd`:

```
//initialize by vect_bnd
vect_bnd::vect_bnd(vect_bnd& v);

//initialize by array
vect_bnd::vect_bnd(int a[], int l, int u);
```

5. Develop a type `matrix_bnd`

```
class matrix_bnd : public matrix {
    int lb1, lb2, ub1, ub2;
    int size1, size2;
public:
    matrix_bnd(matrix_bnd& m); //copy existing matrix
    matrix_bnd();               //5 × 5 matrix
    matrix_bnd(int l1, int u1, int l2, int u2);
    void print();
    . . .
};
```

This is a two-dimensional safe array type that has both upper and lower bounds for each index. Write constructors for this type and a print member function. You should write a member function

```
//reference to an individual element
int& element(int i, int j);
```

that accesses individual elements because overloading [] will not work. *Hint:* You can start by modifying the basic matrix class in Chapter 7, exercise 4, or see the matrix code in Section 7.7.

6. For student and grad_student as defined in Section 8.4, code respective input member functions read that input data for each data member in their class. Use student::read to implement grad_student::read.

7. Pointer conversions, scope resolution, and explicit casting create a wide selection of possibilities. Using main in Section 8.4, which of the following work and what is printed?

```
((grad_student *)ps) -> print();
((student *)pgs) -> print();     //grad_student::print
pgs -> student::print();
ps -> grad_student::print();
```

Print out and explain the results.

8. Modify class D2 in Section 8.5 to be

```
class D2 : private B {
public:
   B::i;
   void print_i()
   {
      cout << i << " inside D2 and B::i is "
           << B::i << "\n";
   }
};
```

What is changed in the output from that program?

9. Add a `virtual` function to the `class proc_data` in Section 8.6 called `read` to be used in reading in values to the various data members in the class hierarchy:

```
class proc_data {
public:
    virtual void read() {}
      . . .
};
```

A different member function `read` should be in each of the three classes `X_data`, `Y_data`, and `Z_data`. For example,

```
void X_data::read()
{
    cout << "\nEnter name and age: ";
    cin >> d -> name >> d -> age;
}
```

10. The following uses `class s_tree`:

```
main()
{
    s_tree t;
    char    dat[80], *p;

    cout << "\nEnter strings; exit with an end-of-file\n";
    while ( cin >> dat, cin.rdstate() == _good) {
        p = new char[strlen(dat) + 1];
        strcpy(p, dat);
        t.insert(p);
    }
    t.print();
    cout << "\n\n\n";
}
```

Use this with redirection to produce an ordered count of each string occurrence in a file. The expression `cin.rdstate() == _good` tests to see that we still have input to read. It is part of the stream input/output library that will be discussed in detail in the next chapter.

11. For `class bstree`, write a destructor. Remember this must traverse and individually delete nodes.

12. For `class s_tree` write a destructor.

13. The traverse routine as written in this chapter is an *inorder* tree traversal.

```
void bstree::traverse(bnode* r, pfct f)
{
    if (r != 0) {
        traverse (r -> left, f);
        (*f)(r);                        //inorder
        traverse (r -> right, f);
    }
}
```

Run the previous program using both *preorder* and *postorder* traversal. For preorder the statement `(*f)(r)` goes first and for postorder it goes last.

14. Develop a `class gen_vect` that is a safe array of generic pointers. Derive a `class s_vect` that is a safe array of `char*`.

15. (Difficult) Using `bstree` derive a `class itree` that stores a vector of type `int` pointed at by the `data` member of each node. You must write an appropriate `comp` function.

16. Rewrite the code for `bstree::insert` to be more efficient. Do this by assigning the value of `comp(temp -> data, d)` to a temporary variable. This avoids the recomputation of a potentially expensive function call.

CHAPTER 9

Input/Output

This chapter describes input/output in C++. The software for C++ includes a standard library that contains functions commonly used by the C++ community. The standard input/output library for C, described by the header *stdio.h*, is still available in C++. However, C++ introduces *stream.h*, which implements its own collection of input/output functions. The header *iostream.h,* on newer systems, is also available (see exercise 16).

The stream I/O is described as a set of classes in *stream.h*. These classes overload the "put to" and "get from" operators << and >>. Streams can be associated with files, and examples of file processing using streams are given and discussed. Much of file processing requires character handling macros that are found in *ctype.h*. These are also discussed.

235

In OOP, objects should know how to print themselves, and we have frequently made `print` a member function of a class. Notationally, it is also useful to overload `<<` for user-defined ADTs. In this chapter we develop output functions for `card` and `deck` that illustrate these techniques.

9.1. The Output Class `ostream`

Output is returned to an object of type `ostream` as described in *stream.h*. An operator `<<` is overloaded in this class to perform output conversions from standard types. The operator is left associative and returns a value of type `ostream&`. The standard output `ostream` corresponding to `stdout` is `cout` and the standard output `ostream` corresponding to `stderr` is `cerr`.

The effect of executing a simple output statement such as

```
cout << "x = " << x << "\n";
```

is to print to the screen first a string of four characters followed by an appropriate representation for the output of `x` followed by a new line. The representation depends on which overloaded version of `<<` is invoked. For example, on some systems if `x` is of type `char`, its integer representation is printed. This is because type `char` is converted to `int` and `<<` is not explicitly overloaded with `char` as an argument type. It is also the case that on some systems the overloading mechanism does not discriminate between `char` and `int`.

The class `ostream` contains public members such as

```
ostream& operator<<(int i);
ostream& operator<<(long i);
ostream& operator<<(double x);
ostream& operator<<(char* s);
ostream& put(char c);
```

The member function `put` outputs the character representation of `c`. Since this is an ordinary member function, it would be used as follows:

```
c = 'A';
cout.put('B');        //output B
cout.put(99);         //output c   ascii value 99
cout.put(c + 3);      //output D
```

9.2. Formatted Output `form()`

As given, the *put to* operator `<<` does not produce formatted output. A typical program error is seen in the following:

```
int   i = 8, j = 9;
cout << i << j ;             //prints 89
cout << i << "   " << j;    //prints 8    9
```

It is inconvenient to always be inserting padding space explicitly when needed. So, to remedy this, *stream.h* imports six functions that perform formatting. These return a `char*` to the generated output string, and this string gets explicitly printed by `<<`. (Also see exercise 16.)

```
format functions

char*   dec (long  d, int width = 0);   decimal
char*   oct (long  o, int width = 0);   octal
char*   hex (long  x, int width = 0);   hexadecimal
char*   chr (int   c, int width = 0);   character
char*   str (char* s, int width = 0);   string
char*   form (const char*, ...);        general facility
```

The first five functions print an appropriate string of length `width`. It is right justified and padded on the left with blanks. If the `width` is omitted, the default value 0 produces a string that is exactly the width of the output representation without blanks.

The `form` function has two nice properties that allow flexible use at a high level. First, a list of arguments of arbitrary length can be printed, and second, the printing is controlled by simple formats. This is analogous to the `printf` function in *stdio.h*. The argument list to `form` has two parts:

    control_string   and   *other_arguments*

In the example

```
form ("%d / %f = %f", 9, 3.3, 9 / 3.3);
```

we have

> *control_string:*   `"%d / %f  =   %f "`
> *other_arguments:*   `9,  3.3,  9 / 3.3`

The expressions in *other_arguments* are evaluated and converted according to the formats in the control string, and then placed in the output stream. Characters in the control string that are not part of a format are placed directly in the output stream. The % symbol introduces a format, or conversion specification. A single conversion specification is a string that begins with % and ends with a conversion character. The conversion characters and other formatting commands are the same as those used in C by `printf`. We review them here.

Conversion character	How the corresponding argument is printed
c	character
d	decimal integer
i	decimal integer
u	unsigned decimal integer
o	unsigned octal integer
x	unsigned hexadecimal integer
X	unsigned hexadecimal integer
e	floating point number; example: `6.310000e+01`
E	floating point number; example: `6.310000E+01`
f	floating point number; example: `63.10000`
g	e-format or f-format, whichever is shorter
G	E-format or f-format, whichever is shorter
s	string
p	pointer in hexadecimal

Explicit formatting information may be included in a conversion specification. If it is not included, then certain defaults occur. For example, the format %f is printed with six digits to the right of the decimal point by default. Explicit formatting information is specified as follows. Between the % sign and the conversion character there may be

- a minus sign, which means that the converted argument is to be *left adjusted* in its field. If there is no minus sign, then the converted argument is to be *right adjusted* in its field. The place where an argument is printed is called its *field*, and the number of spaces used to print an argument is called its *field width*.

- a plus sign, which means that a nonnegative number is to have a + prepended. This works with the conversion characters d, i, e, E, f, g, and G. All negative numbers automatically have a - prepended.

- a blank instead of a plus sign, which means that a nonnegative number is to have a blank prepended. This works with the conversion characters d, i, e, E, f, g, and G.

- a #, which has a meaning that depends on the conversion character. In an o-format it causes o to be prepended to the octal number being printed. In an x- or x-format it causes 0x or 0x to be prepended to the hexadecimal number being printed. In a g- or G-format it causes trailing zeros to be printed. In an e-, E-, f-, g-, or G-format, it causes a decimal point to be printed, even with precision 0.

- a positive integer, which defines the *field width* of the converted argument. If the converted argument has fewer characters than the specified field width, then it will be padded with blanks on the left or right, depending on whether the converted argument is right or left adjusted. If the converted argument has more characters than the specified field width, then the field width will be extended to "whatever is required." If the integer defining the field width begins with 0, and the argument being printed is right adjusted in its field, then 0s rather than blanks will be used for padding.

- a period, which separates *field width* from *precision*.

- a nonnegative integer, which defines the *precision* of the converted argument. For an e, E, f, g, or G conversion this is the number of digits to the right of the decimal point. For an s conversion it is the maximum number of characters to be printed from a string.

- the character l, which specifies that the conversion character d, i, o, x, or u that follows corresponds to an argument of type long or that the conversion character e, E, f, g, or G that follows corresponds to an argument of type double. Similarly, the character h specifies that the conversion character d, i, o, x, or u that follows corresponds to an argument of type short.

- a *, which indicates that a value is to be obtained from the argument list. The field width or precision or both may be indicated by a * instead of by a nonnegative integer.

The field width is the minimum number of spaces that must be used to print the expression. The default is whatever is required to properly display the argument. Thus the integer value 102 (decimal) will require three spaces for decimal conversion d or octal conversion o, but only two spaces for hexadecimal conversion x. These digits will appear right adjusted unless the minus sign is present. If the field width is too short to properly display the value of the corresponding argument, the field width will be increased to the default. If the entire field is not needed to display the converted argument, then the remaining part of the field is padded with blanks on the left or right, depending on whether the converted argument is right or left adjusted. The padding character on the left can be made o by specifying the field width with a leading zero.

The precision is specified by a nonnegative number that occurs to the right of the period. For string conversions this is the maximum number of characters to be printed from the string. For floating point conversions this is the number of digits to be printed to the right of the decimal point. Examples of formats are given in the table that follows. We use double quote characters to visually delimit the field. They are not part of what gets printed.

The function form() is not supported in *iostream.h*. Instead the header file *strstream.h* includes functions that can be used for converting I/O values to strings.

Declarations and initializations

```
char      c = 'w';
int       i = 1, j = 29;
float     x = 333.12345678901234567890;
double    y = 333.12345678901234567890;
char      s1[] = "she sells sea shells";
```

Format	Expression	How it is printed in its field	Remarks
%c	c	"w"	field length 1 by default
%2c	c	" w"	right adjusted
%-3c	c	"w "	left adjusted
%d	-j	"-29"	field length 3 by default
%010d	i	"0000000001"	padded with zeros
%-12d	j	"29 "	left adjusted
%12o	j	" 35"	octal, right adjusted
%-12x	j	"1d "	hexadecimal, left adjusted
%f	x	"333.123444"	precision 6 by default
%.1f	x	"333.1"	precision 1
%20.3f	x	" 333.123"	right adjusted
%-20.3e	y	"3.331e+002 "	left adjusted
%s	s1	"she sells sea shells"	field length 20 by default
%7s	s1	"she sells sea shells"	more space needed

To print the character % in the output stream one can use the conversion specification %%, which prints a single percent symbol. Of course, the conversion specification %c can be used to print the expression '%' in the argument list.

9.3. User-Defined Types: Output

User-defined types have been printed by typically creating a member function print. Let us use the types card and deck of Section 5.9 as an example of a simple user-defined type. We write out a set of output routines for displaying cards.

```
//card output

#include  <stream.h>

char pips_symbol[14] = { '?', 'A', '2', '3', '4', '5', '6',
                         '7', '8', '9', 'T', 'J', 'Q', 'K'};
char suit_symbol[4] = { 'c', 'd', 'h', 's'};

enum suit {clubs, diamonds, hearts, spades};

class pips {
   int  p;
public:
   void assign(int n) { p = n % 13 + 1; }
   void print() { cout << chr(pips_symbol[p], 2); }
};

class card {
   int  cd;          //a cd is from 0 to 51
public:
   suit s;
   pips p;
   void assign(int n) { cd = n; s = n / 13; p.assign(n); }
   void pr_card() { p.print(); cout << chr(suit_symbol[s]); }
};

class deck {
   card d[52];
public:
   void init_deck();
   void shuffle();
   void deal(int, int, card*);
   void pr_deck();
};

void deck::pr_deck()
{
   for (int i = 0; i < 52; ++i) {
      if (i % 13 == 0)          //13 cards to a line
         cout << "\n";
      d[i].pr_card();
   }
}
```

In this solution we use the format function chr. Each card will be printed out in three characters. If d is a variable of type deck, then d.pr_deck() will print out the entire deck, 13 cards to a line.

In keeping with the spirit of OOP, it would also be nice to overload << to accomplish the same aims. The operator << has two arguments, an ostream and the ADT, and it must produce an ostream. Let us write these functions for the types card and deck.

```
ostream& operator<<(ostream& out, pips x)
{
    return (out << chr(pips_symbol[x.p], 2));
}

ostream& operator<<(ostream& out, card cd)
{
    return (out << cd.p << chr(suit_symbol[cd.s]));
}

ostream& operator<<(ostream& out, deck x)
{
    for (int i = 0; i < 52; ++i) {
        if (i % 13 == 0)                //13 cards to a line
            out << "\n";
        out << x.d[i];
    }
    return (out);
}
```

The functions that operate on pips and deck need to be friends of the corresponding class because they access private members.

A second solution for providing user-defined output for ostreams is to convert a representation of the object to char*, which can be used as is with <<. This solution typically uses form.

```
#include <string.h>

char* pips::ostring(char* f)
{
    return (form(f, pips_symbol[p]));
}
```

```
//find position of 2nd c in string s
int arg1(char* s, char c)
{
    int  i = 0, cnt = 0;

    while ((cnt += (*s++ == c)) < 2)
        i++;
    return (i);
}

char* card::ostring(char* f)
{
    char f1[40], f2[40];
    int i;

    strncpy(f1, f, i = arg1(f, '%'));
    strcpy(f2, f + i);
    return (strcat(p.ostring(f1), form(f2, suit_symbol[s])));
}

void deck::pr_deck()
{
    for (int i = 0; i < 52; ++i) {
        if (i % 13 == 0)            //13 cards to a line
            cout << "\n";
        cout << d[i].ostring("%2c%c");
    }
}
```

What is interesting here is that a `card` is printed out by a user-defined format. The format string `"%2c%c"` is passed to `card::ostring`, where it is converted into two separate strings `f1` and `f2`. The first format is used by `pips::ostring` and the second by `form`. In this code, `pips` are printed in a two-character width field and `suit` in a single-character width.

9.4. The Input Class `istream`

Input is returned to an object of type `istream` as described in *stream.h*. An operator `>>` is overloaded in this class to perform input conversions to standard types. The standard input `istream` corresponding to `stdin` is `cin`.

The effect of executing a simple input statement such as

```
cin >> x >> i;
```

is to read from standard input, normally the keyboard, a value for x and then a value for i. White space is ignored.

The class istream contains public members such as

```
istream& operator>>(int& i);
istream& operator>>(long& i);
istream& operator>>(double& x);
istream& operator>>(char& c);
istream& operator>>(char* s);
istream& get(char& c);
istream& get(char* s, int n, int c = '\n');
```

The member function get(char& c) inputs, white space characters included, the character representation to c. The member function get(char* s, int n, int c = '\n') inputs into the string pointed at by s at most n characters, white space characters included. The optionally specified default character acts as a terminator. If not specified, the input is read up to the next newline. Since this is an ordinary member function it would be used as follows:

```
cin.get(c);          //one character
cin.get(s, 40);      //length 40 or terminated by '\n'
cin.get(s, 10, '*'); //length 10 or terminated by *
```

When overloading the operator >> to produce input to a user-defined type, the typical form of such a function prototype is:

```
istream& operator>>(istream& p, user-defined type& x)
```

If the function needs access to private members of x, it must be made a friend of its class. A key point is to make x a reference parameter so its value can be modified.

9.5. Files

C systems have stdin, stdout, and stderr as standard files. In addition, systems may define other standard files, such as stdprn and stdaux. Abstractly, a file may be thought of as a stream of characters that are processed sequentially.

Written in C	Name	Remark
stdin	standard input file	connected to the keyboard
stdout	standard output file	connected to the screen
stderr	standard error file	connected to the screen
stdprn	standard printer file	connected to the printer
stdaux	standard auxiliary file	connected to an auxiliary port

The C++ stream input/output ties the first three of these standard files to cin, cout, and cerr, respectively. Typically, C++ ties cprn and caux to their corresponding standard files stdprn and stdaux. Other files can be opened or created by the programmer. We shall show how to do this in the context of writing a program to double-space an existing file into an existing or new file. The file names will be specified on the command line and passed in to argv.

The class ostream and the class istream both have constructors. One such constructor, ostream::ostream(streambuf* s), allows a buffer to be associated with a stream. The class filebuf is a special case of streambuf used by files. To properly open and manage an istream or ostream related to a system file, you

1. Declare a filebuf.

2. Open the corresponding file for input or output.

3. Call a constructor with the address of the filebuf.

The function filebuf::filebuf* open(char*, open_mode) is used to open the file named in the first argument. The second argument is an enumerated type

```
enum open_mode {input, output, append};
```

and specifies what mode is required. If file opening fails, the value 0 is returned.

As an alternative to the older scheme found in *stream.h*, version 2.0 has the header *fstream.h* to provide file manipulation (see Appendix C, Section 11.2).

```
//dbl_sp: a program to double space a file
//Usage: executable  f1 f2
//f1 must be present and readable
//f2 must be writable if it exists

#include <stream.h>

main(int argc, char** argv)
{
   void       double_space(istream&, ostream&);
   filebuf    f_in, f_out;

   if (argc != 3) {
      cout << "\nUsage: " << argv[0]
           << "  infile  outfile\n";
      exit(1);
   }
   if (!f_in.open(argv[1], input)) {
      cerr << "cannot open " << argv[1];
      exit(1);
   }
   istream  in(&f_in);
   if (!f_out.open(argv[2], output)) {
      cerr << "cannot open " << argv[2];
      exit(1);
   }
   ostream  out(&f_out);
   double_space(in, out);
}

void double_space(istream& f, ostream& t)
{
   char  c;

   while (f.get(c)) {
      t.put(c);
      if (c == '\n')
         t.put(c);
   }
}
```

■ DISSECTION OF THE *dbl_sp* PROGRAM

```
filebuf    f_in, f_out;
```

- The variable f_in is used for input and the variable f_out is used for output. They are used to create corresponding istream and ostream variables.

```
if (!f_in.open(argv[1], input)) {
   cerr << "cannot open " << argv[1];
   exit(1);
}
istream   in(&f_in);
```

- The member function open is invoked to open for input the command line argument argv[1], which names the input file. If this fails—for example, if the file does not exist or is unreadable—then an error exit is executed. If opening succeeds, the istream in is constructed connected to the filebuf f_in. At this point f_in can be used analogously to cin.

```
if (!f_out.open(argv[2], output)) {
   cerr << "cannot open " << argv[2];
   exit(1);
}
ostream   out(&f_out);
```

- The file named in argv[2] is either opened for writing or is created with write permission. If opening succeeds, the ostream out is constructed connected to the filebuf f_out. At this point f_out can be used analogously to cout.

```
double_space(in, out);
```

- The actual double spacing from the input file to the output file occurs here.

```
void double_space(istream& f, ostream& t)
{
    char  c;

    while (f.get(c)) {
        t.put(c);
        if (c == '\n')
            t.put(c);
    }
}
```

● The get member function gets a character from an istream.
   The put member function puts a character to an ostream.
   The newline character is outputted twice, creating the desired
   double spacing in the output file.

9.6. The Functions and Macros in *ctype.h*

The system provides a standard header file *ctype.h*, which contains a set
of macros that are used to test characters and a set of functions that are
used to convert characters. This is a standard C header file but is mentioned here because of its usefulness in C++ input/output. Those macros
that only test a character return an int value that is nonzero (*true*) or 0
(*false*). The argument is type int.

Macro	Nonzero (true) is returned if:
isalpha(c)	c is a letter
isupper(c)	c is an uppercase letter
islower(c)	c is a lowercase letter
isdigit(c)	c is a digit
isxdigit(c)	c is a hexadecimal digit
isspace(c)	c is a white space character
isalnum(c)	c is a letter or digit
ispunct(c)	c is a punctuation character
isprint(c)	c is a printable character
iscntrl(c)	c is a control character
isascii(c)	c is an ASCII code

Other functions provide for the appropriate conversion of a character value. Note carefully that these functions do not change the value of c stored in memory.

Function	Effect
toupper(c)	changes c from lowercase to uppercase
tolower(c)	changes c from uppercase to lowercase
toascii(c)	changes c to ASCII code

9.7. Using Stream States

Each istream or ostream has an associated state that can be tested. The states are as follows:

```
enum stream_state {_good, _eof, _fail, _bad};
```

This value is held in the private member variable state. The values for a particular stream can be tested using the overloaded public member function rdstate. The state can also be tested by using member functions good, eof, fail, and bad to test these conditions separately.

Applying input/output operations to streams not in the state _good leads to a null operation, and can cause a program to hang up. The member function clear can reset a stream to _good.

A stream state of _good means the previous input/output operation worked and the next operation should succeed. A stream state of _eof means the previous input operation returned an end-of-file condition. A stream state of _fail means the previous input/output operation failed but did not lose any characters in the stream. And a stream state of _bad means the previous input/output operation failed but may have lost some characters in the stream.

The following program counts the number of words coming from the standard input. Normally this would be redirected to use an existing file. It illustrates ideas discussed in this and the last two sections.

```
//A word count program
//Usage: executable < file
#include    <stream.h>
#include    <ctype.h>

main()
{
    int    word_cnt = -1;
    void   found_next_word(void);

    while (cin.good()) {
        ++word_cnt;
        found_next_word();
    }
    cout << "word count is " << word_cnt << "\n";
}

void found_next_word(void)
{
    char    c;

    cin >> c;
    while (!isspace(c))
        cin.get(c);
}
```

■ DISSECTION OF THE *word_cnt* PROGRAM

```
int    word_cnt = -1;
```

- The `int` variable `word_cnt` is initialized to −1. The program will count one extra before detecting an end-of-file condition.

```
while (cin.good()) {
    ++word_cnt;
    found_next_word();
}
```

- As long as the input stream state associated with `cin` is `_good`, the body of the `while` loop is executed, causing word_cnt to be incremented. The function found_next_word attempts to read the next word.

```
void found_next_word(void)
{
    char    c;

    cin >> c;
    while (!isspace(c))
        cin.get(c);
}
```

- A non—white space character is gotten from the input stream and assigned to c. The while loop tests that adjacent characters are not white space. The loop terminates when a white space character is found, because this indicates that a word has been found. If the function encounters an end-of-file, it sets the stream state for cin and causes cin.good() in main to terminate its while loop. One last point: The loop cannot be rewritten

```
while (!isspace(c))
    cin >> c;
```

because this would skip white space.

■ _____

9.8. Summary

1. C++ introduces *stream.h*, which implements a wide range of input/output functions, many of which overload the operators << and >>.

2. Output is returned to an object of type ostream. An operator << is overloaded in this class to perform output conversions from standard types. The standard output ostream corresponding to stdout is cout and the standard output ostream corresponding to stderr is cerr.

3. Formatted output is produced by using one of six standard functions: dec, oct, hex, chr, str, and form. They all return strings with the appropriate output representation.

4. The function `char* form(const char*, ...);` has two nice properties that allow flexible use at a high level. First, a list of arguments of arbitrary length can be printed, and second, the printing is controlled by simple formats. The argument list to `form` has two parts:

   control_string and *other_arguments*

   It acts analogously to `printf` in C.

5. One can overload `<<` to output user-defined types. The operator `<<` has two arguments: an `ostream` and the user-defined type. It must produce an `ostream`. A typical function that does this is

   ```
   ostream& operator<<(ostream& out, user-defined type x)
   {
       return (out << form(. . .));
   }
   ```

6. C systems have `stdin`, `stdout`, and `stderr` as standard files. In addition, systems may define other standard files, such as `stdprn` and `stdaux`. Abstractly, a file may be thought of as a stream of characters that are processed sequentially. The standard files are defined in *stdio.h*. The C++ stream input/output ties the first three of these standard files to `cin`, `cout`, and `cerr`, respectively. C++ ties `cprn` and `caux` to their corresponding standard files `stdprn` and `stdaux`. Other files can be opened or created by the programmer.

7. To properly open and manage an `istream` or `ostream` related to a system file, you

   Declare a `filebuf`.

   Open the corresponding file for input or output.

   Call a constructor with the address of the `filebuf`.

8. The function `filebuf::filebuf* open(char*, open_mode)` is used to open the file named in the first argument. The second argument is an enumerated type

   ```
   enum open_mode {input, output, append};
   ```

   and specifies what mode is required. If file opening fails, the value 0 is returned.

9. Input is returned to an object of type `istream` as described in *stream.h*. An operator `>>` is overloaded in this class to perform input conversions to standard types. The standard input `istream` corresponding to `stdin` is `cin`.

10. Each `istream` or `ostream` has an associated state that can be tested. The states are as follows:

```
enum stream_state {_good, _eof, _fail, _bad};
```

This value is held in the private member variable `state`. The values for a particular stream can be tested using the overloaded public member function `rdstate`. The state can also be tested by using member functions `good`, `eof`, `fail`, and `bad` to test these conditions separately.

9.9. Exercises

1. Experiment with your system by defining the following:

```
const double e = 2.718281828459045235360287471352;
```

Now print this out using:

```
cout << e;
cout << float(e);
cout << form("%f : %g : %25.20fl : %25.20\n", e, e, e, e);
```

Remember that floating point precision cannot be exact.

2. See if `float` and `double` are stored differently on your machine by repeating the above experiment with e declared as `float`.

3. Use the format functions `dec`, `oct`, `hex`, and `chr` to write out a table that displays 0–255 in each of these representations. Print each value in a field six characters wide. Some sample output follows from our system:

dec	oct	hex	chr
0	0	0	
1	1	1	.
2	2	2	
. . .			
32	40	20	
33	41	21	!
34	42	22	"
. . .			
65	101	41	A
66	102	42	B
67	103	43	C
. . .			
253	375	fd	
254	376	fe	
255	377	ff	

Explain why the `chr` column does not always print.

4. Exercises 4−6 use the `class clock` from Section 7.6. Overload `<<` to print a standard representation of a `clock` value. Its function prototype should be a friend function of `clock`:

```
friend ostream& operator<<(ostream& out, clock x);
```

5. Write a `clock` member function to produce a string as an output representation of `clock` based on a format. Its prototype is

```
char* ostring(char* f);
```

The format string `f` should be broken into four integer formats to be used to format the four data members `secs`, `mins`, `hours`, and `days`.

6. Overload `>>` to read a standard representation of a `clock` value. Its function prototype should be a friend function of `clock`:

```
friend istream& operator>>(istream& in, clock& x);
```

7. Use the `class complex` from Section 7.3. Overload both `<<` and `>>` to work with `complex` values.

8. Rewrite the *dbl_sp* program so that it gets the name of the input file as a command line argument and writes to `cout`. After this has been done, the command

   dbl_sp infile > outfile

   can be used to double-space whatever is in *infile*, with the output being written into *outfile*.

9. Rewrite the *dbl_sp* program so that it uses a command line option of the form − *n*, where *n* can be 1, 2, or 3. If *n* is 1, then the output should be single-spaced. That is, two or more contiguous newline characters in the input file should be written as a single newline character in the output file. If *n* is 2, then the output file should be strictly double-spaced. That is, one or more contiguous newline characters in the input file should be rewritten as a pair of newline characters in the output file. If *n* is 3, the output file should be strictly triple-spaced. Note, some systems use \r\n (carriage return, newline) to terminate lines.

10. Write a program to number the lines in a file. The input file name should be passed to the program as a command line argument. The program should write to `cout`. Each line in the input file should be written to the output file, with the line number and a space prepended.

11. Read about the system function `unlink()`, on page 320 of *A Book on C* by Al Kelley and Ira Pohl (Benjamin/Cummings, Menlo Park, Calif., 1984). The following program uses this function to remove a file. It is a simple version of the MS-DOS command *del*, which is used to remove files. Modify the program to remove one or more files obtained as command line arguments.

    ```
    main(int argc, char** argv)
    {
        unlink(argv[1]);
    }
    ```

12. The `istream` member function `istream& putback(char c)` is used to push one character back into the stream. Write a program to test this. Can you describe a situation where this would be useful?

13. Write a program that displays a file on the screen 20 lines at a time, with a maximum length of 80 characters per line. The input file should be given as a command line argument. The program should display the next 20 lines after a carriage return has been typed.

14. Modify the previous exercise to display one or more files given as command line arguments. Also, allow a command line option of the form $-n$ to be used, where n is a positive integer specifying the number of lines that are to be displayed at one time.

15. Since cout and cerr are both an ostream, what is the effect of the assignment

```
cerr = cout;
```

16. A library is not directly part of the language. It is only a standard when the programming community agrees to its use. On AT&T C++ Release 2.0 or compatible products, you should have *stream.h, Ostream.h,* and *iostream.h* as distinct standard headers (see Appendix C, Section 11.1). Check the definition of *Ostream.h* on your system. See how it differs from *iostream.h.* Using *iostream.h* formatting can be indicated with the use of *format states.* For example:

```
int i = 16;
cout << i;          //prints 16
cout << hex << i;   //prints 10
cout << ++i;        //prints 11
cout << oct << i;   //prints 21
cout << dec;        //format state becomes decimal
```

Recode exercise 3 using this technique, if available.

CHAPTER 10

Advanced Features

This chapter describes some advanced features of C++ and recent additions to the language. Many of these changes are described in *The Evolution of C++ : 1985 to 1987* by Bjarne Stroustrup (USENIX C++ Papers, Santa Fe, N.M., 1987, pp. 1–21). These changes are incorporated into the AT&T version 2.0 compiler.

Chief among these advanced features is multiple inheritance, which allows a derived class to include inherited members from more than one ancestor class. Pure virtual functions are used to develop *abstract* base classes. Another change is that default assignment and initialization is no longer bitwise copy. These and other advanced topics will be discussed. The chapter concludes with an overview of the OOP design process.

259

10.1. MULTIPLE INHERITANCE

The examples in the text thus far require only single inheritance; that is, they require that a class be derived from a single base class. This feature can lead to a chain of derivations wherein class B is derived from class A and class C is derived from class B, . . . , and class N is derived from class M. In effect, N ends up being based on A, B, . . . , M. This chain must not be circular, however, so a class cannot have itself as an ancestor.

Multiple inheritance allows a derived class to be derived from more than one base class. The syntax of class headers is extended to allow a list of base classes and their privacy designation. An example is

```
class tools {
    . . .

};

class parts {
    . . .

};

class labor {
    . . .

};

class plans : public tools, public parts, public labor {
    . . .

};
```

In this example, the derived class plans publicly inherits the members of all three base classes. This parental relationship is described by the inheritance *directed acyclic graph* (DAG). The DAG is a graph structure whose nodes are classes and whose directed edges point from base to derived class. To be legal it cannot be circular, so no class may, through its inheritance chain, inherit from itself.

In deriving an identically named member from different classes, ambiguities may arise. These derivations are allowed provided the user does not make an ambiguous reference to such a member. For example,

```
class tools {
public:
    int cost();
    . . .
};

class labor {
public:
    int cost();
    . . .
};

class parts {
public:
    int cost();
    . . .
};

class plans : public tools, public parts, public labor {
public:
    int tot_cost() { return (parts::cost() + labor::cost()); }
    . . .
};

int foo()
{
    int  price;
    plans* ptr;

    price = ptr -> cost();
    . . .
}
```

In the body of foo, the reference to cost is inherently ambiguous. It can be resolved by either properly qualifying cost using the scope resolution operator or adding a member cost to the derived class plans.

One further modification to the original inheritance scheme has been made: virtual inheritance. With multiple inheritance, two base classes can be derived themselves from a common ancestor. If both base classes are used in the ordinary way by their derived class, that class will have two subobjects of the common ancestor. This duplication, if not desirable, can be eliminated by using `virtual` inheritance. An example is

```
class under_grad : public virtual student {
   . . .

};

class grad : public virtual student {
   . . .

};

class department : public under_grad, public grad {
   . . .

};
```

Without the use of `virtual` in this example, `class department` would have objects of `class::under_grad::student` and `class::grad::student`.

The early releases of C++ left unspecified the order of execution for initializing constructors in base and member constructors. Most of the time these constructions were independent of each other, and the results were independent of order. With the addition of multiple inheritance, however, it became unnecessarily hazardous to continue this laxness. Thus the current ordering is

1. Explicit reference to base class constructors in the order in which they are listed after the header colon

2. Unmentioned base classes in the order in which they are declared

3. Explicit reference to member class constructors in the order in which they are listed after the header colon

Virtual base classes have special precedence and are constructed before any of their derived classes. They are constructed before any nonvirtual base classes. Their construction order depends on their DAG. It is a depth-first, left-to-right order. Destructors are invoked in reverse order of constructors. These rules, although complicated, should conform to one's intuition, and a client program's correctness should not depend on constructor/destructor ordering.

A further improvement is that the class name is used for each base class initializer. The old style of just using a parenthesized argument list that implicitly called the base class constructor is allowed for single inheritance, but is poor style even for that case. Finally, the associated destructors are called in the reverse order from constructor invocation.

Let us illustrate by elaborating on a previous example.

```
class tools {
    . . .
public:
    tools(char*);
    ~tools();
    . . .
};

class parts {
    . . .
public:
    parts(char*);
    ~parts();
    . . .
};

class labor {
    . . .
public:
    labor(int);
    ~labor();
    . . .
};

class plans : public tools, public parts, public labor {
    . . .
    special a;   //member class with constructor
public:
    plans(int m) : labor(m), tools("lathe"), a(m), parts("widget")
        { . . . }
    ~plans();
    . . .
};
```

In this case, the member constructor a(m) appears before the base class constructor parts("widget") but by our rules is invoked last. Since its constructor was last, its destructor is invoked first, followed by ~parts, ~tools, ~labor, and ~plans.

For a concrete worked-out example of multiple inheritance, look at *iostream.h*. This contains the class iostream, which is derived from istream and ostream. Exercise 8 is based on this idea.

10.2. ABSTRACT BASE CLASSES

A type hierarchy usually has its root class contain a number of virtual functions. Virtual functions provide for dynamic typing (see Section 8.5). Often these virtual functions in the root class are dummy functions. They have an empty body in the root class, but they will be given specific meanings in the derived classes. In version 2.0 of C++, the *pure virtual function* is introduced for this purpose. A pure virtual function is a virtual member function whose body is undefined. Notationally it is declared inside the class as follows:

> virtual *function prototype* = 0;

A derived class must define or declare each pure virtual function in its immediate base class.

A class that has at least one *pure virtual* function is an *abstract class*. It is useful to have a root class for a type hierarchy be an *abstract class*. It would have the basic common properties of its derived classes, but would not itself be used to declare objects.

We want to design an object-oriented data base (see Section 8.6). The data base will be built-up from a type hierarchy that will have different objects whose root class will be the abstract class object.

```
class data {
        //abstract class - root of type hierarchy
public:
   virtual void print() = 0;
};

class person : public virtual data {
protected:
   char f_name[10], l_name[20];
   int   age;
   int   soc_sec;
public:
   person();
   person(char* fn, char* ln, int a, int ss);
   void print();
};
```

```
class object {
protected:
   data*   record;
   int     key;
public:
   virtual void print() = 0;
   virtual void del(int k) = 0;
   virtual void insert(data* ) = 0;
   int     display_key() { return key; }
};

class read_object : public object {
public:
   void print();
   void del(int k)
      { cerr << "\nError: Attempt to delete read-only data"; }
   void insert(data* d);
};
```

The two classes data and object are abstract base classes. It would be illegal to declare objects of these types. The class data serves as the base class for a type hierarchy that defines the different forms of data objects used in our program. Notice how easy it is to extend this scheme to new forms of data. The class object is an abstract base class used to derive different types of database objects.

Virtual derivation was used in class person. This use anticipates the use of multiple-inheritance at a later point in the development of this database program. A new derived class from data could be a combination of several existing derived classes. A final point: The return type of virtual functions is restricted to be the same in all derived classes. This is a natural restriction since otherwise expression evaluation involving virtuals would have to be dynamic.

10.3. DEFAULT ASSIGNMENT AND OVERLOADING new

In Chapter 7 we discussed overloading the assignment operator. If this operator were not overloaded for a particular user type, then assignment between two objects of that type, for early C++ compilers, was bitwise copy. Current systems default to a more sophisticated member-by-member assignment. This rule is recursive until components that are built-in types are assigned in the usual way.

This rule is safer than the original bitwise copy method. In instances where a class, call it A, had a data member of a different class, call it B, and B had assignment overloaded and A did not, there was a possibility of errors if objects of type A were bitwise copy–assigned.

The same idea applies to default initializations. The user in most cases need not have a constructor of type X(X&) for class X. The compiler is responsible for providing both assignment and initialization based on the recursive member-by-member subassignment rule. Of course, where necessary, the user can still overload these member functions to produce a different result.

A further change allows the operators new and delete to be overloaded. This feature provides a simple mechanism for user-defined manipulation of free store. Older methods for directly controlling allocation involved the explicit manipulation of the this pointer. For example:

```
class X {
    . . .
public:
    void* operator new(unsigned size) { return (malloc(size)); }
    void  operator delete(X* ptr) { free((void*)ptr); }
    X(unsigned size) { new(size); }
    ~X() { delete(this); }
    . . .
};
```

10.4. POINTER OPERATORS

The structure pointer operator -> can be overloaded as a nonstatic class member function. (This restriction also applies to the assignment operator, the subscript operator, and the function call operator.) The overloaded structure pointer operator is a unary operator on its left operand. The argument must be either a class object or a reference of this type. It can return either a pointer to a class object or an object of a class for which operator -> is defined.

In the following example, we overload the structure pointer operator inside the class t_ptr. Objects of type t_ptr act as controlled access pointers to objects of type triple.

```
// Overloading the structure pointer operator.
#include <stream.h>
enum boolean {false, true};
```

```
class triple {
private:
    int       i, j, k;
public:
    triple(int a, int b, int c) { i = a; j = b; k = c; }
    void print() { cout << form("\ni = %d, j = %d, k = %d",
                        i, j, k); }
};

triple    unauthor(0, 0, 0);

class t_ptr {
    boolean   access;
    triple*   ptr;
public:
    t_ptr(boolean f, triple* p) { access = f; ptr = p; }
    triple*   operator ->() ;
};

triple* t_ptr::operator ->()
{
    if (access)
        return (ptr);
    else {
        cout << "\nunauthorized access";
        return (&unauthor);
    }
}
```

The variable t_ptr::access is tested by the overloaded operator -> and
if true access is granted. The following code tests this:

```
main()
{
    triple   a(1, 2, 3), b(4, 5, 6);
    t_ptr ta(false, &a), tb(true, &b);
    ta -> print();   //access denied
    tb -> print();   //access granted
}
```

Pointer to Class Member

A pointer to class member is *distinct* from a pointer to class. A pointer
to class member's type is $T::*$, where T is the class name. C++ has

two operators that act to dereference a pointer to class member. The pointer to member operators are

.*   *and*   ->*

Think of *obj.**ptr_mem as first dereferencing the pointer to obtain a member variable and then accessing the member for the designated *obj*. The following code shows how to use these operators:

```
//Pointer to class member.

#include <stream.h>

class X {
private:
    int  hide;
public:
    int  visible;
    void print()
        { cout << "\nhide = " << hide
               << " visible = " << visible; }
    void reset() { visible = hide; }
    void set(int i) { hide = i; }
};

typedef void (X::*pfcn)();

main()
{
    X  a, b, *pb = &b;
    int X::*pXint = &X::visible;
    pfcn pF = &X::print;

    a.set(8); a.reset();
    b.set(4); b.reset();
    a.print();
    ++a.*pXint;
    a.print();
    cout << "\nb.visible = " << pb ->*pXint;
    (b.*pF)();
    pF = &X::reset;
    (a.*pF)();
    a.print();
    cout << "\n";
}
```

■ DISSECTION OF THE *ptr_to_mem* FUNCTION

```
typedef void (X::*pfcn)();
```

- This says that pfcn is pointer to class x member whose base type is a function of no arguments returning void. Member functions x::print and x::reset match this type.

```
int X::*pXint = &X::visible;
pfcn pF = &X::print;
```

- This declares pXint to be a pointer to class x member whose base type is int. It is initialized to point at the member x::visible. The pointer pF is initialized to point at the member function x::print.

```
++a.*pXint;
```

- This is equivalent to ++a.visible.

```
cout << "\nb.visible = " << pb ->*pXint;
(b.*pF)();
```

- The pointer expression is equivalent to pb -> visible. The function call is equivalent to b.print().

```
pF = &X::reset;
(a.*pF)();
```

- The pointer pf is assigned the address of x::reset. The function call is equivalent to a.reset().

10.5. SCOPE AND LINKAGE

Large C programs are partitioned into multifile units that can be compiled separately. Linking such separate modules requires resolving external references. In C, the rules for resolving external references are frequently system-dependent.

In C++ , these rules are explicit. The key difference is that external nonstatic variables must be defined in exactly one place. As usual, `static extern` constructs can be defined in multiple files because they are local to a given file. Use of the keyword `extern` together with an initializer constitutes defining a variable. Using the keyword `extern` without an initializer constitutes a declaration but not a definition. The following examples illustrate these rules. The first example is legal.

```
//file prog1.c
    char   c;             //definition of c
    . . .


//file prog2.c
    extern char c;        //declaration of c
    . . .
```

The second example is illegal.

```
//file prog1.c
    char   c;
    double x = 0.9;
    . . .


//file prog2.c
    char         c;       //illegal second definition
    extern int   x;       //illegal type mismatch
    extern int   k;       //illegal no declaration
    . . .
```

These two files have three errors. Most C compilers would complain only about the type mismatch. The third error has the variable `k` defined but not declared.

Constant and `inline` declarations at file scope that are not explicitly declared `extern` are local to the file. If these names are to be used in other files, they need to be imported there using the preprocessor directive `include`.

```
//file my_stuff.h
    const double pi = 3.14159;
    inline  double max(double a, double b)
              { return (a < b) ? b : a); }
    . . .


//file main_prog.c
#include <my_stuff.h>
    . . .
```

In general, it is good style to avoid reliance on the #define mechanism to produce simple constants and macros. Macro expansion occurs as string replacement and leads to subtle errors in the source code. For particular applications, it is desirable to place related definitions into header files. Good examples of this are found in the system header files, such as stream.h.

Linkage rules for non-C++ functions can be specified using a *linkage-specification*. Some examples are

```
extern "C" atoi(const char* nptr);   //C linkage

extern "C" {
#include <stdio.h>
}                       //C linkage for these prototypes

extern "Pascal" {
    sin(double);
    cos(double);
    tan(double);
}                       //Pascal linkage
```

This specification is at file scope and is system-dependent as to which languages are supported.

10.6. ITERATORS

Iterators were mentioned briefly in exercises 7.10 and 7.11. An iterator is a mechanism for accessing all components of a given type. The for statement provides a built-in iterator for simple arrays. Classes allow data to be hidden from general access, and, typically, an iterator needs to be either a member function or a friend function of the class. The following example shows an iterator class associated with a safe vector class that provides ordered access to all elements:

```
//iterators : vector class

class  vector {
   friend class vector_iterator;
   int* v;
   int  sz;
public:
   vector(int);
   ~vector() { delete v; }

   int  size()  { return (sz); }
   int& operator[](int);
};

class  vector_iterator {
   int      cur_ind;
   vector* bv;
public:
   vector_iterator(vector& v) { bv = &v; cur_ind = 0; }
   int& next();
};
```

The iterator class vector_iterator has two private data members, both typical of such classes. The variable cur_ind is used to keep track of the ordering of element presentation. It is an index. The pointer variable bv is the reference to the associated vector variable. The constructor initializes these hidden variables. The member function next accesses each element in turn, using cur_ind as its internal protected index into a variable of class vector.

The member function next is written as follows:

```
int& vector_iterator::next()
{
   if (cur_ind < bv -> sz)
      return (bv -> v[cur_ind++]);
   else {
      cur_ind = 0;
      return (bv -> v[cur_ind++]);
   }
}
```

This member function accesses private members of class vector and must be a friend of that class. The pointer variable bv is bound to an instance of class vector. The index variable cur_ind is autoincremented each time next is called, and is tested to make certain it does not exceed the internal vector element bound sz. It wraps around to 0 whenever it gets to this limit.

The following example shows how to use the iterator class to output the individual elements of a vector and contrast this scheme with a traditional iteration:

```
ostream& operator<<(ostream& s, vector& w)
{
    s << "\nVECTOR  0 to " << w.size() - 1 << "\n";
    for(int i = 0; i < w.size(); ++i)
        s << dec(w[i], 8);
    s << "\n";
    return (s);
}
```

This is a standard style for overloading the stream operator << to output a variable of type vector. A traditional for loop is used to access elements of vector using public member functions. Now we will write a main function to output two vector variables:

```
main()
{
    vector          u(25), w(10);
    vector_iterator w_it(w);

    for( int i = 0; i < u.size(); ++i)
        u[i] = i;
    cout << u;

    for( i = 0; i < w.size(); ++i)
        cout << (w_it.next() = 2 * i) << "\t";
}
```

The first for loop is traditional C. It initializes the vector u. The second for loop uses the iterator function next to initialize and print out consecutive values of the associated vector w.

10.7. AN EXAMPLE: WORD FREQUENCY

In this section we develop a multifile program using header files. The program will count the frequency of occurrence of words in a specified file, and will output an alphabetized list with each word's frequency.

Part of our purpose is to show how C++ allows you to write programs quickly and modularly. We will reuse previously developed code. The binary search tree, which was discussed in Chapter 8, is a convenient and efficient means of storing this information.

```
//file bstree.h  binary search tree

typedef void (*pfct) (void*);
typedef void*  p_gen;

class bnode {
    friend class bstree;
    bnode* left;
    bnode* right;
    p_gen  data;
    int    count;
    bnode(p_gen d, bnode* l, bnode* r)
          { data = d; left = l; right = r; count = 1; }
    friend int comp(p_gen a, p_gen b);
    friend void prt(bnode* n);
};

class bstree {
    bnode* root;
public:
    bstree() { root = 0; }
    void  insert(p_gen d);
    p_gen find(p_gen d) { return (find(root, d)); }
    p_gen find(bnode* r, p_gen d);
    void  apply(pfct f) { traverse(root, f); }
    void  traverse(bnode* r, pfct f);
};
```

The class bstree is capable of storing a generic pointer and a count at each node of a binary search tree. It is a prototype class from which other classes are derived as needed.

```
//file stree.h

void prt(bnode* n);

int comp(p_gen i, p_gen j);
```

```
class s_tree : bstree {
public:
    s_tree() {}
    void  insert(char* d) { bstree::insert(p_gen(d)); }
    char* find(char* d)
        { return ((char* )bstree::find(p_gen(d))); }
    void  print() { bstree::apply((pfct)prt); }
};
```

The `class s_tree` uses the `insert` function to store a pointer to `char`. In effect, each node will store a string. Each new word will be inserted as a string into the `s_tree`. The code for implementing these classes is stored in corresponding *.c files in order to allow separate compilation.

```
//file bstree.c
#include "bstree.h"

void bstree::insert(p_gen d)
{
    bnode* temp = root;
    bnode* old;

    if (root == 0) {
        root = new bnode(d, 0, 0);
        return;
    }
    while (temp != 0) {
        old = temp;
        if (comp(temp -> data, d) == 0) {
            (temp -> count)++;
            return;
        }
        if (comp(temp -> data, d) > 0)
            temp = temp -> left;
        else
            temp = temp -> right;
    }
    if (comp(old -> data, d) > 0)
        old -> left = new bnode(d, 0, 0);
    else
        old -> right = new bnode(d, 0, 0);
}
```

```
p_gen bstree::find(bnode* r, p_gen d)
{
    if (r == 0)
        return (0);
    else if (comp(r -> data, d) == comp(d, r -> data))
        return (r -> data);
    else if (comp(r -> data, d))
        return (find( r -> left, d));
    else
        return (find( r -> right, d));
}

void bstree::traverse(bnode* r, pfct f)
{
    if (r != 0) {
        traverse (r -> left, f);
        (*f)(r);
        traverse (r -> right, f);
    }
}
```

We have already discussed this code in Chapter 8.

```
//stree.c

#include "bstree.h"
#include "stree.h"
#include <string.h>
#include <stream.h>

void prt(bnode* n)
{
    cout << (char*)n -> data << "\t" ;
    cout << n -> count << "\t";
}

int comp(p_gen i, p_gen j)
{
    return (strcmp((char*)i, (char*)j));
}
```

The various *.h files are necessary to provide appropriate definitions for these two functions. For example, strcmp is defined in *string.h*
and cout is defined in *stream.h*. The prt function prints out a word, and
its frequency of occurrence as stored in count. The comp function lexi-

cographically compares two strings. It is used for insertion into the binary search tree.

The next header file describes the function and constants related to extracting individual words from an istream:

```
//get_word.h

#include <ctype.h>
#include <stream.h>
enum boolean {false, true};
const maxlen = 80;
boolean get_word(char*, istream&);
```

Its corresponding *.c file is

```
#include "get_word.h"

boolean  get_word(char* word_buf, istream& in)
{
    char    c;
    int     len = 0;

    while(in.get(c), !isalpha(c) && in.good())
        ;
    if (!in.good())
        return (false);
    else {
        word_buf[len++] = (isupper(c) ? tolower(c) : c);
        while (in.get(c), isalpha(c) && in.good())
            if (len < maxlen)
                word_buf[len++] = (isupper(c) ? tolower(c) : c);
        word_buf[len] = '\0';
        return (true);
    }
}
```

■ DISSECTION OF THE get_word FUNCTION

```
#include "get_word.h"
```

- This is the header file needed by this code. By separately compiling this code into an object file—for example, *get_word.o*—this routine can be conveniently used by any file that includes its header.

```
boolean  get_word(char* word_buf, istream& in)
```

- The input will be taken from an `istream`. The output will be a single word. If input fails, then `false` is returned; if a word is found, then `true` is returned.

```
while(in.get(c), !isalpha(c) && in.good())
    ;
```

- The loop continues until an alphabetic character is detected. We use a comma expression. First a character is read into `c`; then it is tested. The loop also detects an end-of-file or an input failure.

```
if (!in.good())
    return (false);
```

- This indicates an input failure, normally an end-of-file.

```
word_buf[len++] = (isupper(c) ? tolower(c) : c);
while (in.get(c), isalpha(c) && in.good())
    if (len < maxlen)
        word_buf[len++] = (isupper(c) ? tolower(c) : c);
word_buf[len] = '\0';
return (true);
```

- This is the loop that collects the alphabetic characters into `word_buf`. A conversion to lowercase is made on all letters.

What remains is to put this all together into `main`.

```
//main for producing word frequencies
//Usage: executable  f1
//f1 must be present and readable
//An alphabetized word list is read to cout
//with frequency counts of all words in f1.
```

```
#include "bstree.h"
#include "stree.h"
#include "get_word.h"
#include <string.h>

main(int argc, char** argv)
{
    filebuf   f_in;

    if (argc != 2) {
        cout << "\nUsage:" << argv[0] << "  infile\n";
        exit(1);
    }
    if (!f_in.open(argv[1], input)) {
        cerr << "cannot open " << argv[1];
        exit(1);
    }

    istream   in(&f_in);
    s_tree    t;
    char      dat[80];
    char*     p;

    while (get_word(dat, in)) {
        p = new char[strlen(dat) + 1];
        strcpy(p, dat);
        t.insert(p);
    }
    t.print();
    cout << "\n\n\n";
}
```

The main function opens the input file for reading. It gets each word and stores it temporarily into dat. It stores the word permanently in a string created by new. This string is inserted into the search tree t. Finally, t.print() outputs the alphabetized word frequencies. Each piece of the code can be compiled separately.

10.8. OOP: OBJECT-ORIENTED PROGRAMMING

The central feature of OOP is its encapsulation of an appropriate set of data types and their operations. The class, with its member functions and operator overloading, provides an appropriate coding tool. An object in this formulation is an instance of a class—in other words a class variable or constant. Classes allow for the implementation of abstract data types.

A second feature is its promotion of code reuse through the inheritance mechanism. Without this reuse mechanism, each minor variation of an ADT would require code replication. Inheritance gives the programmer the ability to build a type hierarchy suitable to a particular problem domain.

A third feature is dynamic binding of types. The `virtual` function provides the ability to bind type at run-time. Thus an object determines how it is acted on. For example, let `shape` be a base class and `draw` and `area` be virtual functions in `shape`. Assume that there is a set of derived classes, such as `rectangle`, `circle`, `pentagon`, and `triangle`, and that each can know how to draw itself or compute its own area. A pointer to type `shape` can be used to dynamically process objects of any of the `shape` subtypes. Code for drawing shapes is more easily maintained because it is highly modular. New `shape` types can readily be added to with inheritance.

A fourth feature is data hiding. Access privileges can be managed and limited to whatever group of functions truly needs access to implementation details. The visibility modifiers `public`, `protected`, and `private` control client access to objects. This control promotes modularity and robustness.

The OOP programming task can be more difficult than normal procedural programming as found in C or Pascal. There is, for example, at least one extra design step before one gets to the coding of algorithms. This extra step involves the hierarchy of types that is useful for the problem at hand. Frequently, one solves a problem more generally than is strictly necessary.

The extra step pays dividends in several ways. The solution is more encapsulated, which makes it more robust and easier to maintain and change, and also more reusable. For example, where the code needs a stack, that stack is easily borrowed from existing code. In an ordinary procedural language, such a data structure is frequently "wired into" the algorithm and cannot be exported. All of these benefits are especially important for large coding projects that require coordination among many programmers. Here the ability to specify general interfaces for different classes allows each programmer to work on individual code segments with a high degree of integrity.

10.9. PLATONISM: OBJECT-ORIENTED DESIGN

C++ gives the programmer the means to implement an OOP design. But how do you develop such a design? No simple methodology exists because each design must be strongly tied to the problem domain and reflect its abstractions. We call this design philosophy "Platonism."

In the Platonic paradigm, there is an ideal object. For example, we imagine an ideal chair in the heavens and attempt to describe its characteristics. These would be characteristics shared by all chairs. Such a chair would be a subcomponent of another ideal—furniture. In turn, it may give rise to subcategories, such as swivel chairs, reclining chairs, beach chairs, and so on. Useful descriptions would require expertise on chairs and agreement among the community of chair users. The Platonic chair should be easily modified to describe most commonly occurring chairs. The Platonic chair should be described in terms consistent with existing chair terminology.

C++ was influenced by Simula 67, a language specifically invented for simulations. The Platonic paradigm is a modeling or simulation of the concrete world. It requires that an extra effort be made in determining a design. The design typically provides a public interface that is convenient, general, and efficient. These considerations can be in conflict. Again, there are no simple rules for deciding such tradeoffs.

The extra effort made should lead to results that offset the increased initial design cost. First and foremost, such effort imposes an additional level of discipline to the programming process. Increasing programmer discipline always pays dividends. Second, it encapsulates into classes meaningful related pieces of code. Encapsulation and decomposition always pay dividends. Third, it enhances code reuse through inheritance and ADTs. Code reuse always pays dividends. Fourth, it improves prototyping by deferring implementation decisions and providing access to large, easily used general libraries. Cheap prototyping always pays dividends.

The Platonic paradigm using OOP techniques is quietly revolutionizing the programming process. It does not displace older techniques, such as structured programming, but instead uses them in the small to effectively manage the composition of large and more robust software.

10.10. Summary

1. Multiple inheritance allows a derived class to inherit from more than one base class. The syntax of class headers is extended to allow a list, after the colon, of base classes and their privacy designation.

2. The early releases of C++ left unspecified the order of execution for initializing constructors in base and member constructors. With the addition of multiple inheritance, however, it became unnecessarily hazardous to continue this laxness. The current ordering is

   - Explicit reference to base class constructors in the order in which they are listed after the header colon

   - Unmentioned base classes in the order in which they are declared

   - Explicit reference to member class constructors in the order in which they are listed after the header colon

3. For early C++ compilers, user types had, by default, bitwise assignment. Current systems default to a more sophisticated member-by-member assignment. This rule is recursive until components that are built-in types are assigned in the usual way. The same idea applies to default initialization.

4. A further change allows the operators `new` and `delete` to be overloaded. This feature provides a simple mechanism for user-defined manipulation of free store. Other technical changes include the ability to overload the operator `->`, distinguishing between signed and unsigned by the overloading selection algorithm, and the use of the scope resolution operator to define pointer to member types.

5. Large C programs are partitioned into multifile units that can be compiled separately. Linking such separate modules requires resolving external references. In C++, these rules are explicit. The key rule is that external nonstatic variables must be defined in exactly one place. Static external constructs are local to a given file. Use of the keyword `extern` together with an initializer constitutes defining a variable. Using the keyword `extern` without an initializer constitutes a declaration but not a definition.

6. An iterator is a mechanism for accessing all components of a given type. The `for` statement provides a built-in iterator for simple arrays.

Classes allow data to be hidden from general access, and, typically, an iterator needs to be either a member function or a friend function of the class.

7. C++ supports object-oriented programming (OOP). The central feature of this method is its encapsulation of an appropriate set of data types and their operations (ADTs). The class, with its member functions and operator overloading, provides an appropriate coding tool. A further key idea in OOP is its promotion of code reuse through the inheritance mechanism. The `virtual` function also provides the ability to bind type at run-time. Classes also provide data hiding. Access privileges can be managed and limited to whatever group of functions truly needs access to implementation details.

8. C++ was influenced by Simula 67, a language specifically invented for simulations. The Platonic paradigm is a modeling or simulation of the concrete world. It requires that an extra effort be made in determining a design. The design typically provides a public interface that is convenient, general, and efficient.

10.11. Exercises

1. What happens if you attempt to compile

```
struct A : B {
    int i;
};

struct B : A {
    int j;
};
```

2. From Section 10.1, use the `class plans` and the function `foo` to see how your compiler detects the inherent ambiguous reference to `cost`. Change the example to avoid this problem.

3. Among the useful standard headers is *assert.h*. It provides an assertion mechanism:

```
assert(expression);
```

If the *expression* evaluates to false, the program terminates with an error indication that includes the file name and source line of the failure.

We want to write a portable factorial program. As written, the following program overflows on most machines:

```
#include <stream.h>
#include <limits.h>
#include <assert.h>

long fact(int n)
{
    if (n <= 1)
        return (1);
    else
        return (fact(n - 1) * n);
}

main()
{
    for (int i = 0; i < 25; ++i)
        cout << i << "  fact  " << fact(i) << "\n";
}
```

Add assertions to protect against system-dependent integer overflow.

4. The *assert.h* has the lines:

```
#ifdef NDEBUG
#define assert(EX)
    . . .
```

Explain how this allows a compiler flag to turn off the assertion mechanism.

5. If your system has a graphics library, see if you can draw a square on your screen.

6. From Section 10.6, we change the second `for` statement in `main` to the following:

```
for ( i = 0; i < w.size(); i += 2)
    cout << (w_it.next() = 2 * i) << "\t";
```

Explain what gets printed.

7. What if the `for` loop in the previous exercise were changed to the following:

```
for (i = 0; i < w.size(); ++i) {
  w_it.next() = 2 * i;
  cout << w_it.next() << "\t";
}
cout << w;
```

Explain what gets printed.

8. The following example shows a genuine use for multiple inheritance:

```
// Create an iostream for standard I/O.

#include <stream.h>

class iostream : public istream, public ostream {
public:
  iostream();
};

iostream::iostream() : istream(stdin), ostream(stdout) { }

main()
{
  char str[255];
  iostream screen_console;

  screen_console << "INPUT STRING :   ";
  screen_console >> str;
  screen_console << "DISPLAY INPUT:   " << str << "\n";
}
```

Use `class iostream` to write a program that would double space a file redirected from `stdin`.

APPENDIX A

ASCII Character Codes

Left/Right Digits	ASCII American Standard Code for Information Interchange									
	0	1	2	3	4	5	6	7	8	9
0	nul	soh	stx	etx	eot	enq	ack	bel	bs	ht
1	nl	vt	np	cr	so	si	dle	dc1	dc2	dc3
2	dc4	nak	syn	etb	can	em	sub	esc	fs	gs
3	rs	us	sp	!	"	#	$	%	&	'
4	(	)	*	+	,	−	.	/	0	1
5	2	3	4	5	6	7	8	9	:	;
6	<	=	>	?	@	A	B	C	D	E
7	F	G	H	I	J	K	L	M	N	O
8	P	Q	R	S	T	U	V	W	X	Y
9	Z	[	\	]	^	_	`	a	b	c
10	d	e	f	g	h	i	j	k	l	m
11	n	o	p	q	r	s	t	u	v	w
12	x	y	z	{	|	}	~	del		

Some Observations

1. Character codes 0–31 and 127 are nonprinting.
2. Character code 32 prints a single space.
3. Character codes for digits 0 through 9 are contiguous.
4. Character codes for letters A through Z are contiguous.
5. Character codes for letters a through z are contiguous.

6. The difference between a capital letter and the corresponding lowercase letter is 32.

The Meaning of Some of the Abbreviations

nul	null	bel	bell	bs	backspace
ht	horizontal tab	nl	newline	vt	vertical tab
cr	carriage return	esc	escape		

APPENDIX B

Operator Precedence and Associativity

The following is the precedence and associativity table for all the C++ operators.

Operators	Associativity
::	left to right
() [] -> . *postfix* ++ *postfix* --	left to right
++ -- ! ~ sizeof (*type*) + (unary) - (unary) * (indirection) & (address) new delete	right to left
.* ->*	left to right
* / %	left to right
+ -	left to right
<< >>	left to right
< <= > >=	left to right
== !=	left to right
&	left to right
^	left to right
|	left to right
&&	left to right
||	left to right
? :	right to left
= += -= *= /= *etc*	right to left
, (comma operator)	left to right

In case of doubt, parenthesize.

APPENDIX C

A Concise Guide for Pascal Programmers

This appendix is a concise guide to C++. It summarizes many of the key language elements of C++ that are not found in older procedural languages, such as Pascal and C. It is intended as a convenient guide to the language for Pascal programmers who have read this text.

1. KEYWORDS

Keywords are explicitly reserved identifiers that have a strict meaning in C++. They cannot be redefined or used in other contexts.

Keywords

asm	continue	float	new	signed	union
auto	default	for	operator	sizeof	unsigned
break	delete	friend	private	static	virtual
case	do	goto	protected	struct	void
catch	double	if	public	switch	volatile
char	else	inline	register	template	while
class	enum	int	return	this	
const	extern	long	short	typedef	

C++ implementations can have the additional keyword

```
overload
```

291

This is considered an anachronism in version 2.0.
The keywords

```
catch      template      throw      try
```

are experimental and reserved for implementing exception handling and parameterized types.

2. CONSTANTS

Enumerations (Section 4.3) define named int constants. These are similar to enumerated types in Pascal. They can be anonymous, as in:

```
enum {false, true};
```

The keyword const (Section 4.2) is used to declare that an object's value is constant throughout its scope.

```
const int N = 100;
double w[N];      //N may be used in a constant expression

const  int bus_stops[5] = {23, 44, 57, 59, 83};
//The separate array elements, bus_stops[i], are constant.
```

The use of const differs from the use of constant definitions in Pascal. In Pascal, constant definitions are identifiers that stand in place of literal values. This is similar to the use of #define, as in:

```
#define N   100
```


3. COMMENTS

C++ has a one-line comment symbol // (Section 4.1).

```
//Compile with version 1.2 or later
const float pi = 3.14159;   //pi accurate to six places
```

C-style comments are also available.

```
/*    *   *   *   *   *
    C++   v2.0
    Demonstrate Multiple-Inheritence
    OOP - Platonic Designs
  *   *   *   *   *   *   */
```

Comments do not nest. This style of comments is equivalent to the brace-enclosed comments in Pascal.

4. SCOPE RULES

C++ has file scope, function scope, block scope, class scope, and function prototype scope. File scope extends from the point of declaration in a file to the end of that file. Function prototype scope is the scope of identifiers in the function prototype argument list and extends to the end of the declaration. Function scope and block scope are similar to the corresponding scope rules in Pascal. Blocks nest in a conventional way, but, unlike Pascal, functions cannot be declared inside other functions or blocks.

Declarations can occur anywhere in a block (Sections 3.2, 4.3).

```
for (int i = 0; i < N; ++i) {
    . . .
```

Class member identifiers are local to that class. The scope resolution operator :: can be used to resolve ambiguities (Section 4.5). A nested class declaration belongs to the same scope as the class it is nested within (Section 5.8). Beware! Nested class declaration scope rules are expected to change.

```
class A {
public:
    int  i;
    void foo();
};

class B {
public:
    char i;
    void foo() {  A :: foo(); . . .}
};
```

A hidden external name can be accessed using the scope resolution operator.

```
int   i;
void  foo(int   i)
{
    i = ::i;
    . . .
}
```

A hidden `class`, `struct`, `union`, or `enum` identifier can be accessed by using its respective keyword.

```
static union u {
    . . .
};

void foo(int u)
{
    union u U;
    . . .
}
```

5. LINKAGE RULES

Pascal views a program as monolithic. This is not practical for modern software development. Modern systems are built around multifile inclusion, compilation, and linkage. For C and C++, it is necessary to understand how multifile programs are combined. Linking separate modules requires resolving external references. The key rule is that external nonstatic variables must be defined in exactly one place (Section 10.5). Use of the keyword `extern` together with an initializer constitutes defining a variable. Using the keyword `extern` without an initializer constitutes a declaration but not a definition. The following example illustrates these rules:

```
//file prog1.c
   char   c;           //definition of c
   . . .

//file prog2.c
   extern char c;      //declaration of c
   . . .
```

```
//file prog3.c
   extern int n = 5;  //definition of n
   . . .

//file prog4.c
   char         c;    //illegal second definition
   extern float n;    //illegal type mismatch
   extern int   k;    //illegal no declaration
   . . .
```

Constant definitions and `inline` definitions at file scope are local to that file unless explicitly declared `extern`. It is usual to place such definitions in a header file to be included with any code that needs these definitions.

A `typedef` declaration is local to its file. It is a synonym for the type it defines.

```
typedef char *c_string;    //c_string is pointer to char
typedef void (*ptr_f)();   //pointer to function
                           //of no arguments returning void
```

Enumerators are local to their file. Enumerators and typedefs that are needed in a multifile program should be placed in a header file. Enumerators defined within a class are local to that class. Access to them requires the scope resolution operator.

```
//types.h    header file
typedef char *c_string;    //c_string is pointer to char
typedef void (*ptr_f)();   //pointer to function

void foo(c_string s);      //function prototypes
void title();
void pr_onoff();

enum {OFF, ON};
extern int x;

//fcns.c to be separately compiled
#include <stream.h>
#include "types.h"

typedef char *c_string;    //c_string is pointer to char
typedef void (*ptr_f)();   //pointer to function
```

```
void foo(c_string s)
{
   cout <<"\noutput: " << s;
}

void title()
{
   cout << "\nTEST TYPEDEFS";
}

void pr_onoff()
{
   if (x == OFF)
      cout << "\nOFF";
   else
      cout << "\nON";
}

//linkage_ex.c   main program file  CC fcns.o linkage_ex.c
#include <stream.h>
#include "types.h"
int x = 0;

main()
{
   c_string f = "foo on you";
   ptr_f    pf = &pr_onoff;

   foo("ENTER 0 or 1:");
   if (( cin >> x) == ON)
      pf = &title;
   pr_onoff();
   pf();
   x = !x;
   pf();
   foo(f);
}
```

6. TYPES

C and Pascal have similar built-in types although C does not have a built-in Boolean type. C generally has more ways of modifying a type declaration; for example, both int and double can be long. The fundamental types in C++ are the same as those in C, with the following ANSI C extensions (Sections 4.3, 4.4, 4.6). Both `signed` and `void` types are available.

The derived types have significant extensions, including generic pointer type `void*`. Both anonymous unions and anonymous enumerations are allowed, and there is also a reference type. The `class` type (Chapter 5) is another extension, and the `struct` is extended to be a variant of the `class`. Union, enumeration, and class names are type-names.

```
void*    gen_ptr;                    //a generic pointer
int      i, &ref_i = i;              //ref_i is an alias for i
enum     boolean {false, true};      //enumeration
boolean  flag;                       //boolean is now a type-name

class    card {                      //user-defined type
   int   cd;                         //private data member
public:
   suit  s;                          //public data member
   pips  p;
   void  pr_card();                  //member function
};
```

7. CONVERSION RULES

In general, C and C++ have far more conversion possibilities than Pascal. Many of these conversions are implicit, which makes C convenient but potentially dangerous for the novice. Implicit conversions can induce hard to detect run-time bugs.

The standard C conversions apply in C++. Implicit pointer conversions also occur in C++ (Section 7.1). Any pointer type can be converted to a generic pointer of type `void*`. The name of an array is a pointer to its base element. The null pointer value can be converted to any type. A pointer to a class can be converted to a pointer to a publicly derived base class (Section 8.4). This also applies to references. C++ is generally stricter than traditional C and does not allow mixing of pointer types unless they are correctly cast. As in ANSI C, float expressions need not be automatically converted to `double`.

Traditional C casts are augmented in C++ by a functional notation as a syntactic alternative (Section 7.2). A functional notation of the form

type-name (*expression*)

is equivalent to a cast. The type must be expressible as an identifier. Thus the two expressions

```
x = float(i);    //C++ functional notation
x = (float) i;   //C  cast notation
```

are equivalent. Functional notation is the preferred style.

A constructor of one argument is de facto a type conversion from the argument's type to the constructor's class type. Consider an example of a class string constructor (Section 6.3):

```
string::string(char* p)
{
    len = strlen(p);
    s = new char[len + 1];
    strcpy(s, p);
}
```

This is automatically a type transfer from char* to string. These conversions are from an already defined type to a user-defined type. However, it is not possible for the user to add a constructor to a built-in type—for example, to int or double. In the string example, one may also want a conversion from string to char*. This can be done by defining a special conversion function inside the string class as follows:

```
operator (char *)() { return s; }    //recall char *s; is a member
```

The general form of such a member function is

```
operator type() { ... }
```

These conversions occur implicitly in assignment expressions and in argument and return conversions from functions.

8. EXPRESSIONS AND OPERATORS

C and C++ have far more operators than Pascal. They also have a large number of precedence levels. Operators also can have side effects. Appendix B lists their precedence and associativity. As explained in Chapter 1, most of the Pascal operators have analogs in C. In general,

C code is far terser than Pascal because complicated expressions can replace lines of Pascal code.

In addition, C makes assignment an operator and couples assignment with many other operators to produce assignment operators, such as +=, *=, <<=, and so on. Thus the expression

a *= b + c;   *is equivalent to*   a = a * (b + c);

C++ has additional novel operators not found in C. C++ introduces the operator :: , called the scope resolution operator. When used in the form :: *variable*, it allows access to the externally named variable (Section 4.5). Other uses of this notation are important for classes.

The unary operators new and delete are available to manipulate *free store* (Section 4.10). Free store is a system-provided memory pool for objects whose lifetime is directly managed by the programmer. The programmer creates the object by using new and destroys the object by using delete.

The operator new is used in the following forms:

new *type-name*
new *type-name initializer*
new (*type-name*)

In each case there are at least two effects. First, an appropriate amount of store is allocated from free store to contain the named type. Second, the base address of the object is returned as the value of the new expression. The expression is of type void* and can be assigned to any pointer type variable. The operator delete destroys an object created by new, in effect returning its allocated storage to free store for reuse. The following example uses these constructs to dynamically allocate an array:

```
//Use of new operator to dynamically allocate an array.

#include <stream.h>

main()
{
    int* data;
    int  size;

    cout << "\nEnter array size: ";
    cin >> size;
```

```
        data = new int[size];
        for (int j = 0; j < size; ++j)
            cout << (data[j] = j) << "\t";
        cout << "\n\n";
        delete data;
        . . .
}
```

The pointer variable `data` is used as the base address of a dynamically allocated array whose number of elements is the value of `size`. The `new` operator is used to allocate from free store sufficient storage for an object of type `int[size]`. The operator `delete` returns to free store the storage associated with the pointer variable `data`. This can only be done with objects allocated by `new`. There are no guarantees on what values will appear in objects allocated from free store. The programmer is responsible for properly initializing such objects.

The operator `delete` is used in the following forms:

```
delete expression
delete [ expression ] expression
```

The first form is the most common. The expression is typically a pointer variable used in a previous `new` expression. The second form is occasionally used when returning store that was allocated as an array type. The bracketed expression gives the number of elements of the array. The operator `delete` returns a value of type `void`.

Almost all unary and binary operators may be overloaded. Precedence and associativity are as built in.

9. CLASSES

Pascal has records and C has structures; both are comparable forms of heterogeneous aggregate types. C++ redefines structures to allow data hiding, inheritance, and member functions as major new extensions. In C++, the new keyword `class` (Chapter 5) or the keyword `struct` are used to declare user-defined types. An example is

```
class vect {
    int* p;                                 //base pointer
    int size;                               //number of elements
public:
    //constructors and destructor
    vect() { size = 10; p = new int[10]}    //create a size 10 array
    vect(int n);                            //create a size n array
    vect(vect& v);                          //initialization by vect
    vect(int a[], int n);                   //initialization by array
    ~vect() { delete p; }                   //destructor
    //other member functions
    int  ub() { return (size - 1); }        //upper bound
    int& operator [](int i);                //obtain range checked element
};
```

The keywords public, private, and protected indicate the visibility of members that follow (Sections 5.5, 8.2). The default for class is private and for struct is public. In the above example, the data members p and size are private. This makes them visible solely to member functions of the same class.

9.1. Constructors and Destructors

A constructor is a member function whose name is the same as the class name (Section 6.1). It *constructs* objects of the class type. This involves initialization of data members and frequently free store allocation using new. For classes with constructors, if they have a constructor with a void argument list, then they can be a base type of an array declaration.

A destructor is a member function whose name is the class name preceded by the character ~ (Section 6.2). Its usual purpose is to *destroy* values of the class type. This is typically accomplished by using delete.

A constructor of the form

type::*type*(*type*& x)

is used to perform copying of one *type* value into another when:

A *type* variable is initialized by a *type* value.

A *type* value is passed as an argument in a function.

A *type* value is returned from a function.

In older C++ systems, if this constructor was not present, then these operations were bitwise copy. In newer systems, the default is member-by-member assignment of value.

Classes with constructors having an empty argument list can have a derived array type. For example,

```
vect a[5];
```

is a declaration that uses the empty argument constructor to create an array a of five objects, each of which is a size 10 vect.

A class having members whose type requires a constructor may have these specified after the argument list for its own constructor (Section 6.5). The constructor has a comma-separated list of constructor calls following a colon. The constructor is invoked by using the member name followed by a parenthesized argument list.

9.2. Member Functions

Member functions are functions declared within a class and, as a consequence, have access to private, protected, and public members of that class (Section 5.4). If defined inside the class, they are treated as inline functions and are also treated when necessary as overloaded functions. In the class vect, the member function

```
int  ub() { return (size - 1); }          //upper bound
```

is defined. In this example, the member function ub is inline and has access to the private member size.

Member functions are invoked normally by use of the "." or -> operators, as in

```
vect   a(20), b;              //invoke appropriate constructor
vect* ptr_v = &b;
int    uba = a.ub(), ubb;     //invoke member ub
ubb = ptr_v -> ub();          //invoke member ub
```

9.3. Inheritance

Inheritance is the mechanism of *deriving* a new class from an old one (Chapter 8). The existing class can be added to or altered to create the derived class. A class can be derived from an existing class using the form:

```
class class-name : (public/private)optional base-class-name
{
      member declarations
};
```

As usual, the keyword `class` can be replaced by the keyword `struct`, with the usual implication that members are default `public`. The keywords `public`, `private`, and `protected` are available as visibility modifiers for class members (Section 8.2). A `public` member is visible throughout its scope. A `private` member is visible to other member functions within its own class. A `protected` member is visible to other member functions within its class and any class immediately derived from it. These visibility modifiers can be used within a class declaration in any order and with any frequency.

A base class having a constructor with arguments requires that a class derived from it have a constructor. The form of such a constructor is

```
class-name(argument list) : (base-class-name) :
(base class argument list)
{
       . . .
};
```

The base class argument list is used when invoking the appropriate base class constructor and is executed before the body of the derived class constructor is executed.

A publicly derived class is a *subtype* of its base class (Section 8.4). A variable of the derived class can in many ways be treated as if it were the base class type. A pointer whose type is pointer to base class can point to objects having the publicly derived class type. A reference to the derived class, when meaningful, may be implicitly converted to a reference to the public base class. It is possible to declare a reference to a base class and initialize it to an object of the publicly derived class.

The following is an example of a derived class:

```
class vect_bnd : public vect {
    int l_bnd, u_bnd;
public:
    vect_bnd();
    vect_bnd(int, int);
    int& operator[] (int);
    int  ub() { return (u_bnd); }
    int  lb() { return (l_bnd); }
};

vect_bnd::vect_bnd() : vect(10)
{
    l_bnd = 0;
    u_bnd = 9;
}

vect_bnd::vect_bnd(int lb, int ub) : vect(ub - lb + 1)
{
    l_bnd = lb;
    u_bnd = ub;
}
```

In this example, the constructors for the derived class invoke a constructor in the base class with argument list following the colon.

9.4. Multiple Inheritance

Multiple inheritance allows a derived class to be derived from more than one base class. The syntax of class headers is extended to allow a list of base classes and their privacy designation. An example is

```
class tools {
    . . .

};

class parts {
    . . .

};
```

```
class labor {
    . . .

};

class plans : public tools, public parts, public labor {
    . . .

};
```

In this example, the derived class `plans` publicly inherits the members of all three base classes. This parental relationship is described by the inheritance *directed acyclic graph* (DAG). The DAG is a graph structure whose nodes are classes and whose directed edges point from base to derived class.

In deriving an identically named member from different classes, ambiguities may arise. These derivations are allowed provided the user does not make an ambiguous reference to such a member.

With multiple inheritance, two base classes can be derived themselves from a common ancestor. If both base classes are used in the ordinary way by their derived class, that class will have two subobjects of the common ancestor. This duplication, if not desirable, can be eliminated by using `virtual` inheritance (Section 10.1).

9.5. Constructor Invocation

The early releases of C++ left unspecified the order of execution for initializing constructors in base and member constructors. Most of the time these constructions were independent of each other, and the results were independent of order. With the addition of multiple inheritance, however, it became unnecessarily hazardous to continue this laxness. Thus the current ordering is

1. Explicit reference to base class constructors in the order in which they are listed after the header colon

2. Unmentioned base classes in the order in which they are declared

3. Explicit reference to member class constructors in the order in which they are listed after the header colon

Virtual base classes have special precedence and are constructed before any of their derived classes. They are constructed before any nonvirtual base classes. Their construction order depends on their DAG. It is a depth-first, left-to-right order. Destructors are invoked in reverse order of constructors. These rules, although complicated, should conform to one's intuition, and a client program's correctness should not depend on constructor/destructor ordering. Finally, the associated destructors are called in the reverse order from constructor invocation.

Let us illustrate by elaborating on a previous example.

```
class tools {
    . . .
public:
    tools(char*);
    ~tools();
    . . .
};

class parts {
    . . .
public:
    parts(char*);
    ~parts();
    . . .
};

class labor {
    . . .
public:
    labor(int);
    ~labor();
    . . .
};

class plans : public tools, public parts, public labor {
    . . .
    special a;   //member class with constructor
public:
    plans(int m) : labor(m), tools("lathe"), a(m), parts("widget")
        { . . . }
    ~plans();
    . . .
};
```

In this case, the member constructor a(m) appears before the base class constructor parts("widget") but by our rules is invoked last. Since its constructor was last, its destructor is invoked first, followed by ~parts, ~tools, ~labor, and ~plans.

9.6. Abstract Base Classes

A pure virtual function is a virtual member function whose body is undefined. Notationally, it is declared inside the class as follows:

virtual *function prototype* = 0;

A derived class must define or declare each pure virtual function in its immediate base class. A class that has at least one *pure virtual* function is an *abstract class*.

9.7. Pointer to Class Member

C, much like Pascal, uses pointers to structures and a simple accessing scheme to pick off a member value.

In C++, pointer to class member is *distinct* from a pointer to class. A pointer to class member has type $T::*$, where T is the class name. C++ has two operators that act to dereference a pointer to class member. The pointer to member operators are:

.*   *and*   ->*

Think of *obj.*ptr_mem* as first dereferencing the pointer to obtain a member variable and then accessing the member for the designated *obj* (Section 10.4).

10. FUNCTIONS

In C, functions are strictly call-by-value. They are not allowed to nest and exist at file scope. The Pascal function/procedure distinction is not made, but instead is indicated by having pure procedures be of type returning void.

Changes in C++ to how functions work include use of function prototypes, overloading, call-by-reference, default arguments, and the effects of the keywords inline, friend, and virtual.

10.1. Prototypes

In C++, the prototype form is (Section 4.6)

type name (argument-declaration-list) ;

Examples are:

```
double sqrt(double x);
void   pr_int(char*, int);        //definition contains names
void   ring_bell(void);           //function of no arguments
int    printf(char* format, ...); //variable number of args.
```

With the above `sqrt` prototype definition, invoking `sqrt` guarantees that, if feasible, an argument will be converted to type `double`. Prototypes are also found in ANSI C and greatly improve type checking.

10.2. Overloading

The term *overloading* refers to use of the same name for multiple meanings of an operator or a function (Section 4.9). The meaning selected will depend on the types of the arguments used by the operator or function (Section 7.3).

Consider a function that averages the values in an array of `double` versus one that averages the values in an array of `int`. Both are conveniently named `avg_arr`.

```
double   avg_arr(double a[], int size);
double   avg_arr(int a[], int size);

double avg_arr(int a[], int size)
{
   int  sum = 0;

   for (int i = 0; i < size; ++i)
     sum += a[i];                 //performs int arithmetic
   return ((double) sum / size);
}
```

```
double avg_arr(double a[], int size)
{
    double  sum = 0.0;
    for (int i = 0; i < size; ++i)
        sum += a[i];                 //performs double arithmetic
    return (sum / size);
}
```

In early systems, the keyword overload was used to declare a non-member function name as overloadable. This practice is allowed but obsolete.

Whichever overloaded function is to be invoked, the invocation argument list must be matched to the declaration parameter list. The matching algorithm is as follows:

Overloaded Function Selection Algorithm

1. Use an exact match if found.

2. Try standard type promotions.

3. Try standard conversions without temporaries.

4. Try standard conversions with temporaries.

5. Try user-defined conversions.

6. Use a match to ellipsis if found.

An exact match is clearly best. Casts can be used to force such a match. A conversion such as float to double is a promotion. A type capable of storing more values is wider than a type storing fewer values. Going from a narrower type to a wider type is a promotion. In some cases, converting from a type T to a type T& requires using a temporary.

A complete explanation of this algorithm would require many pages. The compiler will complain about ambiguous situations. Thus, it is poor practice to rely on subtle type distinctions and implicit conversions that obscure the overloaded function that is called. When in doubt use explicit conversions to provide an exact match.

10.3. Call-by-Reference

Reference declarations allow C++ to have *call-by-reference* arguments (Section 4.7). In this regard, it is easier to recode more directly into C++ than into C a Pascal procedure having VAR arguments. Let us use this mechanism to write a function `greater` that exchanges two values if the first is greater than the second.

```
int greater(int& a, int& b)
{
   if (a > b) {              //exchange
      int temp = a;
      a = b;
      b = temp;
      return (1);
   }
   else
      return (0);
}
```

Now, if `i` and `j` are two `int` variables, then

```
greater(i, j)
```

will use the reference to `i` and the reference to `j` to exchange, if necessary, their two values. In traditional C, this must be accomplished using pointers and indirection.

```
/* traditional C greater  */
int greater(int* a, int* b)
{
   if (*a > *b) {            //exchange
      int temp = *a;
      *a = *b;
      *b = temp;
      return (1);
   }
   else
      return (0);
}
```

10.4. Inline

The keyword `inline` suggests to the compiler that the function be converted to inline code (Section 4.2). This keyword is used for the sake of efficiency and generally with short functions, and is implicit for member functions that are defined within their class. A compiler can ignore this directive for a variety of reasons, including the fact that the function is too long. In those cases, the `inline` function is compiled as an ordinary function. An example is

```
inline float circum(float rad) { return (pi * 2 * rad); }
```

Inline functions are of file scope unless explicitly declared `extern`.

10.5. Default Arguments

A formal parameter can be given a default argument (Section 4.8). However, this can be done only with contiguous formal parameters that are right-most in the parameter list. A default value is usually an appropriate constant that occurs frequently when the function is called. The following function illustrates this point:

```
int mult(int n, int k = 2)              //k = 2 is default
{
    if (k == 2)
        return (n * n);
    else
        return (mult(n, k - 1) * n);
}
```

We assume that most of the time the function is used to return the value of n squared.

10.6. Friend Functions

The keyword `friend` is a function specifier (Section 7.4). It allows a nonmember function access to the hidden members of the class of which it is a friend. Its use is a method of escaping the strict strong typing and data hiding restrictions of C++. A `friend` function must appear inside the class declaration of which it is a friend. It is prefaced by the keyword `friend` and can appear anywhere in the class. Member functions of one class can be `friend` functions of another class. In this case, the member function is written in the friend's class using the scope resolution operator to qualify its function name. If all member functions of one class are friend functions of a second class, this can be specified by writing `friend` `class` *class name*.

The following declarations are typical:

```
class tweedledee {
   . . .
   friend void alice();         //friend function
   int           cheshire();    //member function
   . . .
};

class tweedledum {
   . . .
   friend int tweedledee::cheshire();
   . . .
};

class tweedledumber {
   . . .
   friend class tweedledee;     //all member functions
                                //of tweedledee have access
   . . .
};
```

10.7. Operator Overloading

A special case of function overloading is operator overloading (Section 7.5). The keyword operator is used to overload the built-in C operators. Just as a function name, such as print, can be given a variety of meanings that depend on its arguments, so can an operator, such as +, be given additional meanings. This allows infix expressions of both user types and built-in types to be written. The precedence and associativity remain fixed.

Operator overloading typically uses either member functions or friend functions because they both have privileged access. Overloading a unary operator using a member function has an empty argument list because the single operator argument is the implicit argument (Section 7.6). For binary operators, member function operator overloading has, as the first argument, the implicitly passed class variable and, as a second argument, the lone argument list parameter (Section 7.7). Friend functions or ordinary functions have both arguments specified in the parameter list.

We will demonstrate how to overload a unary operator, using ++ as an example. We define the class clock that can store time as days, hours, minutes, and seconds.

```
class clock {
    unsigned int  tot_secs,  secs,  mins,  hours,  days;
public:
    clock(unsigned int i);      //constructor and conversion
    void print();               //formatted printout
    void tick();                //add one second
    clock operator ++() { this -> tick(); return(*this); }
};
```

This class overloads the autoincrement operator. It is a member function and can be invoked on its implicit single argument. The member function tick adds one second to the implicit argument of the overloaded ++ operator.

The ternary conditional operator ?: , the scope resolution operator :: , and the two member operators . .* cannot be overloaded.

10.8. Virtual Functions

The keyword virtual is a function specifier that provides a mechanism for dynamically selecting at run-time the appropriate member function from among base and derived class functions (Section 8.5). It may be used only to modify member function declarations. A virtual function must be executable code. When invoked, its semantics are the same as other functions. In a derived class, its name can be overloaded, and the function prototype of the derived function must have matching type. The selection of which function to invoke from among a group of overloaded virtual functions is dynamic. The typical case is where a base class has a virtual function and derived classes have their versions of this function. A pointer to a base class type can point at either a base class object or a derived class object. The member function to be invoked is selected at run-time. It corresponds to the object's type not the pointer's type. In the absence of a derived type member, the base class virtual function is used by default.

Consider the following example:

```
//virtual function selection
#include <stream.h>

class B {
public:
    int  i;
    virtual void print_i() { cout << i << " inside B\n"; }
};
```

```
class D : public B {
public:
    void print_i() { cout << i << " inside D\n"; }
};

main()
{
    B   b, *pb = &b;
    D   f;

    f.i = 1 + (b.i = 1);
    pb -> print_i();
    pb = &f;
    pb -> print_i();
}
```

The output from this program is

```
1 inside B
2 inside D
```

In each case a different version of `print_i` is executed. Selection depends dynamically on the object being pointed at.

10.9. Type-Safe Linkage

Linkage rules for non-C++ functions can be specified using a *linkage-specification*. Some examples are

```
extern "C" atoi(const char* nptr);   //C linkage

extern "C" {
#include <stdio.h>
}                       //C linkage for these prototypes

extern "Pascal" {
    sin(double);
    cos(double);
    tan(double);
}                       //Pascal linkage
```

This specification is at file scope and is system-dependent as to which languages are supported.

11. I/O

Pascal has input/output built in to the language. C and C++ import I/O as library functions. This latter approach is more portable. For it to work well, however, the programming community must agree to a basic standard collection of library functions. In C, this library is described by stdio.h. It has been in wide use since the mid-1970s and is available for use in C++ programs.

C++ has been developing its own libraries distinct from C. The most important of these is described by stream.h (Chapter 9) and the newer iostream.h (in 2.0 releases).

Output is returned to an object of type ostream. An operator << is overloaded in this class to perform output conversions from standard types. The standard output ostream corresponding to stdout is cout and the standard output ostream corresponding to stderr is cerr.

Input is returned to an object of type istream as described in *stream.h* (Section 9.4). An operator >> is overloaded in this class to perform input conversions to standard types. The standard input istream corresponding to stdin is cin.

11.1. Iostream I/O

The header iostream.h extends the earlier stream I/O library. It also changes some behaviors. It defines the iostream class, which inherits both istream and ostream properties. Both input and output can be performed on such an object. It no longer supports form(), hex(), and other similar functions for formatting.

Added items include:

- The standard ostream object clog provides buffered output to standard error.

- The format state manipulators dec, hex, and oct change the default integer representation. The stream member function precision(int) can be used to set floating point precision.

- The manipulators flush and endl are used to immediately print buffered output. The endl manipulator also prints a newline.

- Istream functions getline(char Buf[], int Limit, char Delim = '\n') and gcount() are used to extract line-at-a-time input.

The argument Limit is one less than the maximum line length. The delimiter character is by default a newline (also EOF is tested). The line is stored in the character array argument Buf [] . A call to gcount() gets the number of characters extracted from the input by the last call to getline().

● The header file *strstream.h* adds functionality that allows streams to be processed as strings. This allows user-defined formatting to be conveniently coded. The header file *iomanip.h* is also useful for formatting I/O.

11.2 Fstream FILE I/O

In older systems, file I/O was performed using either the C header *stdio.h* or the C++ header *stream.h*. Newer systems include *fstream.h*. Refer to your system manual for documentation.

The following program replaces the double spacing program given in Section 9.5.

```
//dbl_sp: a program to double space a file
//Usage: executable  f1 f2
//f1 must be present and readable
//f2 must be writable if it exists

#include <iostream.h>
#include <fstream.h>
#include <stdlib.h>
```

```
main(int argc, char** argv)
{
    void      double_space(ifstream&, ofstream&);
    ifstream  f_in(argv[1], ios::in);
    ofstream  f_out(argv[2], ios::out);

    if (argc != 3) {
        cout << "\nUsage: " << argv[0]
             << " infile outfile\n";
        exit(1);
    }
    if (!f_in) {
        cerr << "cannot open " << argv[1];
        exit(1);
    }
    if (!f_out) {
        cerr << "cannot open " << argv[2];
        exit(1);
    }
    double_space(f_in, f_out);
}

void double_space(ifstream& f, ofstream& t)
{
    char  c;

    while (f.get(c)) {
        t.put(c);
        if (c == '\n')
            t.put(c);
    }
}
```

Note that `ifstream` and `ofstream` are types used to declare input files and output files, respectively. The input file has a constructor of two arguments—for example,

```
ifstream file_in("my_input", ios::in);
```

The file named `my_input` is opened for reading. The second argument `ios::in` is an enumeration constant. Analogously, `ios::out` and `ios::app` are used to allow writing and appending, respectively. Files that are both read and written to are declared `fstream`.

Standard actions are available such as:

```
file_in.open("my_input", ios::in);   //opens
file_in.close();                      //closes
file_in.seek(10);      //position 10 bytes from beginning
file_in.seek(-10, ios::cur);     //back up 10 bytes
```

INDEX

About the Author

Ira Pohl, Ph.D., is a professor of computer and information sciences at the University of California, Santa Cruz. He has two decades of experience as a software methodologist and is an international authority on C and C++ programming. His teaching and research interests include artificial intelligence and programming languages. Professor Pohl has lectured extensively at U.C. Berkeley, the Courant Institute, Edinburgh University, Stanford, and the Vrije University in Amsterdam. He is the author of the best-selling *C++ for C Programmers* and coauthor, with Al Kelley, of a very successful series of C books: *A Book on C: Programming in C, Second Edition; C by Dissection;* and *Turbo C.* When not programming, he enjoys riding bicycles in Aptos, California, with his wife Debra and daughter Laura.